THE

BEST SHORT PLAYS

1958-1959

THE

BEST SHORT PLAYS

1958-1959

Edited by MARGARET MAYORGA

BEACON PRESS   BEACON HILL   BOSTON

CONTENTS

SHORT PLAY PRODUCTION, 1958-1959

BIBLIOGRAPHIES

PREFACE

In a year when television plays in general seem to have "flatted right down and stayed there" (to use a kind of colloquialism that is becoming more and more the language of TV), it is cheering to note an increasing interest in things poetic among the younger playwrights. Having filled their hands with advertising dollars, some of them are seeking now to fulfill their artistic ambitions. During this past year, poetry of a sort has put down sprangly bushes in many hamlets throughout the land.

As human beings, we all seem to know, in our quieter moments, a few happy if not eternal verities, even though the universe we thought we knew may be rapidly falling away. Yet these happy truths have disappeared from the theatre. Are the playwrights afraid to talk about the saner consequences of living? Must they be steeped in sordid imaginings? (In one off-Broadway show this year, the actors and actresses crawled between decayed timbers, actually as well as symbolically.)

Going to the theatre used to be fun, something to be remembered and enjoyed through memory for years. Too many of today's playbills are tossed into garbage cans by customers who wish they could dispose of their plundered feelings in the same easy way. But drama is experience, and experience cannot be tossed away. Pleasant or sordid, the experience lives on.

It is one thing to read about someone else's neurotic tensions, but it may be degrading to be summoned to participate in them. It can be downright embarrassing to overhear some people's psyches unfold, on- or off-stage. Isn't it time for writers to take good, brisk walks up sunlit avenues, searching for a new look at the world and its ways?

Granted, there has been a flood of poetry of a sort this year. But too much of it is the "sort"—teetering on the brink of poetry, leaving audience eyes dry and nervous systems cold. And merely by framing a play in poetry of a sort, the playwright does not make malignant sentiments palatable. Nor will a counter-attack of slick Fair Ladies and Music Men revive us.

Somewhere beyond the waves of musical entertainment and

rock-bound neuroses lies a land of milk and honey, now sparsely settled, but joyous and inviting. Earnest playwrights can find the way there. But the road is hard:

> It is not enough or a playwright to do something different —or to imitate.
> Success measured in wealth is irrelevant to art.
> To write verse, one must have a new way with words.
> To be a dramatist, one must survive suffering, not just bequeath it.

Margaret Mayorga

GLEN COVE, NEW YORK

AUGUST 1959

THE COW-CATCHER ON THE CABOOSE

By

Edward H. Devany

(Published here for the first time)

For My Father and Mother

CAST

Columbus Styles
Mr. Thomas White
Mrs. Mag Pickens
Bill Dudley
Eddie Burns
Colonel Dick Borden
Mr. Cullamen

Time: A summer day in the early fifties.

Place: The supply room office of a large southern railroad.

THE COW-CATCHER ON THE CABOOSE

SCENE 1

The scene is the supply room office of a large southern railroad. The place hasn't seen fresh paint in years. Most of the wall space is lined with shelves loaded with dusty stacks of tariffs, old files, and other papers. At one end of this room is a door which opens to a hall. Beside the door is a water cooler. A little farther along this wall is a mimeograph machine and a small table roughly divided into sections for the sorting of mail. In the center of the room is a large multigraph machine, above which is suspended an old ceiling fan with its huge naked blades spinning lazily. The other end of the room is occupied by a large desk with a swivel chair behind it. This part of the room is even more filthy and disordered than the rest. Stacks of papers, some as high as three feet, are piled on the desk, along with ash trays, weights, three jars filled with pencils, and other assorted junk. On top of the file cabinets around the desk are old Coke bottles, paper cups, and lunch bags which have been folded and bundled together with rubber bands. To one side of the desk is an unpolished spittoon. And near the wall is a coat rack which is loaded with old coats of varying types, and several hats, including a winter cap with attached ear muffs. On the wall a clock reads 8:07 A.M.

As the houselights dim, we hear the eight o'clock whistle, then almost instantaneously, the combined sounds of typewriters, telephones, a small press, footsteps, and other sounds of a large and busy office.

These sounds fade into the background, their source being a big office behind the one we see on stage. Here everything is quiet. COLUMBUS STYLES, *aging Negro, is carefully polishing the multigraph machine. He is dressed in old work clothes. While he works, he occasionally glances up at the clock on the wall and shakes his head sadly.*

3

A moment later, THOMAS WHITE, *office manager, looks into the room. He is a thin man, in his late fifties, with a sharp face and a long beak of a nose. In his hand he carries a big pocket watch, which he compares with the clock on the wall.*

MR. WHITE. [*Chuckling.*] Looks like Colonel and Virginia Transit didn't hit it off again, eh, Columbus?

COLUMBUS. [*Grinning.*] No, suh.

MR. WHITE. Forty-eight years, and he hasn't gotten in here on time two days in a row since he's been here. Well, after today . . .

COLUMBUS. They ain' gonna give him no more time?

MR. WHITE. All depends on what Mister Cullamen says. But frankly, Colonel better come up with a good one this time, Columbus. He's already . . .

[MAG PICKENS, *a short, dumpy little woman in her forties, enters.*]

MAG. Mister White, some of us would like to . . .

[*She stands on tiptoe to whisper the rest of it in* MR. WHITE'S *ear. He chuckles, nods his head.*]

MR. WHITE. [*Starting out the door with* MAG.] Well, since it's probably his last day . . .

[*They exit together, talking. A moment later* BILL DUDLEY, *a mild-mannered little man in his late fifties, pokes his head in the door.*]

BILL. Columbus?

COLUMBUS. Yes, suh.

BILL. Colonel in yet?

COLUMBUS. No, suh.

BILL. [*Holding up a little box.*] I got something for him.

COLUMBUS. Present?

BILL. Made it myself.

COLUMBUS. He oughta be in soon, Mister Dudley.

BILL. Don't tell him about it. I want to surprise him.

COLUMBUS. Yes, suh, Mister Dudley.

[BILL DUDLEY *starts out. At the doorway, he stops, looks back in.*]

BILL. Don't you tell him now . . .

COLUMBUS. No, suh.

[BILL *exits.* EDDIE BURNS, *the office boy, eighteen years old, enters as unobtrusively as possible. He wears a Panama hat, white shirt, bow tie, seersucker trousers a little worse for wear. Avoiding* COLUMBUS' *stare, he hangs up his hat, takes two black rubber bands and rolls them up his sleeves, then quickly moves over to the big desk where he searches for a pile of mail.*]

EDDIE. God, you can't find nothing on this stupid desk.

[*He finds the mail and carries it over to the sorting table on the other side of the room.*]

COLUMBUS. Where you get that hat?

EDDIE. Bought it.

COLUMBUS. Look jes' like the Colonel's Panama.

EDDIE. You kidding? That's a brand-new hat. His is all beat up. [COLUMBUS *cackles shrilly.* EDDIE *glares at him.*] What's so funny?

COLUMBUS. I's jes' thinkin'—if you puts on twenty pounds or so an' lets yo' hair bald back on the top o' yo' head, maybe folks'll start callin' you Colonel Borden.

EDDIE. Ha, ha, ha! Very funny.

COLUMBUS. You's even comin' in late jes' like he do. Late every mornin' . . .

EDDIE. Seven minutes late. Seven minutes. First time in . . .

COLUMBUS. Since day 'fore yesterday.

EDDIE. Now that's a . . .

COLUMBUS. An' Mister White look in here two times, too.

EDDIE. [*Nervously looking toward the door.*] Did he ask . . .

COLUMBUS. I tole him you gone for mail. But I ain' coverin' for you all the time.

EDDIE. Well, I won't be late tomorrow. You just wait and see.

COLUMBUS. Now you's even talkin' like him. Every day he late, and every day he say he ain' gonna be late the next day. The damn Virginia Transit cause it all, he say.

EDDIE. Aw, he's just an old windbag. Nobody listens to all his jazz.

COLUMBUS. Ain' gonna listen to you, neither, if you don' start comin' in on time. You wanna get yo' self sidetracked like they done to him? Spend the rest o' yo' life in here?

EDDIE. Aw, what're you talking about? [*A loud burst of applause is heard from the hallway.*] What's that?

COLUMBUS. I don' know.

EDDIE. [*Peering around the door into the hall.*] Good Lord! [*He ducks back into the room.*] Old lady Pickens has got everybody standing around the elevator. Colonel just got off and he looks madder'n hell.

COLUMBUS. [*Laughing.*] Woo—gonna be some day today!

EDDIE. What are you talking about?

COLUMBUS. Today Colonel's last day with the railroad, Eddie.

EDDIE. They really gonna retire him? Aw, he'll figure some way out of it. [*He moves toward the mimeograph machine, where he takes an almost-at-attention stance.*] You just wait and see! He'll talk 'em out of it again, just like he did last time. [*A crowd is heard approaching. One voice roars out above the murmur of the rest for them to "Go away," "Get back to work." Then the enormous figure of* COLONEL DICK BORDEN *appears in the doorway. He is dressed in a Palm Beach suit, wrinkled, ill-fitting, and blotched with occasional stains. He wears a Panama hat. A tall man, and portly, his great stomach bulges out over his trousers, making it impossible for him to button his coat. His round face is marked with crags, and driblets of sweat which he dabs at with a large white handkerchief. He walks rather stiffly from age, but he possesses still, at sixty-seven, a full, rumbling voice which, when raised, has all the subtlety of a fog horn. He backs in, facing the crowd outside.*]

COLONEL. [*Shouting.*] Go on now, the whole damn shiftless bunch of you! Ain't you got nothing better to do than bother me when I got all the work I got piled up in here?

THE CROWD. [*Men and women chanting outside the doorway.*]

> Eleven minutes late,
> Eleven minutes late,
> You made us stand and wait and wait,
> Eleven minutes late!

COLONEL. [*Trying to hush them up.*] God Almighty, you

trying to get me fired? Now get on out of here, all of you, before Whitey comes along and cans every last one of you!

A VOICE FROM THE CROWD. Mister White's right beside you, Colonel!

[COLONEL BORDEN *turns and sees the office manager.*]

COLONEL. Oh, my God—Mister White—I didn't even . . . [*He draws himself up straight.*] It's that—that damned Virginia Transit Company, Mister White. They couldn't run a bus on time if they had Jesus driving it. I told that fool driver, coming down, I said, "If we tried to run a railroad like you run your bus line, why there wouldn't be no more railroads in this country!" No, sir!

[*Laughter from the crowd.*]

MR. WHITE. Well, we'll let it go this time, Colonel, since it's your last day.

COLONEL. Last day? Now wait a minute . . .

MR. WHITE. [*To the crowd.*] All right. Everyone back to your desks now! Party's over.

[*The crowd breaks up.*]

COLONEL. Just a minute, Mister White . . .

MR. WHITE. I'll be in to see you in a while, Colonel.

COLONEL. But . . . [MR. WHITE *disappears from view.* COLONEL BORDEN *turns into the office.*] What's goin' on around here? God, I come in a couple of minutes late, and things are going on I ain't heard nothing about before. Not one stinking word's been said about "last day" that I've heard anything about. By God, I'm telling you that . . .

[MAG PICKENS *peeks in the doorway.*]

MAG. [*Teasingly.*]
                 Eleven minutes late!
                 Eleven minutes late!

[COLONEL BORDEN *whirls around on her with a roar. Giggling, she runs back out into the hall. After staring at her for a second,* COLONEL BORDEN *turns back into the room.*]

COLONEL. That old pig—Pickens! It's sickenin'—a forty-five-year-old woman with hips as big as a elephant's butt skippin' up and down the hall like she was sixteen years old. Damn woman don't have good sense, that's what. [COLUMBUS *stifles a laugh.* COLONEL BORDEN *glares at him.*] Well, what are you grinnin' at, you devil? I bet you put 'em up to this.

COLUMBUS. I ain' done nothin', Colonel.

COLONEL. Well, stop that grinnin' and get that machine started! First thing you know, Cully's gonna be hollerin' for rates and . . . [*He turns toward his desk, and scowls.*] Damn desk! I'm coming in here tomorrow, Saturday or no Saturday, and clean that junk up. Place looks like a . . . [*He stops, and glares out the doorway.*] Pickens did it, didn't she? [*Turning to* EDDIE.] She put 'em up to all that clapping and singing and everything, didn't she, Eddie?

EDDIE. I guess so, Colonel.

COLONEL. [*Sarcastically mimicking her poem.*] *Eleven minutes late! Eleven minutes late!* Pig-butt! [COLUMBUS *giggles loudly.*] Stop that laughing! [*He settles himself, painfully, into his swivel chair.*] There's nothing funny about her kind, Columbus. Oh, she walks up and down the halls, whistling and sashaying and smiling at everyone like she just couldn't do enough for you. And it's all a part of her game to get ahead in this man's railroad. [EDDIE *picks up the mail and starts toward the door.*] Wait a minute! You think I'm talking through my hat, don't you? [*He throws his hat onto a shelf.*] Just the other day I caught her down in Cully's office, polishing his desk. "What you doing polishin' that damn desk?" I asked her. "Mister Culla-men's coming back from Richmond tomorrow and I want everything spick and span for him," he says. Spick and span! Get that? Spick and span! [*He struggles to take off his coat.*] And don't you think she wasn't down there the next morning, telling Cully, "Just look at that desk, Mister Cullamen, see how nice and polished your desk is. I spent three hours after work yesterday and . . ." [*He stops and stares toward the door.*] Wait a minute! Yeah! Damn it! I got it now!

COLUMBUS. Huh?

EDDIE. What, Colonel?

COLONEL. [*Struggling to open a jammed drawer in his desk.*] She's trying to make me look so bad they'll have to retire me! Ugh! Rotten desk! Ughhh! Draggin' everybody down to that

elevator! God! [*The drawer flies open.* COLONEL *searches it.*]
Trying to use me for laughs so she can get in good with everybody else. Now where in the hell are they? I'll bet she's even
been down to Cully and . . . [*Beginning to search the top of the
desk.*] Can't find a damn thing on this desk. Tried to talk Cully
into letting me go! Well, Cully's too smart for her. He's on to
her tricks. *Spick and span!* Where . . . ? Damn cleaning women
come in here at night and move things around so you can't find
a— Here they are! [*He picks up two arm garters and rolls them
up his sleeves. Then he leans back in his chair with a happy
thought.*] Well, you saw how I handled it. I wasn't letting her
put one over on me. Not for one second. No, sir. I told Whitey
—hell, you heard what I said. "Whitey," I said, "that damned
Virginia Transit Company couldn't run a bus on time if . . ."

COLUMBUS. [*Laughing.*] I bet you's sure surprised to see him
standin' right there beside you.

COLONEL. Ha! You think so? Ha! [*He smashes his fist down
on the desk.*] That burns me up!

EDDIE. What, Colonel?

COLONEL. Draggin' Whitey in on it, too. That was embarrassing. Here I'm trying to get 'em to hold off retiring me, and
she has to fix it up so Whitey sees me coming in late. Trying to
ruin any chance I got of . . .

COLUMBUS. Mister White—he knows you come in late every
day, Colonel.

COLONEL. He what?

COLUMBUS. He knows. He check in here every morning,
eight o'clock, to see who here and who ain't and he know . . .

COLONEL. Are you kidding? Whitey don't . . .

COLUMBUS. He say to me every morning, "Well, Columbus, I
guess the Colonel and Virginia Transit ain't hit it off right
again."

COLONEL. [*Spluttering wildly, staggering to his feet.*] Damn
—I—you—Why, you oughta. Hell fire, you gone too far this
time! Why . . .

EDDIE. [*Trying to make him sit down.*] Take it easy,
Colonel!

COLONEL. You think they'd 've kept me on here all these

years if I wasn't one of the most regular . . . Why, there's men sets their watches by the time I arrive at the door to this building.

COLUMBUS. Then they sets their watches late.

COLONEL. [*Raising a hand.*] Why you . . . ! [*Lowering his hand, smiling.*] You good-for-nothing, you're razzing me, ain't you?

COLUMBUS. No, suh, Colonel, I . . .

COLONEL. Come here!

[*He falls, exhausted, back into his chair.*]

COLUMBUS. What you wan', Colonel?

COLONEL. Don't give me that *"What you wan', Colonel"* business! Just come here.

COLUMBUS. But Colonel, you say, "Get the multigraph runnin'."

COLONEL. It can wait. [COLUMBUS *walks over to the desk.*] Damn, I nearly overslept this morning. Missed my breakfast, and I'm about to starve to death. [*He fishes in his pocket and pulls out a little purse, which he opens. He takes out coins and gives them to* COLUMBUS.] Sausage biscuit and coffee.

COLUMBUS. Yes, suh.

COLONEL. [*Digging into his purse again.*] No. Make that two sausage biscuits and coffee. My stomach's hurtin', I'm so damned hungry. [*Roaring out again.*] Damn the Virginia Transit Company! If they ran their buses on time, I'd get a chance to eat a decent meal in the mornings. [COLUMBUS *grins.*] Now what you grinnin' about?

COLUMBUS. Colonel, you knows—an' I knows—you gonna have that sausage biscuit and coffee if you gets yo' breakfast at home or not. You gonna have . . .

COLONEL. Get on outa here! [COLUMBUS *starts toward the door.*] And don't go wasting half the morning, either. We got work piled up in here to . . .

[MAG PICKENS *appears in the doorway, with a cardboard box. She hands it to* COLUMBUS.]

MAG. Here it is, Columbus.

[COLUMBUS *looks down at the box. His face contorts. He rushes to the desk and dumps the box, then dashes to the multigraph machine, which he ducks behind, stuffing a rag into his twitching mouth.*]

COLONEL. [*Glaring down at the box.*] What is this? What is this?

MAG. [*Moving into the room.*] Sausage biscuit and coffee, Colonel.

COLONEL. Pickens, you're off your rocker. I always knew you'd crack up sooner or later. Now you done it. [MAG *giggles happily. She obviously enjoys every minute of this.*] Listen to her! Listen to her laughing like a loon. Bringing this crap in here . . . You know that eating on the job's against the rules. Now you just pick this right back up again and . . .

MAG. [*Winking at* EDDIE, *who refuses to acknowledge her.*] But wasn't Columbus going down to get it for you?

COLONEL. What! [*He draws himself up full in his chair.* MAG *giggles again.*] Columbus was—well, listen to me, you laughing hyena! Columbus was going down to Mister Cullamen's office for copies of the tariffs of the day. If you knew half as much about this man's railroad as you think you know, you'd know he goes there, for the same reason, at the same time, every morning.

MAG. But I thought he . . .

COLONEL. You thought nothing! You don't fool me. I'm on to you, Pickens. I've figured out what you're up to. Well, get this straight: nobody's wrecking me with this railroad. You hear me? I've put too many years, too much work, for you or anybody else to . . .

MAG. Aw, Colonel, what are you talking about? I'm not trying to wreck you, or anything else. Just trying to have a little fun.

COLONEL. Fun! FUN? This here's an office, not a fun house. Now get on outa here! We got work to do.

MAG. [*A little hurt, she moves to his desk, then brightens.*] And it looked so good, too, when they were fixing it.

COLONEL. [*After eyeing the box, hungrily, for a second.*] Well, if it looked so good, why don't you take it down to Cully Cullamen's office, and sit on the desk and eat it there? [*He roars with laughter.*]

MAG. [*Reaching over and chucking him under the chin.*] That's just what I'll do, honey.

COLONEL. Don't you *honey* me!

[*Taking the box,* MAG *runs, squealing and giggling, from the room.*]

EDDIE. Good God, Colonel, she's getting crazier every day.

COLONEL. [*Glaring after her.*] She don't fool me, not for one minute. Comin' in here with that damn food and . . . I told you what she was up to. I told you she . . . [*He looks over, sees* EDDIE *and* COLUMBUS. *Anger reddens his face.*] All right! [*He pushes himself up out of the chair.*] Which one of you told her? Come on! I'm waiting for an answer. Which one of you rats told Pickens? [*A muffled choking issues from behind the multigraph machine.*] COLUMBUS!

[COLUMBUS, *his face streaked with tears, his body still quivering with laughter, peeks up from behind the machine.*]

COLUMBUS. Gawd, Colonel, you know we ain' never gonna tell nothing on you.

COLONEL. Oh, no. Not much! Don't you see that . . . [MR. WHITE *appears in the doorway. He has his hands behind him.*] Oh—Oh—Mister White. Come on in, sir. We was just . . .

MR. WHITE. [*Pulling a cardboard carton from behind his back, and holding it out to the* COLONEL.] I brought you a sausage biscuit and coffee, Colonel.

[COLUMBUS *disappears behind the multigraph machine again.*]

COLUMBUS. [*Trying to muffle the sounds.*] Oh, Lawd— Oooh, Laawwdd! Hehehehehehehehehehe!

COLONEL. [*Glaring at the machine.*] Columbus! [*He turns to* MR. WHITE. *His face is serious now, eyes moist.*] I don't know what you mean, Mister White. I don't believe food's allowed on this floor during working hours, sir.

MR. WHITE. [*His face distorted in an effort not to smile; his eyes darting to the multigraph machine.*] Well, it seems fair enough to make an exception in the case of a man with the number of years' service to the railroad that you have, Colonel.

COLONEL. That's mighty thoughtful of you, Mister White, but I don't know if I could break the rules—even under them conditions.

MR. WHITE. [*His face twitching now; his shoulders trembling.*] Well, I'll leave them here, at any rate. [*He moves to the desk and sets the box down.*] Perhaps later . . .

[*He turns to go.* COLONEL *rushes to him and shakes his hand.*]

COLONEL. Mister White! I just want to say that I appreciate the gesture, sir. I appreciate the gesture.

MR. WHITE. Glad to do it, Colonel.

COLONEL. Mister White?

MR. WHITE. Yes, Colonel?

COLONEL. About that retirement business . . .

MR. WHITE. Colonel, I wish I could tell you, but you know Mister Cullamen has to make the final decision on that.

COLONEL. It's just that—maybe you could talk to him, first. I mean—well, you know him right well and—after all, I have been with the railroad forty-eight years now . . .

MR. WHITE. Two years past retirement age.

COLONEL. Past *voluntary* retirement.

MR. WHITE. And two months past compulsory.

COLONEL. I don't feel a day over fifty, Mister White. If you could just . . .

MR. WHITE. I'll talk to him, Colonel.

COLONEL. I sure would appreciate that, Mister White. I tell you, that sure would be a big help. I know it would.

[MR. WHITE *starts out. Then he turns back again.*]

MR. WHITE. Colonel, if I was you, I'd clean this place up some, before Cully comes down.

COLONEL. Yes, sir! That's just what I was thinking. [MR. WHITE *smiles, exits.*] Thank you again, Mister White. [*He disappears from view.*] I remember the day Whitey come to work for this railroad.

COLUMBUS. Yea, Colonel, so do I. He always was a good man.

COLONEL. Yeah. Had your job once, Eddie. That man's a worker, too.

EDDIE. I never thought I'd see the day he'd come in here and kid around like that.

COLONEL. What're you talking about: *kid around?*

EDDIE. Bringing that sausage biscuit in here.

COLONEL. You think that was kidding around? Boy, you got a lot to learn about people. Didn't you hear what he said? He wouldn't do something like that for just anybody. Why . . . [*He looks up suddenly.*] Wait a minute! Maybe Pickens put him up to it. Somebody had to tell him. [*Glaring at the multigraph machine, and* COLUMBUS.] COLUMBUS! [COLUMBUS *steps toward the desk.*] I'm not through with you two yet. I want to know how the hell Pickens found out, in the first place.

EDDIE. About the sausage biscuit?

COLONEL. Yes. How do you think that's gonna look if Cully hears about it?

EDDIE. Aw, she's known about it all along, Colonel.

COLONEL. What the hell are you talking about? I keep the things out of sight, in my desk drawer, don't I? Nobody's ever seen me so somebody had to tell her. Or else—yeah—she probably seen one of you dumb nuts bringing the stuff in here.

COLUMBUS. Everybody know, Colonel.

COLONEL. You're crazy!

COLUMBUS. Well, they mos' all does the same thing theirselves, so . . .

COLONEL. So that makes it all right for me! Oh, a fine sense of honor you have: want your friends traveling in the company of sneaks, people disloyal to the railroad's rules. You think they make those rules for nothing?

COLUMBUS. No, suh, Colonel, but . . .

COLONEL. You think I'd do it, if I wasn't so hungry I couldn't lift a hand to do my work? [*He lifts a wax-paper-wrapped package from the box and opens a drawer to his desk.*] Well, do you?

COLUMBUS. No, suh, Colonel.

COLONEL. A man's gotta eat a good breakfast to do a good day's work. Right? [*He takes the coffee cup from the box and sets it in the drawer. Then, looking out to see that no one is looking from the hall, he begins unwrapping the package.*] Now, some people up here just do it to try and get away with something, and that's something else again. [*He starts to take a bite of the biscuit, then stops.*] Pickens probably poisoned the thing before she give it to Whitey to bring in here. [*He takes a cautious bite, then begins eating with relish. He stops, looking up at* COLUMBUS.] Well, go on, Columbus, get on downstairs! I said I wanted two biscuits, didn't I? [COLUMBUS *starts toward the door.*] Wait a minute! You got more money'n you need there. You get me another coffee, and one of those little fried peach pies.

COLUMBUS. Yessuh.

[*He exits.*]

COLONEL. [*Sipping his coffee.*] I swear, the way everybody's carrying on around here today . . . There's something goin' on. Eddie?

EDDIE. Yeah, Colonel.

COLONEL. We got to toe the mark today—keep one step ahead of 'em. I want you to get that mail out fast, then get on back down here and give me a hand cleaning out this room. First thing you know, Cully'll be down here, and I want this place in perfect order when he comes. 'Cause you know damn well that Pickens is gonna be down there telling him about this . . . [*He points to the coffee cup.*] and anything else she can think of to make me look bad. I'm telling you, I wish to hell it was up to Whitey to decide. Then I wouldn't have nothing to worry about. But Cully's different. He didn't work his way up like most of 'em around here. He went to college, and all that mess. And when he come to work for the railroad, it was in the passenger department. He don't have any idea what we got to put up with in freight.

EDDIE. I swear if I was you, Colonel, I'd want to retire. I'd be damn glad to get outa this joint.

COLONEL. Well, you ain't me. The trouble with you is: you think this whole damn railroad's one big joke. Well, I'm gonna tell you something, Eddie. You come walking in this room here five days a week, but you don't stop to realize what's really going on in this room.

EDDIE. Nothing.

COLONEL. You kidding? See these orders? That's one week's orders. One week's, Eddie. And see this stack over here? That's supplies coming in. And here's tariffs. And rates. Billing, here. It all goes through this desk, right here, Eddie. You want to know something? All I gotta do is get up outa this chair and walk over to that door, right there, and shut it, and hold my foot against it so nobody could get in. You know what would happen then?

EDDIE. Sure. Whitey'd blow his stack.

COLONEL. That ain't the point. The point is, this railroad would come to a standstill. And not just here. All up and down the line. Eight thousand miles of track, without an engine running on it, or a freight car, or a passenger car. That's what would happen, Eddie.

EDDIE. That's a bunch of stuff.

COLONEL. Right here's the only multigraph machine! Mail for fourteen major departments is handled through this office. Every tariff, every rate change, every freight bill, every . . . [COLUMBUS enters with a cardboard carton.]

COLUMBUS. Didn't have no peach pie, Colonel, so I got you pineapple.

COLONEL. God Almighty, Columbus, you gotta tell the world?

COLUMBUS. I jes' say that . . .

COLONEL. All right! I heard you the first time. Now bring it over here away from the damn door where everybody can see you. [COLUMBUS brings the carton to the desk.] And you two telling me everybody knows! If everybody knows, that's how they know—right there! [He slips the carton to the desk drawer.] God! Before you two and Pickens get finished with me, I'll be washed up with this man's railroad for good. You just don't use your heads. All Cully's got to do is walk in here and— Come on, Columbus, get that multigraph running! The rest of the office's been at work an hour already. Eddie! Finish up that mail! [BILL DUDLEY walks in.] What do you want?

BILL. I just came in to say hello, Colonel.

COLONEL. Well, we ain't got time for that this morning. We're up to our ears in work here.

BILL. I wanted to show you something.

COLONEL. Later! COLUMBUS!

COLUMBUS. [At the machine.] We ain' got tariffs yet, Colonel.

COLONEL. Then run off yesterday's again. All Pickens wants to do is catch us loafing in here, and she'll run down to Cully . . .

BILL. [*Closer to the desk.*] Just take a peek at this, Colonel.

COLONEL. Bill, I ain't got time. I told you, once. [BILL *opens up the case and shows it to the* COLONEL.] Say—that's a beauty, Bill. [*He takes the case, and removes a fishing lure from it.*] Where'd you get that little thing, the shiny one there?—EDDIE!

EDDIE. All right, Colonel, I'm going.

[*He starts out the door with the mail basket.*]

COLONEL. And don't dawdle talking to the rate clerks.

EDDIE. Yeah, yeah.

COLONEL. Wait a minute, Eddie.

EDDIE. Well, what do you want?

COLONEL. Listen, when you go by Cully's office, you sneak a look in there and see if you can tell what kind of mood he's in. Hear?

EDDIE. Okay.

[*He exits.*]

BILL. [*Pointing to the lure.*] I swiped that piece there out of my wife's jewelry box.

COLONEL. Just a minute, Bill. COLUMBUS!

COLUMBUS. I's looking, Colonel.

COLONEL. Bill, you oughta catch some big ones with this.

BILL. It's for you, Colonel.

COLONEL. For me?

BILL. I made it for you, special.

COLONEL. Well, I'll be damned. [*He looks at it again. Then a thought occurs to him.*] Hey, wait a minute! What's this for?

BILL. Just a present, Colonel.

COLONEL. How come you bringin' it in here now?

BILL. It's your last day, Colonel.

COLONEL. Who says so? Pickens?

BILL. Everybody says so, Colonel.

COLONEL. Who? Whitey ain't said so. Cully ain't.

BILL. Well, maybe I heard wrong, Colonel.

COLONEL. You're damn right, you did! You think I'm just

gonna sit back and let Pickens and her crew push me outa my job?

BILL. It wasn't Pickens said it, Colonel.

COLONEL. She started it! She don't fool me for a minute. All the years of service I put in with this man's railroad, and now, because she thinks it's my last day . . . You know what that damn woman done this morning?

BILL. You mean about the coffee and biscuit?

COLONEL. You mean she's told everybody, *already?* By God, I'll . . . [*He rises, in rage.*] Now that's—hear that, Columbus? Didn't I tell you? Didn't I say she was trying to ruin my reputation with everybody up here? By God, I'll show her! I'll go right down to Cully right this minute and tell him just what the hell she's up to.

[*He starts toward the door.*]

BILL. Listen, Colonel, I wouldn't go rampaging down to Cully about that. You're liable to put your foot in it. Suppose he doesn't know. Pickens is an old fool, but I don't think she really means any harm. And I don't think she'd go down and . . .

COLONEL. Don't try and tell me what she'd do! I know her too damn well.

BILL. I'm telling you, Cully probably doesn't know anything about it.

COLONEL. Yeah?

BILL. Your best bet is to keep quiet about the whole thing. I learned a long time ago with this railroad: the less said, the less people find out, and the less people find out, the less trouble with the man at the top.

COLONEL. [*Starting back to his chair, sitting.*] Yeah, but too much's been said already. Hell! You don't know what Pickens is liable to do. And you know Cully ain't gonna keep me on the job if he hears all that crap about coming in late and eating in the office. Bill, I got too many years with this railroad to stand by and see it all wrecked in just one day.

[*He unconsciously reaches for a biscuit, which he unwraps and starts to munch on.*]

BILL. Well, if you get the room cleaned up, everything looking real nice in here, and talk nice to Cully . . . Colonel, you better keep that biscuit out of sight.

COLONEL. [*Slipping the biscuit back into the drawer.*] God, things is got me so I don't know whether I'm coming or going. Bill, I gotta think of something. I gotta think of something quick.

BLACKOUT

SCENE 2

It is later that afternoon. The lights rise on the same scene. The clock reads 4:50 P.M. Otherwise the room remains unchanged. COLUMBUS *is stacking tariffs which he has run off the multigraph.* EDDIE *is having a drink at the water cooler.* COLONEL *sips a milk shake out of a large paper cup.*

EDDIE. Hey, Colonel, it's ten minutes of five.

COLONEL. I know what time it is.

COLUMBUS. Colonel, ain' we gonna clean your corner?

COLONEL. Soon as I finish this milk shake. God! Four-thirty around here and I get so damned hungry and thirsty I can't even move.

EDDIE. You reckon Cully's coming, Colonel?

COLONEL. [*Snappishly.*] Yes, I reckon Cully's coming. Whitey said he was coming. He'll be here.

COLUMBUS. Colonel, it's ten minutes o' five. We don' get that desk cleaned up now we ain' gonna . . .

COLONEL. All right! All right! If you'd be quiet half a minute, I could think of what to do. But I can't think of nothing with you butting in on my thoughts every two minutes.

COLUMBUS. I jes' thinkin' 'bout you, Colonel.

COLONEL. I'm gonna straighten out this desk—right now. Grab yourselves some dust rags and come on over here. [*They start looking for rags.* COLONEL *finishes his milk shake with a sigh of pleasure.*] That was good. I could drink me three or four of them shakes. Eddie!

EDDIE. Yeah, Colonel?

COLONEL. Maybe you oughta run down the hall again and see what kind of mood Cully's in now.

EDDIE. God, Colonel, I been down the hall twenty times already. All he's done since lunch is sit there scratching on that old yellow pad of paper.

COLONEL. Hhm! That don't tell us too much, but it might be an encouraging sign. [*He lifts the cup again, draining the last drop. Then wearily, he puts it down carefully on his desk.* EDDIE *resumes his search for a rag, which he finds. He and* COLUMBUS *come over and start dusting the desk.* COLONEL *stands and begins lifting old coffee cups, looking sadly at each one, then throwing it into the waste basket. He picks up the pile of lunch bags.*] Columbus, you want these lunch bags? They're good as new. [MAG PICKENS *enters. She looks at the activity, and laughs.*] Well, what are you looking at, you giggling idiot?

MAG. You just starting to clean up?

COLONEL. I been waiting for you, Pickens. I thought you was gonna clean it up for me. Ain't you gonna polish my desk spick and span?

MAG. Mister Cullamen's on his way down here right now.

COLONEL. You better not let him catch you loafing in here. You're liable to get yourself fired. [*He roars with laughter.*]

MAG. Colonel, I'm not kidding. He's on his way . . .

COLONEL. It ain't worrying you, is it?

MAG. It's not my little red wagon.

COLONEL. You damn right: it ain't. Pickens, you don't fool me for one minute. I know what's bothering you. That scheming brain of yours is figuring like crazy to know what I'm gonna do. Maybe I got a secret plan, Pickens. And you can't figure it out. This time I'm one up on you, Pickens. I got aces up my sleeve you ain't even dreamed of.

MAG. You're just an old silly, Colonel. Nobody's scheming anything, unless it's you.

COLONEL. You'd like to know what it is, wouldn't you?

MAG. Oh, you haven't got any plan. [*She giggles happily, and rushes out of the room.*]

COLONEL. Oh, no? Go on, laugh! We'll see who has the last

laugh, though. Columbus, I bet I just added twenty years to old pig-butt's life. She'll give herself an ulcer, trying to figure out what I'm gonna do.

[*He chuckles with satisfaction.*]

COLUMBUS. What you gonna do, Colonel?

COLONEL. [*Sobering.*] I got to figure something out quick. I swear, an idea keeps coming right up to where I think I got it, then just when I think I got it, I can't figure out what it is. Don't just stand there starin'. Let's get this mess up outa here. [EDDIE *and* COLUMBUS *start to move a stack of papers from the filing cabinet. Under them is an old newspaper, which* COLONEL *picks up and opens. He chuckles, turning the paper around so* COLUMBUS *and* EDDIE *can read the headlines:* ARMISTICE DECLARED IN EUROPE, KAISER'S TROOPS SURRENDER.] I knew I'd saved that thing. Been looking for it for a couple of years.

EDDIE. God, Colonel. That's World War I.

COLONEL. And this paper here come out just two days after I was promoted to this job. Right, Columbus?

COLUMBUS. I don' know, Colonel, you 'member better'n I does.

[MR. WHITE *appears in the doorway.*]

MR. WHITE. Good Lord! Are you just starting?

COLONEL. Doin' a little spring cleanin', Mister White.

MR. WHITE. You should've done that this morning, Colonel. Cullamen's on his way down here right now.

COLONEL. Oh, God, I thought Pickens was . . . Well, hold him off just a minute, will you? We been up to our ears in work all day and just ain't had a chance to . . . [MR. WHITE *ducks back out again as* COLUMBUS *and* EDDIE *move furiously.* COLONEL *gives them confusing directions with flailing arms. They don't even start on the desk.*] Over there! No, over there, Columbus! Here, Eddie, get this stack here . . . Dust the top. DUST THE TOP!

COLUMBUS. Ain' no more room, Colonel!

COLONEL. Shove some of it under Eddie's table over there! Come on! I swear, the way they sneak up on you around here— not a bit of warning.

EDDIE. What about that junk on the window sill, Colonel? And your desk?

COLONEL. Never mind that now! Just finish up the top of them cabinets. And don't mix everything up, either. I gotta be able to find things Monday.

[MR. CULLAMEN *appears in the doorway. He is a fairly short man in his fifties, rather stout, with a kindly face. He looks at the confusion, and smiles.* COLONEL *is still waving the paper.* MR. CULLAMEN *notes the headlines, and walks in.*]

MR. CULLAMEN. Colonel, that's a collector's item.

COLONEL. [*Looking up and seeing him.*] Mister Cullamen— I—come right in, sir. We're just cleaning up a few things. I— Eddie, why don't you go pick up the mail?

EDDIE. All right, Colonel. [*He starts out and, on passing* MR. CULLAMEN, *nods respectfully.*] Afternoon, Mister Cullamen.

MR. CULLAMEN. Eddie . . .

COLONEL. Columbus, check with Mister White on that form he wanted run off.

COLUMBUS. Yes, suh, Colonel. [COLUMBUS *starts out.*] Afternoon, Mister Cullamen.

MR. CULLAMEN. Columbus . . .

COLONEL. Excuse me, Mister Cullamen, but I had to get the boys working. No matter what else happens on this floor, this department here keeps at it. That's the way I've run it, Mister Cullamen, for forty-eight years now, and that's the way I'll always run it.

MR. CULLAMEN. [*Turns away, coughing.*] Well . . . [*He goes over to the desk; picks up the paper.*] Say, where on earth did you get this?

COLONEL. Oh, I've been saving that, Mister Cullamen. Yes, sir. I was promoted to this job two days before that paper come out, so it means right much to me.

MR. CULLAMEN. It certainly should. [*He looks at the paper, and chuckles.*] Well, it just goes to show you how time passes.

COLONEL. Yes, sir, Mister Cullamen. Now, Mister Cullamen . . .

MR. CULLAMEN. You know, Colonel, I was just seventeen

years old when this paper came out. Nineteen eighteen. Tch! Started with the passenger department in . . .

COLONEL. Nineteen twenty-four.

MR. CULLAMEN. You remember that? Colonel, you're amazing.

[*He puts down the paper.*]

COLONEL. It's nothing, really. You gotta be able to remember a lot of things on this job. Wouldn't you like to have a seat, Mister Cullamen?

MR. CULLAMEN. No, thanks, Colonel. You go on sit down, though.

COLONEL. [*Proudly.*] Sitting gets on my nerves, Mister Cullamen. I'm a standing man, myself. I always have said that what this railroad needed was some good old stand-up desks.

MR. CULLAMEN. Not for me, thanks. Now, Colonel— We had our last little chat about two months ago.

COLONEL. Yes, sir, Mister Cullamen.

MR. CULLAMEN. And, at that time, you asked for two months more of service in order to get things in your department under more control, before relinquishing your job to your successor.

COLONEL. Yes, sir, Mister Cullamen.

MR. CULLAMEN. And at the same time we discussed the possibility of a full year's extension.

COLONEL. That's right, Mister Cullamen. You see, this department here's not exactly one of the easiest departments to run. More papers, more orders go through this department here than . . .

MR. CULLAMEN. Yes, Colonel. However, as I told you before, my decision would be based upon two things.

COLONEL. Mister Cullamen, I'd just like to . . .

MR. CULLAMEN. Two things, Colonel: first your efforts to shape up the department which, you admitted at the time, has become a little—uhh—disorderly.

COLONEL. Well, that's just the point, Mister Cullamen.

MR. CULLAMEN. The other thing was the union. You know how strict they are about retirement. As a matter of fact, I was taking a small risk in giving you a two months' extension.

COLONEL. You see, Mister Cullamen, when I said it'd take two months, I didn't have any idea how many back orders and everything we had piled up on us. You can just ask Columbus and he'll tell you he's been running tariffs off at the rate of five to ten thousand copies a day. And Eddie— Well, just the other morning Pickens give him fifteen sheets to mimeograph for the big office. So you can see . . .

MR. CULLAMEN. Colonel, we made a bargain. And as I just said, I was risking trouble with the union because of it.

COLONEL. Oh, don't think I don't appreciate that, Mister Cullamen. But I was just trying to show you how . . .

MR. CULLAMEN. Colonel, now you wait just a minute. I want to ask you a question.

COLONEL. Yes, sir, Mister Cullamen. You just go right ahead and . . .

MR. CULLAMEN. [*Looking around the room, which isn't any neater than it was before their efforts.*] Can you honestly say, Colonel, that you have taken advantage of those two months?

COLONEL. Oh, yes, sir, Mister Cullamen, without any question.

MR. CULLAMEN. Everything is in order here?

COLONEL. Well—well—now not exactly. Like I said before, my boys 's overworked. Just keeping in step half kills 'em. Now catching up, that's something else. But we've been working at it, Mister Cullamen. Why, when you come in, just now, you saw how . . .

MR. CULLAMEN. What about the inventory you promised me? Have you done that?

COLONEL. I'm glad you brought that up. Just yesterday I was counting packs of stencils. Day before that, pencil sharpeners.

MR. CULLAMEN. Pencil sharpeners? A whole day? How many were there?

COLONEL. Now that's the strangest part of it, Mister Cullamen. Did you know we got thirty-two pencil sharpeners in that case up there?

MR. CULLAMEN. And all you inventoried in one day was thirty-two pencil sharpeners?

COLONEL. Oh, no, Mister Cullamen. I done my regular duties, too. That's why it's taking longer'n I expected it to. You see, we gotta squeeze the extras in between the regulars, and that's a job in itself, just figuring out how to do it.

MR. CULLAMEN. Colonel, I think I try to understand these things, to be sympathetic. But I simply cannot understand it when a man gives me his word and then makes no effort to keep that word.

COLONEL. Now that ain't fair, Mister Cullamen! I been working my head off. But I can't bleed my boys. Columbus ain't no spring chicken. And Eddie— Well, Eddie's even getting bags under his eyes from so much work. It ain't myself I been thinking about, Mister Cullamen. I can stay here half the night if I have to, but . . .

MR. CULLAMEN. Well, maybe you have made an effort.

COLONEL. Oh, yes, sir, Mister Cullamen. I wouldn't try to . . .

MR. CULLAMEN. But Colonel— Well, frankly, it's out of my hands now anyway. Even if I felt I could grant you an extension, the union . . .

[*He reaches into his coat pocket and takes out an envelope.*]

COLONEL. Well, if that's all's worrying you, Mister Cullamen, I know the boys up at the union hall and . . . [MR. CULLAMEN *hands the letter to* COLONEL.] What's this?

MR. CULLAMEN. Their decision, Colonel.

COLONEL. [*Starting to open it.*] But, what . . . ?

MR. CULLAMEN. It's "No," Colonel.

COLONEL. You can't let 'em do that, Mister Cullamen. It ain't fair! I mean— Well, who's running this man's railroad, anyway? You know more about what's needed up here than that bunch of bus drivers at the union hall. Half of 'em never even been on a train.

MR. CULLAMEN. Colonel, it's not just the union. It's the company, too. You're sixty-seven years old.

COLONEL. You can't go on that! I don't feel a day over fifty, Mister Cullamen. I swear to God, just last night I ate me a whole fried chicken and two baskets of french fries, and six biscuits, two glasses of iced tea, and a slice of blueberry pie the size . . .

MR. CULLAMEN. Colonel, I . . .

COLONEL. The size of my fist. I'm in the pink.

MR. CULLAMEN. I don't doubt that, Colonel. But the fact is you've reached the age of compulsory retirement.

COLONEL. Don't all I've done for this man's railroad count for nothing?

MR. CULLAMEN. Certainly it does. That's precisely the reason for retiring you. The railroad owes you these years.

COLONEL. Then I ought to be able to do what I want to with 'em. If I want to stay on the job, then . . .

MR. CULLAMEN. Colonel, I can't.

COLONEL. It just ain't right. It just ain't right to take a man and throw him out and— Wait a minute! Mister Cullamen, I'll tell you why you can't do it.

MR. CULLAMEN. Colonel, you'll have to hurry. There's a little presentation planned in just a few minutes, and I've got to . . .

COLONEL. Just a minute, Mister Cullamen, you gotta hear this. You started in the passenger department, right?

MR. CULLAMEN. Yes, but . . .

COLONEL. And in the passenger department, if you miss a day's work, you got to make up a day's work. Right?

MR. CULLAMEN. Yes, Colonel. But I don't see what that has to do with . . .

COLONEL. Mister Cullamen, there's something I got to tell you. I didn't say this last time, Mister Cullamen, because—I—because this ain't the kind of thing a man likes to come out and say about himself—because it ain't easy for a man to admit to himself— Well, anyway, Mister Cullamen, I started seeing the truth today about a lot of things.

MR. CULLAMEN. Yes, Colonel?

COLONEL. Maybe some people's already told you about it. Well, that don't make no difference either, because I'm gonna say it myself.

MR. CULLAMEN. What are you talking about, Colonel?

COLONEL. It's just that— This ain't easy for me to say,

Mister Cullamen. Well, the truth is I've broke a lot of the railroad's rules, right here in this office: drinking milk shakes, eating on the job, in other words—sausage biscuits and coffee, and those little doughnuts they got downstairs with the white icing on the top. [*He sighs.*] And coming in late. Almost every day, if you want to know the truth.

MR. CULLAMEN. I appreciate your telling me that, Colonel. But I wouldn't feel too badly, if I were you. Everybody up here has . . .

COLONEL. The point is, Mister Cullamen, that all that time adds up to time missed from work. The way I figure it, Mister Cullamen, I owe the railroad another year at least. It's the least I can do.

MR. CULLAMEN. But Colonel, I . . .

COLONEL. I just couldn't walk out of here, knowing I'd cheated the railroad out of all that time, Mister Cullamen. I just couldn't . . .

MR. CULLAMEN. Isn't that sort of like putting the cow-catcher on the caboose? It's too late for that now, Colonel.

COLONEL. No, it ain't, Mister Cullamen. A man's gotta pay for what he done wrong.

MR. CULLAMEN. [*Smiling.*] I guess you've done enough for the railroad so that the company can afford to forgive a few slip-ups. For the record, Colonel, you're in the clear.

COLONEL. But Mister Cullamen, I got to make up that time.

MR. CULLAMEN. [*Patting him on the shoulder.*] You go on and get into your coat now and get ready for the presentation. Everybody's looking forward to it, Colonel. I'll be right back for you as soon as I pick up—the watch.

[*He starts toward the door.* COLONEL *follows him.*]

COLONEL. Just a minute, Mister Cullamen. You got to let me explain this thing now. The way I see it— Well, even in a couple of weeks I could— Just to get the room here cleaned up good so I could at least say I . . .

[MR. CULLAMEN *stops in the doorway. He turns back.*]

MR. CULLAMEN. I'm sorry, Colonel. If there were any way to do it . . . but there isn't.

[*He exits.* COLONEL *stares after him. A second later,* EDDIE *comes in with a basket of mail.*]

EDDIE. What'd he say, Colonel?

COLONEL. You pick up the mail?

EDDIE. Yeah. What'd he say?

[COLONEL *starts back toward his desk.*]

COLONEL. Cow-catcher on the caboose! Whoever heard of . . . ? What's he know about a train? [*He plops down into his chair.* COLUMBUS *enters. He just looks at* COLONEL *and doesn't have to ask anything. He motions* EDDIE *toward the mail table.*] Well, let him try to run the place any better, if he thinks he can. Let him try keeping it clean and— Ha! Let him try keeping this place running with not enough help and not enough time. He knows so much about railroads. Let him try it!

COLUMBUS. Colonel, how 'bout I run downstairs an' get you a large limeade?

COLONEL. *"Put your coat on for the presentation."* Gonna give me a watch, I guess, like they always do. What's he think I am? A big soggy piece of crappy cake that they can smother with icing and top off with a candle, so everybody can get to stand around and sing and laugh and say "It ended well"? 'S that what he thinks I am?

COLUMBUS. Now, Colonel, you ain' gonna go frettin' way all the good times jes' 'cause . . .

COLONEL. Good times! This here's the end of the line and I got nothing to show for it.

COLUMBUS. How 'bout a nice ham on rye, with mustard, Colonel?

COLONEL. That all you can think about? Food? I put forty-eight years of my life into this place. That's a lot of time for a man to give—to anything. Now I gotta go home, for the few years that's left me, and have nothing to think about but how everybody up here thinks I've wasted all them years.

COLUMBUS. Nobody think that, Colonel.

COLONEL. The hell they don't! Cully, Whitey, all of you— Think I'm a big, fat joke, just somebody for Pickens to stand around and laugh at.

EDDIE. Aw, Colonel . . .

COLONEL. Here I thought I had friends up here in this office. And every one of you, every last one of you was in on it.

COLUMBUS. Colonel, that ain't true.

COLONEL. Don't tell me you two ain't played right into her hands! Standin' around tellin' me Whitey knows this, and Cully knows that! I bet you been runnin' around tellin' everybody up here what I . . . [*He stands up.*] *Cow-catcher on the caboose!* You think I don't get nothing done. Well, by God, I'll show you bunch of know-it-alls what work really looks like. I'll get this place straightened up if it's the last thing I do. [*He grabs a stack of files from his desk, but this causes another stack to give way, and stack after stack of papers crashes down off the desk on to the floor.*] Damn! I swear . . . [*He tries again, causing the remaining piles of paper to crash to the floor. Angrily, he drops the stack in his arms.*] Aw, God, what's the use? [*He plops back into his chair.*] When stuff's been piling up as long as this has, the only thing to do is let it set. [*He stares down at the floor. Then he notices something lying in the mess, and straining, bends over to pick it up. It is a small wooden pass which he looks at, smiling.*] Hey, Columbus! You know what this is? [*He holds it up.*]

COLUMBUS. No, Colonel.

COLONEL. Aw, sure you do. Remember back in 'twenty-six when we used to have a pass?

COLUMBUS. [*Moving in for a closer look.*] Oh, yeah. What are you doing with that, Colonel?

COLONEL. That was when old crap-head Johnson was office manager. [*He hands the pass to* COLUMBUS. COLONEL *notices something else, and picks it up. It is a popsicle wrapper.*] Ha! I was trying to save enough of these here popsicle wrappers to get myself a fishing rod. You had to have seven hundred and fifty. And if you look in one of the file cabinet drawers around here, somewheres, you'll find six hundred and twenty-two wrappers. That's how many I got before the offer run out.

COLUMBUS. Colonel, how 'bout we lend you a hand straightening up?

COLONEL. [*Reminded, looking around.*] I don't want no help! I said I'd do it and by God . . .

EDDIE. [*Wading into the mess.*] We don't mind, Colonel.

COLONEL. Well, when stuff gets piled this high— No! Eddie, I want this railroad to remember my name—with respect. And I got to do this . . .

[MR. CULLAMEN *and* MR. WHITE *appear in the doorway.*]

MR. WHITE. [*Laughing.*] Colonel, what on earth happened in here?

COLONEL. Pile slipped on me! But I'm gonna get this room cleaned up if I got to stay all weekend.

MR. CULLAMEN. You'll have to take a minute off, Colonel. It's time to . . .

COLONEL. Mister Cullamen, I just wish that . . .

[*He sighs and reaches for his coat from the hanger. As he takes it, the ear-muff cap falls to the floor.* COLONEL *bends down and picks it up, as the bell, outside, rings, and the sounds in the big office offstage die out.*]

CULLAMEN. That's it, Colonel. Come on. Everybody'll be waiting.

COLONEL. [*Hanging up his cap.*] Wore this old hat in 'thirty-three. Worse winter we ever had. [*He starts to put on his coat.* EDDIE *helps him.*] That was before Sid opened up the luncheonette on the first floor, and you had to go across the street, through the snow, to eat. But that place over there made the best durn barbecued spare ribs you've ever put in your mouth. [*He sighs, then starts slowly, sadly, toward the door.*] Well, when you come in here Monday morning, you won't know this office.

[*They lead him out of the room.*]

COLUMBUS. Eddie, how 'bout we kinda clean things up for Colonel? Goin' 'way present!

EDDIE. Sure, Columbus. It's the only way it'll ever get done. [*They move toward the piles of paper on the floor. From the distance comes a loud burst of applause and wild shouts of "Colonel Dick Borden." "Hooray! Hooray! Hooray!"* COLUMBUS *looks toward the door.* EDDIE *shakes his head sadly. Then he notices a book lying in the mess. He picks it up and opens it.*] Hey, Columbus! Look at this.

COLUMBUS. What is it, Eddie?

EDDIE. [*Reading from the book.*] "Dick Borden, Rate-Tariff School, Seaboard Airline Railroad, 1917."

COLUMBUS. [*Taking the book.*] I never know Colonel gone to Rate School, studyin' an' all.

EDDIE. Yeah. How about that? I didn't think he'd ever do anything he didn't have to. [*He laughs.*] Can't you just see it? He probably had big plans when he started here. He probably pictured himself riding around the whole country in a private car, a vice-president, or something.

COLUMBUS. Yeah. [*He puts the book down and begins to pick up the files.*] You gonna help, or you gonna stand there laughin'? [EDDIE, *still chuckling, joins in the work.*] Yeah, Eddie, old Colonel had him some plans— Always did, that man!

CURTAIN

THE TINY CLOSET

By

William Inge

(Published here for the first time)

CAST

The Tiny Closet was originally produced at Pennsylvania State University as one of a bill of five short Inge plays in the Mateer Playhouse, July 28 to August 2, 1958, with the following cast:

Mr. Newbold .... Laurence Kabat
Mrs. Crosby .... Charlotte Jones
Mrs. Hergesheimer .... Jo Laing

Director .... Max Fischer
Managing Director .... Warren S. Smith
Stage Manager .... Delmar Hendrick
Production Manager .... Russ Whaley
Technical Directors .... William B. DeLaney
Cameron Iseman

Time: The present.

Place: A boarding house in a Midwestern city.

THE TINY CLOSET

The scene is laid in a boarding-rooming house somewhere in a Midwestern city. On stage we see the big living room of the house, which is Victorian in design, with ornate woodwork and high ceiling. The furnishings, too, are Victorian. An ornate wooden stairway is at the right. The outside entrance is down right. When the curtain is up, MR. NEWBOLD *is seen coming down the stairs. He is a man of about fifty, a large man and rather nice looking. He is always impeccably dressed in the most conservative clothes, a dark blue suit, white shirt, modest tie, a high shine on his black shoes, and his thinning hair carefully combed. He is the sort of man who takes great pride in his grooming. Something now seems to be bothering him. When he gets to the bottom of the stairs, he stops a moment and thinks. Then he calls his landlady.*

MR. NEWBOLD. Mrs. Crosby! [*No response.*] Mrs. Crosby!

MRS. CROSBY. [*Coming from the kitchen.*] Yes, Mr. Newbold. I was just straightening up after breakfast. I'm afraid none of the guests like the new bacon I got. It's just as expensive as the other bacon I was serving. On my word it is. Every bit. I didn't buy it to bring down expenses. Not at all. It's *fine* bacon. Hickory smoked. Only it's the kind you slice yourself. That's why I got it. You can cut yourself a good thick slice of bacon that you can really get your teeth into, instead of that other stuff that shrivels up like tissue paper . . .

[*She is the sort of woman who continues talking until someone stops her.*]

MR. NEWBOLD. Mrs. Crosby . . .

MRS. CROSBY. Yes, Mr. Newbold?

MR. NEWBOLD. Mrs. Crosby, you remember, before I moved in, I specified that no one was to enter my closet . . .

MRS. CROSBY. Indeed I remember, Mr. Newbold. And I told you, you could have your own lock on the closet, like you asked me. No one around here has any keys to your closet but *you*, Mr. Newbold.

MR. NEWBOLD. Nevertheless, Mrs. Crosby . . .

MRS. CROSBY. And I told the colored woman, "Elsie, you're not to enter Mr. Newbold's closet. Mr. Newbold," I told her, "is a perfectly orderly gentleman who is perfectly capable of keeping his own closet, and you're not to bother it." I gave her strict orders, Mr. Newbold.

MR. NEWBOLD. Nevertheless, Mrs. Crosby . . .

MRS. CROSBY. And as for me, goodness, I never go near the rooms. I got enough on my hands downstairs without bothering about the upstairs. I leave all that to Elsie. I don't suppose I been upstairs now in almost . . .

MR. NEWBOLD. Mrs. Crosby, a closet is a very small space. That's all I ask in this life. That's all I ask, is just that tiny closet to call my own, my very own.

MRS. CROSBY. I quite understand, Mr. Newbold. We all have to have some place that's private to us, where we don't invite the world to see. I quite understand.

MR. NEWBOLD. But someone has been monkeying with the lock on the door, Mrs. Crosby.

MRS. CROSBY. [*Shocked.*] You don't say!

MR. NEWBOLD. I *do* say, Mrs. Crosby. Someone has been monkeying with that expensive Yale lock I had put on the door.

MRS. CROSBY. Do you suppose someone coulda got up there when no one was around and . . .

MR. NEWBOLD. I'm sure I don't know, but I won't stand for anyone's monkeying with that lock, Mrs. Crosby. That room, while I rent it, is my private property, and I gave strict instructions that no one was to go near the closet, and I expect my orders to be respected.

MRS. CROSBY. Of course, Mr. Newbold; you're my favorite of all the roomers. Oh, I wish they was all like you. You keep your room spotless and you're always so correct around the house. My, you're a model guest. You really are. You should open up a class out here at that night school they have for adults and teach 'em how to behave in their rooming houses. The landladies in this town would get together and thank you.

MR. NEWBOLD. Thank you, Mrs. Crosby. Nevertheless, I must repeat that that closet is my personal property. There is nothing inside I am ashamed of. It's not that. It's only that I have *some* place, just some little place, that's completely private, that no one has access to. That's all I ask, Mrs. Crosby.

MRS. CROSBY. And I quite understand, Mr. Newbold.

MR. NEWBOLD. Very well. As long as that is clearly understood, I hope I'll not have to bring the subject up again, Mrs. Crosby.

MRS. CROSBY. I'll tell Elsie again, Mr. Newbold. I'll give special emphasis that no one is to go near that closet.

MR. NEWBOLD. Thank you, Mrs. Crosby. [*Looks at his watch.*] Goodness! I mustn't dally another minute.

MRS. CROSBY. Did you see Mrs. Hergesheimer in your store yesterday, Mr. Newbold?

MR. NEWBOLD. Mrs. Hergesheimer? Oh, yes, I believe I did.

MRS. CROSBY. She called me yesterday and told me she seen you. "Whata fine man that Mr. Newbold is!" she says. "You're a lucky woman, Mrs. Crosby, to have such a fine guest. All I got in my house is a lotta old-maid schoolteachers, and I'm always cleanin' up after 'em." That's what she says. "Oh, men are much tidier than women," I told her. I kept schoolteachers once and they was always in the bathroom, curling their hair in there or giving themselves shampoos, or shaving their legs on my nice bedspreads. *Mr.* Crosby was alive then, and it almost drove him crazy. He never could get to the bathroom when he wanted to, because of them schoolteachers.

MR. NEWBOLD. Good day, Mrs. Crosby.
[*He puts on his hat and goes out the door.*]

MRS. CROSBY. Good day, Mr. Newbold! [*Calling to him outside the door.*] You be here for dinner tonight, won't you?

MR. NEWBOLD. [*Off.*] I intend to be.

MRS. CROSBY. [*Closing the door.*] Good day, Mr. Newbold. [*Now she comes back inside the room. Curiosity is about to kill her. She is childishly excited. She goes back to the door and peers out to make sure that* MR. NEWBOLD *is on his way. Then she comes back inside the room and goes to the telephone, dialing her number.*] Mrs. Hergesheimer? Have you got a minute?

He's just left. "You're not to go into my room," he says to me again, for the two-hundredth time. "Someone's been playing with the lock on my door and you're not to go near that closet," he says, like it was his house and he was ordering me about. Can you beat it? Now what do you suppose he's got hid away in that closet? [*She listens a while.*] No, I can't think he'd be a Communist, Mrs. Hergesheimer. Of course, he *might* be. You never can tell. But I don't think that's it, somehow. [*She listens again.*] Love letters? But why would he need a whole closet for his love letters?— If he's got any. Besides, I don't think he's the type of man that has love letters. [*She listens.*] It's certainly a mystery. I confess, it's certainly a mystery. What would *you* do, Mrs. Hergesheimer? [*A pause.*] You would? Well, hurry over, why don't you, and we'll try again. Hurry! [*She hangs up, then calls out to the kitchen.*] Elsie, you're not to go upstairs for a while. Mrs. Hergesheimer is comin' over and she and I have some things we wanta do up there, so you're to keep busy with the washin'. Understand?

ELSIE. [*Off.*] Yes, Mrs. Crosby.

[*Now* MRS. CROSBY *spends a few minutes of nervous activity. Her conscience bothers her some, but primarily she is afraid of being caught. She looks out the door again, then out of each window, then calls out to the kitchen again.*]

MRS. CROSBY. Remember, Elsie, you're not to bother me for a while. I'll let you know when I want you, Elsie. You're to stay out there till I call you.

[*Now* MRS. HERGESHEIMER *hurries into the house.*]

MRS. HERGESHEIMER. I think you've got every *right,* Mrs. Crosby. Every right.

MRS. CROSBY. That's what I've been telling myself, Mrs. Hergesheimer. I've got every right. For all I know, I may be harboring a *spy,* or a criminal, or a lunatic. What's he got in that closet that he don't want anyone to see? Can you tell me? It must be something he's ashamed of, or he wouldn't mind if anyone saw. Isn't that what you say? And if it's something he's ashamed of, I think we should find out what it is. You can't tell: he might have a bomb in there he meant to destroy us with. I'm not gonna set idly by while someone is plotting something, Mrs. Hergesheimer. I pride myself, I'm a real American, and I say if anyone's got any secrets he wants to keep hid, let 'm come out into the open and declare himself. Mr. Newbold has always seemed like a fine man, and I got nothin' against him personally, and he's the best roomer I ever had; keeps his room spotless. Elsie don't have to do anything but make the bed. And I appreciate that, but if you ask me, it's kinda unnatural for a man to be so tidy. Isn't that what you say? There's been something suspicious about him from the very first.

MRS. HERGESHEIMER. I made a point of talking to him when I was shopping in Baumgarden's yesterday. My, he struts around that floor. You'd think he was president instead of a floorwalker. I asked him where they kept the artificial flowers. I knew, but I just wanted to see if he'd recognize me. He smiled and made a lordly gesture with his hand, showin' me the way. You'd have thought he was the king of Persia, with all his fine manners.

MRS. CROSBY. He belongs to the Lions' Club. Do you think he'd be a Communist and still belong to the Lions' Club?

MRS. HERGESHEIMER. You can't tell. Lots of them join clubs like that just as a cover-up. That schoolteacher I got: she's a Red and I know it. Brings home all kinds of books to read. Yes. Dangerous books. But she goes to church every Sunday morning, just as big as you please, just to pretend she's *not* a Red.

MRS. CROSBY. Forevermore!

MRS. HERGESHEIMER. I think you've got every right to go into that closet, Mrs. Crosby.

MRS. CROSBY. Yes, I think so, too. Well— Well, you come with me!

MRS. HERGESHEIMER. Oh, Mrs. Crosby, honey, I don't think it's right for me to do it. I'll stay down here and see that Elsie doesn't bother you.

MRS. CROSBY. I'm not going to do it, if you don't come with me.

MRS. HERGESHEIMER. Well . . .

MRS. CROSBY. After all, you've been just as curious about this as I've been, and I think you owe it to me to come along.

MRS. HERGESHEIMER. Well, if that's the way you feel about it, Mrs. Crosby, I'll come along. After all, it's not as though we were doing anything criminal.

MRS. CROSBY. Indeed it's not. Come on then.

[*She starts toward the stairs, taking a final look toward the kitchen to make sure that* ELSIE *is occupied.*]

MRS. HERGESHEIMER. [*Following with some trepidation.*] Oh dear, I hope he doesn't find out.

MRS. CROSBY. We can get that lock off this time without making any more scratches than we made yesterday. He won't notice.

MRS. HERGESHEIMER. Oh, I bet he does. He's got a sharp eye.

MRS. CROSBY. Well, I don't care if he does. I've got a right to see what's in that closet.

MRS. HERGESHEIMER. Yes. Well—go on, Mrs. Crosby. I'm right behind you.

[*Slowly, cautiously, the two women go up the stairs together. The stage is empty for a few moments, then* ELSIE *comes in from the kitchen, looks up the stairs with curiosity. Then, as though the behavior of the two women was too much for her to understand, she shrugs her shoulders, laughs gently, and returns to the kitchen. The stage is empty again for a few moments. Then, slowly, the front door opens and* MR. NEWBOLD *returns inside the house. He has suspected the two women to do exactly what they're doing. He is very nervous. His heart is pounding. He starts up the stairs and then comes down again. He can't seem to get the courage to confront the women. The starch he showed earlier in the play has dissolved. He is perspiring heavily and twisting his hands in fear and excitement. In a few moments we hear the women on their way downstairs.* MR. NEWBOLD *hurriedly finds a closet to hide in. The women come down the stairs slowly, holding an awed silence.* MRS. CROSBY *carries a woman's hat, a large hat, the kind a graceful lady might wear to a garden party. It is quite a lovely hat, in a light pastel color with great flowers in its limber brim, and sleek satin ribbons. They come center together,* MRS. CROSBY *holding the hat, both of them studying it with bafflement.*]

MRS. CROSBY. Hats! Dozens of hats! I can't believe it.

MRS. HERGESHEIMER. He must have brought them home from the store, don't you think?

MRS. CROSBY. But there was all that sewing equipment on a shelf.

MRS. HERGESHEIMER. But no man could make hats as lovely as these.

MRS. CROSBY. I don't know. There's something kinda unusual about Mr. Newbold. I think he might have made them. I—I know he did. [*She suddenly recalls a clue.*] I remember now how he was always looking through the fashion magazines. Sometimes he'd take them up to his room. He'd *study* them. I always wondered why.

MRS. HERGESHEIMER. But why would he stay up in his room making hats—and then keep them locked in his closet?

MRS. CROSBY. He—he's just peculiar. That's all. He's just peculiar. I thought so, the first time I saw the man. He's too prim for a man. He's too tidy, the way he keeps his room. It's just not natural.

MRS. HERGESHEIMER. Oh, I wish now we hadn't looked.

MRS. CROSBY. I had a perfect right.

MRS. HERGESHEIMER. I know, but . . .

MRS. CROSBY. Why, I think he's the most peculiar man I ever heard of. Why, I'd rather be harboring a Communist.

MRS. HERGESHEIMER. Oh, Mrs. Crosby, don't say that.

MRS. CROSBY. I would. I'd rather be harboring a Communist than a man who makes hats.

MRS. HERGESHEIMER. Why, there's nothing wrong with making hats. I don't see anything wrong with it. Why, lots of men make hats. Some of the finest designers there are, are men. Why, of course.

MRS. CROSBY. But he kept them locked in his closet. He was ashamed of them.

MRS. HERGESHEIMER. Maybe it's just a hobby with him. Some men knit, you know, because it helps their nerves.

MRS. CROSBY. I'm going to ask him to leave.

MRS. HERGESHEIMER. Oh, no, Mrs. Crosby. Don't do that.

MRS. CROSBY. I am. I'm going to ask him to leave. And I'm

going to call the store he works at, and tell them what kind of a freak they have working for them. Indeed I am.

MRS. HERGESHEIMER. Oh, I wouldn't do that. It's not against the law for a man to make hats. He hasn't done anything really wrong.

MRS. CROSBY. Why, a man who'd make hats, and lock them up in his closet, there's no telling what kind of a person he is. He might do any kind of dangerous, crazy thing.

MRS. HERGESHEIMER. Oh, I don't think so, Mrs. Crosby. Really I don't.

MRS. CROSBY. I'd rather he was a communist. At least you know what a communist is up to. But a man that makes hats! What can you tell about such a creature?

MRS. HERGESHEIMER. I wouldn't give it another thought, if I was you.

MRS. CROSBY. Well, I guess it takes all kinds of people to make a world.

MRS. HERGESHEIMER. Of course. That's the way to look at it.

MRS. CROSBY. Hats! Hats! Hats! With *flowers* on them!

MRS. HERGESHEIMER. I must run along now.

MRS. CROSBY. Hats!

MRS. HERGESHEIMER. Goodness, I hope he never finds out . . .

MRS. CROSBY. I don't care if he does. Just let him try to scold me, in that superior way of his. [*Imitating* MR. NEWBOLD.] "Mrs. Crosby, someone's been tampering with the lock on my closet. I demand privacy, Mrs. Crosby. That's all I ask, is just one tiny closet to call my own. That's all I ask." Hmm. I'll have an answer for him: "What in God's name does a grown-up man like you mean by making hats, Mr. Newbold? Shame!" That's what I'll tell him. And he won't act so superior then.

[MRS. HERGESHEIMER *flutters out of the house as though wanting to avoid further involvement.* MRS. CROSBY *studies the hat again, taking it to the mirror to try it on. She deliberately burlesques its elegance and all that it signifies of feminine daintiness and beauty. Then she tosses it onto a chair and returns to the kitchen. Stealthily,* MR. NEWBOLD *comes from the closet in which he has been hiding. He is a shattered man. His stiff pride, his erect authority are destroyed. He picks up the hat lovingly, hold-*

ing it in the air to admire again its loveliness. He even weeps. Finally, his courage restored, he determines on a course of action. Twisting a great, beaded hat-pin from the feathers and furbelows of his creation, he walks boldly to the kitchen door and stands, holding the pin behind his back, and calling in a voice that is eerie with its dire purpose.]

MR. NEWBOLD. Mrs. Crosby! Could you come here a moment, please? Could you come here a moment, Mrs. Crosby?

CURTAIN

CASTLE IN THE VILLAGE

By

Verna Woskoff

(Published here for the first time)

CAST

LYDIA
MR. LLEWELLYN
MRS. GOLDFINE
MR. HILL
MRS. HILL
AN ARTIST
A MOVING MAN

TIME: The present.

PLACE: A tenement apartment in New York City.

CASTLE IN THE VILLAGE

The scene is a dingy tenement apartment in the chaos of moving.
LYDIA *is packing belongings into a barrel. She is glamorous but unaware of it, a warm-hearted and genuine person. She takes time out from packing to feed her fish, which are swimming in a small bowl on top of a packing case. She is recommencing to pack when the phone rings. She answers it.*

LYDIA. Hell-o? [*Matter-of-factly.*] Oh, hello, Mom. Yeah. Yeah, I'm almost all packed. I just have to figure out what to do with the fishbowl . . . I *am* relaxed . . . It's just that moving is a rather hectic period in anyone's life . . . I told you a million times why I can't live home. We agreed that when I was twenty-five I could lead a life of my own and have a place of my own. What's wrong with *this* apartment? If you had an hour to kill I could tell you. The place I'm going is very nice, and as soon as I'm settled you'll come up to see it. How am I supposed to know if there are any young doctors in the building? Of course, I care about getting married—but does it have to be a doctor and does it have to be this week? . . . Twenty-five is *not* old. So I won't be a child bride! . . . Yes, I went to the dance last week. [*Bored.*] A rat-race. Like musical chairs! . . . Yeah, an accountant. No, there's nothing wrong with an accountant, but he was such a no-account accountant. He had about as much sex appeal as an IBM Univac . . . Univac! Never mind . . . No, I don't want an Arab chieftain. But Mother, you don't understand: Marjorie Morningstar was different from the way I am. All she really wanted in life was to get married, so whatever she got was okay. But to me, other things are equally important, such as—such as my job on the magazine, and my ideals . . . Yes, but I haven't reached the point yet where I'm willing to compromise to the extent of a monosyllabic accountant with clammy hands . . . Yes, I'll keep an open mind. Don't worry, Mom; when I get engaged, you'll be the first person I'll call. [*The doorbell rings.*] Mom, there's someone at the door. It

47

must be that fellow who's taking over this apartment when I leave. Oh, *Mother!* He's about forty-five years old! Yeah, yeah, I'm getting enough sleep. I've got to go now. Love to Pop. 'Bye.

[*She hangs up, goes to the door.* MR. LLEWELLYN *enters. He is a mousy, well-behaved little man with an attaché case.*]

MR. LLEWELLYN. Hell, I'm sorry I'm late. You said to come at four, but I got on the wrong train at Times Square.

LYDIA. Oh, is it after four? I still haven't decided how to pack my guppies. [*To the fish.*] Don't worry, babies, I won't leave you behind.

MR. LLEWELLYN. Yes, I hurried as fast as I could because I simply *must* have this apartment. They're tearing down my building to build a new office building and if I don't move by the fifteenth of the month I shall be put out on the street. Isn't that embarrassing? Sometimes I wish I were a machine. They'd think twice before they'd put a machine out on the street. The fifteenth of the month! What's today?

LYDIA. Today is the thirteenth.

MR. LLEWELLYN. Oh, dear! It's not myself I'm worried about, you understand. *I* don't mind being put out on the street. But it's Joseph—he's my parakeet. He will perish. Parakeets are not accustomed to severe changes of temperature.

LYDIA. I'm sorry I couldn't let you know sooner, but I've been trying to make up my mind. You see, so many people answered my ad. I didn't know the *Village Voice* had such a large circulation. So I have to decide who needs the apartment most, and that's taking me a long time to figure out. Let's see, first came a couple named Hill. They've been waiting a year for an apartment in this building to become available. But then they said they'd let me know, and I was surprised I never heard from them. Next came an artist—a real one—not the kind that are so that their hair stands up in peaks. He said he needed a place with northern light. Imagine! For seventy dollars a month he expects an aurora borealis! Next came a Mr. Llewellyn. I can't quite remember what he was like . . . Oh, that's you? I'm sorry.

MR. LLEWELLYN. Yes, it's me—I—me, although I really don't feel like the same person I was a few weeks ago. If there is one thing I cannot bear, it is uncertainty. Is it uncertainty or in-certitude? Anyway, I cannot bear not knowing where I shall sleep next week. I suppose, if worse came to worst, I could sleep in the park. I could become a vagabond, a gypsy. But I really don't feel I have the physical constitution for it. I catch cold so easily.

LYDIA. You poor thing! Have you tried to find any other apartment?

MR. LLEWELLYN. Oh, my goodness, yes. But someone is always there ahead of me. I've also tried to get into a coopera-tive. But they wanted a year's rent as a deposit. The deposit is not returnable, and does not gather interest. I don't call that being very cooperative, do you? Besides, the building won't be finished for another five years. You are my last hope, Miss . . . [He fumbles for her name.]

LYDIA. Just Lydia.

MR. LLEWELLYN. Please, just Lydia, is this apartment defi-nitely mine?

LYDIA. I guess so, if you really want it.

MR. LLEWELLYN. Oh, I do, I do. In fact, I can't understand why *you* don't want it.

LYDIA. Well— I feel I should warn you. There are several inconveniences. Like the night visitors, for instance.

MR. LLEWELLYN. What do you mean? Prowlers?

LYDIA. Sort of. Roaches, to be exact.

MR. LLEWELLYN. [*Stunned.*] Are you sure?

LYDIA. My dear man, in the past five months I have become an expert on their sex life and tribal customs. Did you know there are three distinct species in this very house? You can recognize the German ones by their . . .

MR. LLEWELLYN. Couldn't—couldn't the landlady call an exterminator?

LYDIA. It's against her principles. She's an anti-vivisection-ist. I finally called one myself, but he gave up in despair. He said the entire building should be exterminated permanently.

MR. LLEWELLYN. [*Laughs nonchalantly.*] Well, I suppose it could be worse. After all, they are very small. It's better than having—say, rats.

LYDIA. Oh, we have them, too! Are you all right?

MR. LLEWELLYN. [*Holding a handkerchief to his nose.*] Yes. Only a slight nose bleed! I get them from time to time, under stress.

LYDIA. Oh, that reminds me: the pilot light of the stove keeps going off, and you have to take special care not to be asphyxiated.

MR. LLEWELLYN. I see. How often?

LYDIA. Every time you light the oven.

MR. LLEWELLYN. Oh! Thank you. Well, if that's all . . .

LYDIA. But it's not all. The bathroom sink is stopped up, and the refrigerator is broken. Oh, and another thing: in the morning, if the steam doesn't come up, just take a spoon and bang it on the pipe for about a half an hour. That usually wakes up the janitor, if he's home.

MR. LLEWELLYN. Oh, I wouldn't want to disturb him. I'll put on a sweater. You see, despite its few little quirks, this apartment has one main advantage for me: it has a roof. I am therefore ready to sublet it from you immediately.

LYDIA. Okay, if you want it, you are welcome to it. But subletting is not what I had in mind. I want to break my lease entirely, and have you sign an entirely new lease. That way, I'm not responsible for anything that should go wrong with you or the apartment, like, for instance, if you shouldn't pay your rent on time.

MR. LLEWELLYN. But my goodness, I always pay my rent. I have been in my apartment for fifteen years, and I always paid my rent promptly three days before it is due. I assure you I have a very steady job; in fact I have just been promoted. I am now the Assistant Executive Checker in the systems department of the Eastern branch of the Testing Division of IBM.

LYDIA. I only mean I would prefer a re-lease to a sublease.

MR. LLEWELLYN. I'm agreeable to that. In fact, I'll give you a deposit in advance. Then we'll both know that everything is definite.

LYDIA. Very well. I'll be leaving today, and you can move here on the fifteenth—and since I've paid for the entire month on the first, you can reimburse me for half a month's rent. That's thirty-five dollars.

MR. LLEWELLYN. No, no, I'll give you a full month's rent. [*Taking out the money.*] Seventy dollars! I'm so grateful to have a roof over my head. [*He gives her the money.*] There! Now that settles it.

[*The doorbell rings.*]

LYDIA. I'll give you a receipt. Just a minute! [*The doorbell rings again.*] That must be Mrs. Goldfine, the landlady. She said she would be here to sign the papers.

[*She answers the door.* MRS. GOLDFINE *enters: a stocky widow, wearing a fur stole which she cannot subdue. She is very nervous, cannot sleep at night worrying that someone will sue her for a building violation, or that the Board of Health will have one of her fire-traps condemned. She always sounds out of breath.*]

MRS. GOLDFINE. Oh, my feet! My shoes are too tight, but who can buy new ones? I see the janitor has not been sweeping the stairs like I told him to. I'll have to speak to him again. Oh, my feet! I must sit down.

MR. LLEWELLYN. How do you do! I'm Mr. . . .

MRS. GOLDFINE. [*Ignores him.*] I have consulted my lawyers and have acquired the necessary information. It seems there is a ridiculous law that says every time a lease expires the landlord is entitled to a fifteen per cent increase in rent. A very foolish law, because someone may be living in a very small apartment, but the rent will be higher than the rent in a larger apartment because the people in the smaller apartment have moved more often into larger apartments because the smaller apartment was too small. But what can you do? The law is the law, and we have to abide by it. There's no use crying over sour grapes.

MR. LLEWELLYN. Absolutely.

MRS. GOLDFINE. Now, the lease has not yet expired, but since you are breaking that lease and beginning a new one, my lawyers tell me I am entitled to a fifteen per cent increase right now. I don't want you to think I'm taking advantage. Goodness knows, I understand how the cost of living is. I'm always advising my tenants on how they can save money. Some of them regard me as a mother, practically. But you see, my husband didn't leave me a penny—only real estate—so I have to manage as best I can. And the bills! What the government don't take in taxes, I have to give to the building inspectors. So you see, I have to stick by my rights, after all, because if I don't, then who's going to get stuck by them? I'd like to know!

MR. LLEWELLYN. Of course.

MRS. GOLDFINE. So whoever comes in will pay the increase; and then at the expiration of *that* lease, I must obey the rent commission and increase the rent another fifteen per cent—or whatever the law will allow. Maybe by that time they will remove rent controls altogether. Who knows? [*To* MR. LLEWELLYN.] Are you Mr. Hill?

MR. LLEWELLYN. No, Llewellyn is my name. Descended from Llewellyn, Prince of Wales in the twelfth century, the one who suffered from paralysis.

MRS. GOLDFINE. Tsk! Don't give me no Prince of Wheels, Prince of Schlemiels! What type of work do you do for a living? That's what I want to know.

MR. LLEWELLYN. I guess you might call it administrative work.

MRS. GOLDFINE. Well, I don't know what it means exactly, but it sounds like you'll be able to pay your rent.

MR. LLEWELLYN. Um, how shall we word it—about my taking over the lease?

MRS. GOLDFINE. I don't know why in the world this child wants to give up a perfectly good two-year lease. Young people today have no sense of responsibility. To teach her a lesson, I should make her pay the balance of the rent through next year. [*She notices* LYDIA's *aghast face.*] But of course I wouldn't want to take advantage.

MR. LLEWELLYN. I, the undersigned, do hereby agree . . . Does that sound legal?

MRS. GOLDFINE. Hold your shirt, Mr. Llewellyn! I'm not so sure you're going to be the one to get this apartment. Who told you you could have it? This is a big city, my dear man. You're not the only fish on the beach, you know.

MR. LLEWELLYN. Oh, no, you can't change your minds now!

I've already paid this young lady a full month's rent in advance.

MRS. GOLDFINE. You did what? A full month's rent? But you're moving in on the fifteenth. That's terrible!

MR. LLEWELLYN. Oh, it's all right with me. I offered it to her. Oh, dear, I'm sorry I mentioned it.

MRS. GOLDFINE. She's taking advantage of you, young man. That's not fair! Some people think of nothing but how they can rob other people. Make her give it back!

[*The doorbell rings.* LYDIA *goes to answer it.*]

MR. LLEWELLYN. If she gives it back, then I might not get the apartment . . .

MRS. GOLDFINE. She *must* give it back, or I'll call the police. Robbery, that's what it is—household robbery!

[LYDIA *re-enters with* MR. HILL *and his timid, pregnant wife. He is a young insurance salesman, who makes it a point never to do anything which requires great effort. She is rather bored with him.*]

MR. HILL. Remember me? I'm Mr. Hill, and this is my wife. We're ready to sign the papers.

LYDIA. But what are *you* doing here? You said you'd call back, but you never did.

MRS. HILL. Oh, yes, we did. We called the landlady, God bless her!

[MRS. HILL *sits on the sofa, and starts reading a newspaper.* MR. HILL *stands.*]

LYDIA. But you were going to call *me*! Mrs. Goldfine told me to get another tenant. So when you didn't call back, I went ahead and got someone else [*Waving at him*]—Mr. Llewellyn.

MR. LLEWELLYN. How do you do! [MR. HILL *grunts in response, and paces the floor.*] I knew it! I knew something like this would happen. Everything's been going wrong lately since Mother died.

LYDIA. [*To* MRS. GOLDFINE.] Why did you tell them they had the apartment, when I already told you I had someone?

MRS. GOLDFINE. My dear, I happen to be a business woman, which you definitely are not. How could I be sure that you really did have someone to take over? What if you had forgotten? Or what if you did get someone and he reneged at the last minute?

I would lose perhaps a full month's rent. Think of it! [*Groans.*] A bird in the hand, darling, is worth an ounce of prevention.

LYDIA. You mean you doubted for one minute that you would get someone who wanted the apartment? In New York City? But there are always more people than houses. It's like a gigantic game of musical chairs: you just about sit down when someone pulls another chair away, and off you go again—always more people than there are places for them.

MR. LLEWELLYN. Oh, dear, and some people always get left out. Out in the street, that's where I shall have to live. In the street! What shall I do when it rains? [*Terrorized.*] Or snows?

MR. HILL. Frankly, you might as well face it sooner or later: *nobody cares.* I mean we all have ourselves to worry about. You think you got a sad case. I got the responsibility of two and a half: me, my wife, and in six weeks . . .

MRS. GOLDFINE. Congratulations, Mr. Hill! Isn't that nice! I simply adore small children.

MR. HILL. Fried or broiled?

MRS. GOLDFINE. What?

MR. LLEWELLYN. Oh, dear, I knew the situation would become difficult. I knew it. I shall have to move to the "Y" and put my furniture in storage. If only we could return to the Middle Ages, where every man had his plot of land, and he was either a serf or a vassal or a lord and he knew it, and the neighbors knew it, and life had order and tranquility.

[*There is a loud knocking at the door.* LYDIA *answers it. It is the* ARTIST, *a resourceful young fellow with a sense of his own worth.*]

ARTIST. [*Calmly.*] Hi! I decided I could do without the north light for the time being. I have to have this apartment. I've haunted every borough and burrowed in every haunt. Nothing else fits my price range. Where are the papers I have to sign?

MR. HILL. Hey, hey, cool it, Jack! There's a couple of other people who happened to get here first.

ARTIST. Ah, but you couldn't be as desperate as I am. My roommate went off to Hollywood to make Westerns—omelets, not movies. He's working at a roadside stand; and I've lost my job, and can't pay the entire rent myself. I haven't sold a painting in months. I haven't eaten in two days. If I don't get a less expensive place to live in by the end of the week, I'll starve to death. That's all there is to it!

MR. HILL. Well, why don't you go in for something that pays better, like engineering?

ARTIST. [Shrugging.] Because I'm an artist. I have a talent for the communication of qualities of quintessences. It all started when I was five years old and I smeared streaks of paint upon a piece of paper: sizzling red, orange, incandescent gold. The kindergarten teacher asked, "What is it supposed to be?" and I said, "It is FIRE-ness!" I have been an artist ever since.

MR. HILL. Well, if you're going to be stubborn about it, you deserve to starve to death. Who needs pictures? You know what I mean? Take me, for instance: I figured I wanted to do something there was a steady demand for. Okay, you say: food, clothing, shelter. Nonsense! One thing people always have; it never goes away. And that's fear. Fear of growing old, fear of death, fear of fires and floods and accidents, fear of anything that's unforeseen. That's why I decided I would sell insurance. I represent the Fair and Square Insurance Company. My card. [He passes cards around. The ARTIST does not take one.]

ARTIST. No, thanks. I thrive on the unforeseen. I accept, in fact, enjoy, the possibility of being constantly surprised. The only real security is death, which I carry with me in capsule form. Do you see this tooth? That's not a filling, that's a capsule of cyanide, which I shall take if I do not find an apartment immediately.

[He feigns a Hamlet-like pose.]

MRS. HILL. Oh, no, you mustn't let him do that! We mustn't let him kill himself. He's so young and so handsome! Let's let him have the apartment; he needs it more than anybody.

MR. HILL. Martha, in another minute you can start looking for a one-room-and-a-half!

MRS. HILL. I'm sorry dear, but I felt . . .

MR. HILL. That's the trouble: you keep on allowing your feelings to tell you what to do. Remember, the city we live in is like a jungle. You have to be tough!

MRS. HILL. [*Growls.*]

MR. HILL. That's better.

MRS. HILL. [*Growls louder.*]

MR. HILL. All right, Martha, you don't have to overdo it.

LYDIA. Oh, please don't take the cyanide! I have all kinds of other pills you can take: aspirin, Empirin, Bufferin, Dramamine, Equanil, Miltown, Nodoze. Listen: there's a soothing sound to their names, like a modern incantation against evil spirits. Aspirin! Empirin! Bufferin!

ARTIST. Cyanide! The tranquilizer to end all tranquilizers! [*He poses as if to take it, then gets scared and holds it farther away.*]

LYDIA. Don't!

ARTIST. [*Startled, jumps.*] For Heaven's sake, woman, don't shout like that! You practically made me swallow the stuff.

MR. HILL. Look, Buddy, if you really want to end it all . . . I mean who are we to stand in your way? Live and let live is my motto, or live and let die, as the case may be.

MRS. GOLDFINE. Say, I have an idea! We did this another time in a similar situation. We all cut up pieces of paper and put them in a hat, and drew lots. And whoever got the longest piece of paper, or the shortest—I forget which—won the apartment. Isn't that democratic?

LYDIA, HILL, LLEWELLYN, ARTIST. [*General protest.*] No, that's not fair. First come, first served. What if I lost? You know what you can do with your pieces of paper?

MRS. GOLDFINE. Quiet, everybody! You haven't heard my good news. There's another apartment up on the second floor of this building, which used to be occupied by a rather eccentric gentleman named Mr. Hannington. Mr. Hannington was sick in bed for years and I never could raise the rent. Anyway, Mr. Hannington has finally passed on.

[*They all get up and exchange seats.*]

MRS. HILL. He did? Poor Mr. Hannington. I knew him. He was such a nice man. Poor, poor Mr. Hannington. God rest his soul! Did he have much pain?

MR. HILL. What does that have to do with it? There's another vacant apartment. Let me handle this, dear.

MRS. GOLDFINE. Well, it is not exactly vacant yet, you see. Mr. Hannington's sister has paid the rent through next month. She was very devoted to her brother and she hasn't had the heart to come and pick up his things.

ARTIST. I think I know what might hurry her up.

MRS. GOLDFINE. Yes?

ARTIST. All you have to do is tell her you've been hearing complaints—from your tenants—about strange noises coming from that apartment: footsteps, creaking doors, moans and groans. I think Mr. Hannington's apartment will then become available immediately.

MRS. GOLDFINE. As a matter of fact, a few of the tenants *have* complained lately about that. They say they can hear an old gramophone playing "The Last Rose of Summer" in the middle of the night.

ARTIST. Fine! Then you have a perfect excuse. A gramophone!

MR. HILL. [*After whispering with his wife.*] Look, we've decided we'll take that apartment with or without ghosts. It'll be better than living with my mother-in-law, like we are now.

MRS. GOLDFINE. You'd be getting quite a bargain, you know. The rent is much lower than this one, but of course since the poor sick man was unable to do any cleaning since 1954, the place is slightly dirty, and you would have to redecorate—if not fumigate.

MR. HILL. You mean you won't have it painted?

MRS. GOLDFINE. All my tenants do their own decorating. If you don't like it, my dear man, there are others who will. Choosers can't be beggars!

MRS. HILL. That's all right; we'll decorate. Only because the rent is so low.

MRS. GOLDFINE. Oh, yes, the rent is very reasonable. However, the kitchen stove in the apartment is the same one that was there when the house was first built. [*Defensively.*] Mr. Hannington was such a nostalgic man. A regular antique collector! If you want a new stove, the rent office would allow me to raise the rent another ten dollars a month.

MR. HILL. I feel we're being taken, but I suppose we'll have to agree to that—in order to get this all over with.

MR. LLEWELLYN. Good! Then it's settled.

MRS. GOLDFINE. There's only one difficulty. I've already promised that apartment to somebody else.

HILL, LLEWELLYN, ARTIST, LYDIA. Oh, no!

[*They all get up, pace, and switch seats.*]

MRS. GOLDFINE. Mr. and Mrs. Sanchez, the people on the top floor of this building, have a beautiful apartment—five rooms, very lovely—but they've been complaining that they have to climb all those stairs. I told them, as soon as an apartment becomes available lower down I would let them know. Say, Mr. Hill, maybe you would like their place.

MR. HILL. Oh, no, you don't! I'm not going to have my wife dragging a baby carriage up all those flights of stairs.

MRS. GOLDFINE. Well, Mr. Llewellyn then?

MR. LLEWELLYN. I really have no use for five rooms.

[MRS. GOLDFINE *looks at the* ARTIST *inquiringly.*]

ARTIST. I can barely afford *one* room.

MRS. GOLDFINE. Well, you settle it all among yourselves. I'm sure I don't know what to do. Oh, my head! I have a splitting headache. I have not been well lately. The doctors say it's my nerves. I have so many expenses I can't begin to tell you . . . Oh! I think I'll take one of those aspirins you mentioned, dear.

LYDIA. Certainly. Anyone else?

MR. HILL. Yeah.

MRS. HILL. If it's not too much trouble.

LYDIA. Mr. Llewellyn?

MR. LLEWELLYN. Just one, thank you.

MRS. GOLDFINE. [*To* MRS. HILL.] Don't you get up, dear! I'll go in the kitchen and get the water. I don't like to be a nuisance to anyone, or put anyone to any inconvenience.

[*She exits.*]

MR. LLEWELLYN. I've never seen a more stupid woman in all my life.

ARTIST. She's not so stupid. She's obviously waiting to be bribed.

MR. HILL. Why didn't I think of that!

MR. LLEWELLYN. We wouldn't allow such a thing! How much do you suppose she wants?

ARTIST. I don't think it would do any good to bribe her. She's so clever she would probably forget who gave her the most money. Besides, for all we know, she's got still another prospective tenant lined up.

MR. LLEWELLYN. That's true.

MRS. GOLDFINE. [Re-entering.] Here's some nice cold water. [Pours it into glasses.] Now maybe we'll all feel better. It's too bad you don't have a little snack or something to serve your guests, dear.

LYDIA. Guests! I didn't invite all these people.

MRS. GOLDFINE. Well, sometimes the best parties are the ones that happen spontaneously—when people just drop in. [Clinks glass with MR. LLEWELLYN.] Cheers!

ARTIST. There're still guests missing. The people on the top floor. We still don't know if they want to move. Why don't we invite Mrs. Sanchez to have some aspirins with us?

MRS. GOLDFINE. That's a sweet idea. Oh, but my feet ache so—I'll never make it up those stairs by myself.

MR. HILL. My wife and I will go with you. She needs the exercise for her natural childbirth training.

MR. LLEWELLYN. Hey, wait for me!

[They all leave except LYDIA and the ARTIST.]

ARTIST. Let me help you pack!

[He sits on the sofa and lights his pipe.]

LYDIA. I just have to wrap up these pictures. I don't want any of them to get damaged.

ARTIST. Do you think anyone would notice the difference if they were damaged?

LYDIA. Don't you like them?

ARTIST. No.

LYDIA. Why not?

ARTIST. They have no personality—no individuality. They make no statement, no commitment. They are designed to please, to fit in, to conform.

LYDIA. Who is your favorite artist?

ARTIST. I am.

LYDIA. You're conceited.

ARTIST. No, I just have good taste.

LYDIA. I thought you said you would help me pack.

ARTIST. Where are you going when you leave here?

LYDIA. To another apartment.

ARTIST. Ah! Is it a nice one?

LYDIA. Yes.

ARTIST. Large?

LYDIA. Very.

ARTIST. Nice neighborhood?

LYDIA. Lovely.

ARTIST. Must cost a fortune!

LYDIA. No, it's a steal. I heard about it from a friend who knows a linotype operator on the *New York Times.* He told me, just before the *apartment-to-let* ad was set in type.

ARTIST. Does it—does it have northern light?

LYDIA. Why, yes, I believe it does, as a matter of fact.

ARTIST. Ah!

LYDIA. What?

ARTIST. Nothing. I was just thinking.

LYDIA. Would you hand me those pillows over there?

ARTIST. Of course. You're going to live in this new apartment all by yourself?

LYDIA. I beg your pardon . . .

ARTIST. I mean—you don't have a roommate?

LYDIA. No. For the sort of work I do, I need complete privacy.

ARTIST. Oh? What sort of work is that?

LYDIA. I write for a magazine.

ARTIST. I see. A career girl.

LYDIA. No, not exactly.

ARTIST. I don't see why not. You're not married, and you have a career.

LYDIA. Yes, but I always think of a career girl as someone who would rather have a career than anything else. I, on the other hand, have no objection to getting married.

ARTIST. [*Taking her in his arms.*] Good. Then why don't you marry me?

LYDIA. [*With a panel of curtain in each hand.*] You're not serious?

ARTIST. [*Drapes curtain into bridal veil and holds her at arm's length admiringly.*] I was never more serious.

LYDIA. But we don't even know each other.

ARTIST. So what? Nobody really ever knows anybody else. People who have been living together for years still don't know each other. Besides, even if you thought you knew me, that would take away half the fun of our relationship. There would be no mystery to it. It would be cut and dried. This way—we shall continue to fascinate each other. So what do you say?

LYDIA. Well, for another thing—you're an artist. That means you don't have any money. How would you support me? I have to have a certain amount of—security.

ARTIST. My dear girl, where is your spirit of adventure? New York City was not built by people who were interested in the predictable. Did Henry Hudson know what he was going to find when he sailed the *Half Moon* up the river named in his honor? Did Fulton know that his little steamboat would be so successful that they would name a fish market after him? [LYDIA *laughs appreciatively.*] Right now, I am unknown; that is true. Unknown and unemployed. But the possibilities ahead are infinite. You have to be willing to take chances.

LYDIA. I'm sorry, but that doesn't sound to me like the basis of a stable marriage.

ARTIST. There you go again, searching for stability. My dear fiancée—what is your name, by the way?

LYDIA. Lydia. Hey, wait a minute!

ARTIST. Lydia. Not a bad name. Lydia, you must realize that no marriage is stable. Can you ever depend completely on somebody else? Of course not. Darling, you don't find stability outside of yourself. People who believe that marriage is an answer should never ask the question. Marriage, like everything else, is a gamble. So why not gamble on me?

LYDIA. Perhaps because I am not in love with you.

ARTIST. That can always come later. After all, we already have the most important requisite.

LYDIA. Which is what?

ARTIST. An apartment! Look at the hundreds of couples in this city who fall madly in love with each other, but then can't do anything about it because they are unable to find a place to live. We are probably the only couple in New York smart enough to go about things in the right order. The apartment first, then, when the lease is signed, there's plenty of time to fall in love.

LYDIA. You talk about love as if it could be turned on like an electric blanket.

ARTIST. It can. It can be turned on with a light in your eyes that says "I'm not afraid of you." It can be turned on with a smile that says "I understand you." It can be turned on with a touch that says "I will protect you."

LYDIA. I see. And does it turn off just as easily?

ARTIST. Ah, there you go, expecting a guarantee again. It's a hard thing to face the fact that God is interested in a quick turnover and a volume business. He gives no guarantees on anything. I'll tell you one thing, though. If you're looking for security, love is a pretty good imitation of it. Because as long as you are doing the giving, you are in control of a situation.

LYDIA. You make it all sound so simple . . .

ARTIST. Try it and see!

LYDIA. How?

ARTIST. Well, to begin with . . .

[*He kisses her. The others, meanwhile, re-enter.*]

MRS. GOLDFINE. Well, I see our friend has decided to live, after all!

LYDIA. It's all right. We're in love.

MR. LLEWELLYN. So soon? It can't be . . . How can you be sure?

MRS. GOLDFINE. He must be rich. Maybe he has shares in the stock market.

MR. HILL. So what if they're in love! I couldn't care less.

LYDIA. Well, where is Mrs. Sanchez?

MR. HILL. She has to consult her husband. [*He sits down wearily.*] Why does everything have to be so involved?

MRS. GOLDFINE. I'll have to let you know. You can call me next week. In the afternoon, please—not in the morning. I sleep late because I suffer from insomnia. I never get to sleep before three or four A.M.

MR. HILL. We will *not* call you in the morning, afternoon, or evening. We have been waiting a whole year, and we are going away today with an apartment—either this one or that other one.

MRS. GOLDFINE. Yes? Well, whoever gets the apartment will be very fortunate. It has a very lucky history. The first tenants were a university professor and his wife. He went on to write a book and became very famous. I can't recall his name just now, but he's very famous. Then there was an engineer, and when he left he took another apartment for two hundred fifty a month —so you see he did quite well. [*Everyone begins to squirm uncomfortably as she prattles on.* MR. HILL *gets up, and paces.* LYDIA *sits down where he was sitting.*] Then there was a young architect and his wife. They were a fine couple. Quakers, I believe. They moved to an elegant house in New Jersey.

ARTIST. This is getting us absolutely nowhere. The fact is: we must reach a decision. The question as I see it is this: on what basis shall we decide who is to get which apartment? We are all seeking peace, a place to rest; in other words, a home, a haven, a shelter.

MR. LLEWELLYN. Oh, if only we could return to feudalism!

MRS. HILL. I know! I shall consult the stars.

ARTIST. Oh, do you have contacts in television?

MRS. HILL. No, my dear, I am a student of the occult. Oh, I forgot to bring my astrology guide with me.

MR. HILL. Please, Martha, don't make a scene. Remember your . . . !

MRS. HILL. Oh! That reminds me: I'm late for my natural childbirth class. Where's my pocketbook? Oh, here it is. [*She gets up.*] You must excuse me. What a pity! I have to leave before things are settled.
[*An embarrassed pause.*]

MR. HILL. Allow me to apologize. My wife has been in a rather nervous state lately.

ARTIST. She'd make *any* state she was in—nervous.
[*The phone rings.* LYDIA *gets up to answer it.*]

LYDIA. Hello? Yes? Yes! [*To them.*] It's Mrs. Sanchez, the lady on the top floor, for you, Mrs. Goldfine. She can't come downstairs now because their baby is crying, but she says she spoke to her husband and she wants to tell you their decision. [MRS. GOLDFINE *takes the phone.*]

MRS. GOLDFINE. Hello? Yes, it is a lovely day. It's going to rain this afternoon, though. Maybe not. Nothing is certain, Mrs. Sanchez, but the time and the tide. Oh, yes. And what did he say? [*To them.*] She says they like their place very much. It's big and clean and has a lot of closets—but it's too high to walk. [*Into the phone.*] Exactly. That's why I told you you could have Mr. Hannington's apartment. [*To them.*] She says it would be cheaper to move downstairs—seven dollars a month cheaper. [*Into the phone.*] At seven dollars a month you shouldn't sneeze, Mrs. Sanchez. [*To them.*] She says they have so much furniture, they wouldn't know what to do with it in a smaller apartment. [*Into the phone.*] Sell it, darling, don't be a fool! [*To them.*] She says they would have to fix up the place so much they wouldn't save any money anyway . . .

MR. HILL. Give me that! [*He takes the phone.*] Mrs. Sanchez, are you or are you not going to want Mr. Hannington's apartment? Thank you. Good-bye. [*He hangs up.*] They have decided they do not want the apartment.

MRS. GOLDFINE. Then it's yours, Mr. Hill. You're the lucky couple!

LYDIA. [*Thrusting a paper in front of* MRS. GOLDFINE.] Put that in writing!

MRS. GOLDFINE. Some people are so suspicious. They have no faith in other people. They never rely on a person's wordiness.

LYDIA. [*Dictating.*] As soon as apartment 3A becomes available, I promise to rent it to Mr. and Mrs. Hill. Now sign it! I'll be a witness.

MR. HILL. [*Taking the paper from* MRS. GOLDFINE.] Thank you. Whichever one of you fellas turns out to be our neighbor, I hope you'll come to visit us often, and see our new baby. Good luck to you all! Here is my card, in case anyone has need of my services. [*He hands the cards around again.*] Life insurance, fire and theft, and accident insurance. In these days of fear and anxiety, it's nice to know you can depend on something. Protect yourself from every care with "Fair and Square"! [*He exits.*]

MR. LLEWELLYN. That still leaves two of us—and this one apartment. I suppose we could fight a duel. But then one of us might lose, and that would be dreadful.

ARTIST. The solution is perfectly simple. I shall propose marriage to this young lady, and if she accepts, we can go and live in the apartment which she has already found.

LYDIA. But . . .

ARTIST. I realize it is an impulsive step I am asking you to take, but decisions must be made quickly in times like these. Who knows what the future will bring? War, depression, destruction; we may all be blown to bits by a careless jet pilot tomorrow. Remember what I said: turn on the love.

LYDIA. Yes, but once you turn the love on, what do you live on?

ARTIST. Oh, I forgot to tell you. I happen to have a Ph.D., which at present provides an entrée to practically nowhere except teaching. I shall never make a fat amount of money as a teacher, but I shall keep on painting and trying to sell my paintings. Perhaps I shall be an outstanding success; perhaps I shall not. But I shall find satisfaction in my work, and I shall love you as long as I possibly can. There is the prospectus! Are you brave enough to face the fact that life is an unknown quantity? If so, then marry me, and we shall tackle the unknown together. [*He drops to his knees.*]

LYDIA. It sounds perfectly ridiculous and extremely precarious, and I don't know how in the world we are going to manage. [*Pause.*] I accept.

ARTIST. [*Gets up.*] Of course you do.

MR. LLEWELLYN. Then this apartment is really mine once again. All we have to do is sign the lease.

MRS. GOLDFINE. You'll have to give me some security.

MR. LLEWELLYN. How much do you think is necessary?

MRS. GOLDFINE. How much do you have with you?

MR. LLEWELLYN. About one hundred dollars.

MRS. GOLDFINE. I'd feel more secure with two hundred, but it will have to do. Now, just sign here, please!

MR. LLEWELLYN. [*Reading.*] Agree to pay—fifteen per cent. [*He signs.*] Good! Everything is settled.

MRS. GOLDFINE. But what about your rent? I will not allow that woman to take advantage of you.

LYDIA. Of course not. If you give me back half a month's rent—for the time I will not be staying here, from the fifteenth on—I will reimburse you.

MRS. GOLDFINE. That's only fair. [*She takes out her purse, counts the money, then takes it away again and starts all over.*] That's half of seventy: is thirty-five. Why did I think it was twenty-four? There!

[*She shoves thirty-five dollars at* LYDIA.]

LYDIA. [*Handing the money round the table to* MR. LLEWELLYN.] There!

MRS. GOLDFINE. Wait a minute: I still haven't been paid for half a month's rent.

MR. LLEWELLYN. That's right: I haven't paid you yet. [*He hands the thirty-five dollars back to* MRS. GOLDFINE.] There!

LYDIA. [*To* MRS. GOLDFINE.] May I help you into your coat? [*She does so.*]

MRS. GOLDFINE. Good-bye, my dear. I hope you have a very happy marriage. And if you don't, get all the alimony you can.

LYDIA. Thank you. Good-bye.

MRS. GOLDFINE. [*Confused.*] Wait a minute! I knew something was wrong. You forgot the fifteen per cent increase! [*The* ARTIST *and* LYDIA *motion to* MR. LLEWELLYN *to keep quiet.*]

LYDIA. Ah, yes! Give me back the thirty-five dollars. [MRS. GOLDFINE *gives it to* MR. LLEWELLYN, *who gives it back to* LYDIA.] Now, fifteen per cent of thirty-five dollars is . . . ? How much is fifteen per cent of thirty-five dollars?

ARTIST. Four dollars and twenty-five cents.

LYDIA. [*Proudly.*] Isn't he amazing? Do you have four dollars and twenty-five cents, Mr. Llewellyn?

MR. LLEWELLYN. No, I don't have any change.

ARTIST. Wait! The fifteen per cent bit doesn't start until next month, when the new lease begins.

LYDIA. You're a genius, darling. I don't think we're going to starve, after all. [*To* MR. LLEWELLYN.] So you gave me seventy dollars—a full month's rent—but since you are moving in on the fifteenth, here's half of it back.

MRS. GOLDFINE. [*Protesting.*] But darling, *I* gave you that thirty-five dollars.

LYDIA. Well, here you are getting it back.

[MR. LLEWELLYN *hands the thirty-five dollars back to* MRS. GOLDFINE.]

MRS. GOLDFINE. [*Very bewildered, goes through the motions of pointing to herself, then to* LYDIA, *then to* MR. LLEWELLYN, *and back to herself. She shrugs and puts the money in her purse.*] Him! Her! Me! I don't get it . . . ! My husband couldn't leave me an annuity; he had to go leave me real estate. [*She exits.*]

ARTIST. Poor soul, her insomnia is going to really bother her tonight.

MR. LLEWELLYN. It's okay with me—about the money, I mean. I want you to have that extra half-month's rent as a sort of reward for all your help. I thank you. You have restored to me a sense of—of permanence.

[*The doorbell rings. A voice yells* "Moving man!".]

LYDIA. [*Answering the door.*] Come right in; you're just in time. You can start with that chair over there. Oh, and after you're done, there's another job waiting for you: you can take this man's possessions . . .

ARTIST. Such as they are . . .

LYDIA. To the same address. That reminds me: I have to make a phone call. [*She goes to phone, dials. The* ARTIST *helps the* MOVING MAN.] Hello, Mom? Are you standing up? Well, sit down! Are you sitting down? Okay. I've got news for you. I'm getting married. Mom? . . . Mom? I don't know; we haven't set a date yet. Sometime next week—or maybe tomorrow. No, no trouble! I'm in *love* and I want to get married right away. He's an artist. An *artist*. He paints pictures. No, we don't intend to eat pictures. He's going to get a job, teaching. Of course, you'll meet him. You'll like him. He's very nice. I didn't tell you before because I didn't know before. No, don't tell everybody yet. All right, go ahead, tell everybody! I don't know; maybe tonight for supper? Okay. It doesn't matter: anything you make will be fine. I said *anything;* he's hungry. Yes, it is sudden, but that's how wonderful things happen sometimes, very suddenly, when you don't expect them . . . No, Mother, I'm *not* expecting. Thank you. Thank you, I think so. I think we're going to be very happy. Now, you catch your breath and we'll see you later. 'Bye. [*She hangs up.*] The worst is over.

MR. LLEWELLYN. May I offer my sincere congratulations and felicitations? Marriage is a very wonderful thing, no doubt. I would have tried it myself, but I never could be sure . . . Oh, well, it's too late now. I've found other things to keep me busy: my job, my work at the church, Joseph—that's my parakeet— and now, I'll have the apartment to decorate . . .

LYDIA. Yes, that will certainly keep you busy.

MR. LLEWELLYN. It's such a comfort to know that one has a place to rest.

[*The* MOVING MAN *puts his hand on* MR. LLEWELLYN's *chair.*]

MOVER. Excuse me, Mister. [*He removes the chair.*] Is that it, ma'am?

LYDIA. That's it. Good-bye, Mr. Llewellyn, and good luck! [*They shake hands.*]

MR. LLEWELLYN. Best wishes for the future! I hope it brings you exactly what you expect.

ARTIST. It has to—since all we expect is the unexpected. [*He kisses* LYDIA *and they leave.*]

MR. LLEWELLYN. [*He goes on a small tour of inspection, beaming.*] It's such a relief to know that everything is settled. Knock wood! [*He knocks on a doorjamb, and it falls off. He laughs nervously.*] My, I don't know my own strength. All I did was tap it—like that . . . ! [*He taps the wall, and a piece of plaster falls off. He looks distressed, but shrugs and puts the plaster back with Scotch tape. While he is doing this, "The Last Rose of Summer" starts to play on an old gramophone.*] So it's not the most luxurious apartment in the world, but there's still nothing like a roof over one's head to give one a sense of security. [*The ceiling starts to come down noisily, in large flakes.*]

CURTAIN

GIN AND BITTERNESS

A "5-to-7" Comedy

By

Stanley Richards

(Published here for the first time)

CAST

MRS. QUINCY
GILSON CROFT
ROY RADHAKAMAL
CONSTANCE CROFT
MRS. BENSON ROWE
JULIET PEDDLE
MALCOLM NEWCOMB
JODY MCKENZIE

TIME: The present; the cocktail hour.

PLACE: Mid-Manhattan.

GIN AND BITTERNESS

It is the cocktail hour in the living room of an apartment in Manhattan. A small foyer is downstage, left; a door off the foyer leads to the hall. In the rear wall, a large window offers a panoramic view of Manhattan at dusk. Two doors in the right wall lead, respectively, to the kitchen and bedroom.

The furnishings are tasteful and attractive. With the exception of a piano and an antique desk, the most dominant feature about the room is the extensive library.

The door chimes ring. Simultaneously, MRS. QUINCY, *a part-time domestic in starched maid's uniform and cap, and* GILSON CROFT *promptly appear—she from the kitchen, he from the bedroom.* CROFT, *a lean and attractive forty, carefully closes the bedroom door after him.* MRS. QUINCY *is fifty, and overfed.*

CROFT. Never mind, Mrs. Quincy, I'll get it.

MRS. QUINCY. [*Proceeds toward the door.*] One of your guests, likely, for the cocktail party.

CROFT. [*Leaping in front of her, blocking her line of march.*] Back! To the kitchen!

MRS. QUINCY. [*Stunned.*] Mr. Croft!

CROFT. Arrange the *hors d'oeuvres* . . .

MRS. QUINCY. They're arranged.

CROFT. Then rearrange 'em. Rearrange Mrs. Croft. *Anything!*

MRS. QUINCY. Why, indeed!

[*With a domestic's responsiveness she is about to undo the butterfly bow on her apron belt.*]

CROFT. [*Importantly.*] I'm terribly sorry, Mrs. Quincy, but this is rather private and . . .

MRS. QUINCY. I may only be a "part-time," Mr. Croft, but I got me "full-time" sensitivity.

[*And with this declaration,* MRS. QUINCY *returns to the kitchen. The door chimes ring again.* CROFT *hastens to the door, opens it, admitting* ROY RADHAKAMAL, *a good-looking youth of ambiguous*

Asiatic extraction, somewhere in his mid-twenties. He speaks in a precise, halting manner, occasionally groping for the proper word or phrase, suggesting that he was born in a country other than the United States.]

ROY. Mr. Croft?

CROFT. Yes, yes, come in.

ROY. I am Roy. Radhakamal.

CROFT. [*Closing the door.*] Delighted you're here! My wife's completing her dressing. We have no more than a few seconds.

ROY. Why could you not—brief me—on the telephone?

CROFT. Lobby switchboard! Like women, they can't retain secrets. [*He hastens over to the kitchen door, slams it shut; then returns to* ROY.] Now, all of your instructions are in this letter. And here's the key to the maid's quarters, on the roof, two flights up, first door past the water tank. You'll find the paraphernalia laid out on the bed. [*He hands a sealed envelope and key to* ROY.] Any questions?

ROY. Yes. What is this—please—all about?

CROFT. [*Slightly jarred by* ROY's *question.*] I—intend to prove a personal theory this evening.

ROY. And just what is that?

CROFT. We'll discuss it later, tomorrow, after I *have* proven it. It's almost five. The guests will start pouring in . . .

ROY. If I do not know what I am to—assist—you in proving, how can we prove it?

CROFT. [*Indicating the letter.*] If you'll just follow my instructions . . .

ROY. Instructions without definition, I find—disconcerting. You will excuse my being . . .

CROFT. [*Ruffled.*] I'll excuse nothing! But if you're going to be intractable . . .

ROY. Will you give me definition, please—intractable?

CROFT. Oh, never mind! [*Yielding.*] It's my contention [*Quickly checking himself in order to avert another query from* ROY.]—belief—that cocktail parties are the hypocritical bacchanals of modern civilization: free-loading carnivals created to promote the gullibility of mankind.

ROY. [*Listening intently.*] Yes . . .

CROFT. Give your guests inferior gin and some soggy cheese squares, and you can make 'em believe anything you want them to believe.

ROY. An element of—psy-chology, perhaps?

CROFT. Son, all novelists are psychologists to the extent that they understand human nature. At least, they should.

ROY. [A bit apprehensive.] What if—because of this—experimentation—I lose job at the Rotisserie?

CROFT. My dear fellow, doesn't it seem more fundamental to you to experiment with two-legged humans rather than two-legged chickens?

ROY. But I need job.

CROFT. I'm thoroughly aware of that, else you wouldn't have taken it in the first place. Don't worry, I've arranged it with Ralph.

ROY. He believe I am here to serve.

CROFT. I hope you do, and well! Of course, not serving in a servile manner! You've been engaged to participate in a significant experiment which, I agree, may have selfish ramifications, but I doubt if it will cost you your employment.

ROY. [Digesting the thought.] All people believe, under certain circumstance, what you want them to . . .

CROFT. Ah, you are adept at absorbing.

ROY. [With a touch of pride.] I have little education.

CROFT. Life, I see, has educated you. Now, speak as little as possible, but bow as much as you like! Limit yourself to a single cocktail. Your national customs frown upon more than a single cocktail! Remember?

ROY. What kind?

CROFT. Any kind you choose, but a single cocktail. I will jump into the fray if I detect a bit of difficulty; then, after forty minutes or so, I'll signal to you, like this [He gestures.] and you will leave, and return to Ralph's Rotisserie and barbecue your chickens in triumph.

ROY. And you, Mr. Croft?

CROFT. [With a trace of smugness.] Then I shall substantiate my theory—by revealing the truth.

CONSTANCE. [Calls from the bedroom.] Gilley? Darling?

CROFT. [*With a sudden jolt.*] Quick! My wife . . .

ROY. I meet her now?

CROFT. Later! [*He hustles* ROY *to the door.*] The instructions! Remember! I'll expect you in half an hour.

[*He opens the door, and with a little shove,* ROY *disappears. He closes the door just as* CONSTANCE CROFT *appears from the bedroom. She is a pleasantly attractive woman, a few years younger than her husband.*]

CONSTANCE. Would you be a dear, darling, and zip me up?

CROFT. Huh? Oh, yes. Where's the zipper?

CONSTANCE. Where it's always been, silly! [*She turns her back;* CROFT *tinkers with the zipper.*] Who was that just left?

CROFT. A—salesman.

CONSTANCE. Oh? What was he selling?

CROFT. Chickens.

CONSTANCE. [*Turning slightly.*] Chickens? Door-to-door? Ouch! You've pinched my flesh!

CROFT. [*Lightly.*] I did that years ago.

CONSTANCE. Your hands are terribly unsteady, darling. Perhaps you'd better fortify yourself with a Martini?

CROFT. I can wait. There!

CONSTANCE. Thanks. [*She takes a cigarette from a ceramic box on the table.*] I know how you despise these affairs, Gilley, but this *is* an obligation.

CROFT. [*Jauntily, as he lights her cigarette.*] And the punishment must fit the crime . . .

CONSTANCE. Do promise me, though, that you *will* participate . . .

CROFT. Connie, I give you my word, I shall do my legal utmost to make this your most memorable cocktail party.

CONSTANCE. Mine? It's yours, too, darling.

CROFT. Uh-uh, I'm absolved from blame. I have just a single guest. You're the official keeper for the majority of inmates.

CONSTANCE. I wish you wouldn't be so secretive about your lone guest. I've tried to pump you since breakfast.

CROFT. Just what these tribal rituals need: an element of surprise!

CONSTANCE. [*In a small voice.*] I must confess: he won't be a *complete* surprise. I phoned the others—soon after you'd told me you'd invited someone rather extraordinary . . .

CROFT. I anticipated that.

CONSTANCE. [*Fishing.*] What's he really like?

CROFT. He's an eminent international figure. That's all I plan to reveal—at the moment.

CONSTANCE. Is he attractive?

CROFT. Exceedingly.

CONSTANCE. [*Enormously pleased.*] You certainly knew how to pick your sole guest!

CROFT. [*Lightly.*] It took me days to survey the neighborhood.

CONSTANCE. [*Wrapping her arms about him.*] Oh, Gilley, darling! You've done all this for me?

CROFT. Well, not exactly . . .

CONSTANCE. You realize that a hostess is judged by the importance of her guests! [*A sudden thought.*] Oh, dear! How will we ever explain Juliet and Malcolm to him?

CROFT. Most intellectuals have some awfully dumb friends. For contrast!

CONSTANCE. [*Her mind working rapidly.*] Darling, I have a divine idea. Would your guest be suitable for Mrs. Benson Rowe? She's been in a state of manic depression since the tragedy.

CROFT. He'd be very suitable to her, I'm sure—but would *she* be suitable to him?

CONSTANCE. Perhaps Jody McKenzie, then? You know how she's felt about men, ever since her father had her withdrawn from boarding school . . .

CROFT. That was thirty years ago.

CONSTANCE. It's left a deep emotional scar.

CROFT. [*Firmly.*] Connie, I did not invite my distinguished guest as a panacea for your thwarted women.

CONSTANCE. [*She looks struck.*] Gilley, I only *suggested* . . . [MRS. QUINCY *enters from the kitchen with two dishes of cocktail tidbits.*] Oh, Mrs. Quincy, try to distribute the dishes strategically about the room. Please?

CROFT. For fastest consumption, why not on the bar?

CONSTANCE. The bar's in the kitchen, darling. [*Then speaking again to* MRS. QUINCY.] Mr. Croft, of course, will help you with the drinks. The bottles have been marked A and B. The A's are to be used only for the first two rounds . . .

CROFT. After that, you see, Mrs. Quincy, we switch to the no-name brands and no one is any the wiser.

CONSTANCE. Gilley, that's crude.

CROFT. But true, my love!

CONSTANCE. Well, Mrs. Quincy, everyone does that at cocktail parties—simply everyone.

MRS. QUINCY. [*Places one dish on the table.*] Now, don't go and be apologizin' to me. I'm a beer drinker, m'self.

[*She plunks the second dish down on the antique desk.*]

CROFT. [*Hastening over to the desk.*] Uh-uh, Mrs. Quincy! That desk once belonged to Bernard Shaw, and I gave him my word it'd never be used for anything stronger than writing—and carrot juice.

[*He picks up the dish and hands it back to* MRS. QUINCY, *who gives him a sharp, admonishing look.*]

CONSTANCE. [*Cautioning.*] Gilley, do be careful . . .

MRS. QUINCY. [*Muttering; as she places the dish elsewhere.*] Well, I'm not about to be pressin' carrot juice at this hour.

[*The door chimes ring.* MRS. QUINCY *crosses to the door.*]

CONSTANCE. [*Anxiously.*] How do I look?

CROFT. A bit shabby, but you'll do. [*He kisses her, lightly.*] Regardless of what happens this evening, Connie, promise me one thing?

CONSTANCE. [*Her eyes focused on the door.*] What's that?

CROFT. That you'll always love me.

[*Before* CONSTANCE *has the opportunity to reply to this vital question, the door is opened by* MRS. QUINCY, *and* MRS. BENSON ROWE *sweeps in. She is a somewhat formidable woman, perhaps in her fifties, and quite lavishly garbed in black.*]

CONSTANCE. Reena, darling!

MRS. ROWE. It was so kind of you to ask me.

CONSTANCE. [*As they exchange kisses.*] Nonsense, Reena, we're in your debt.

[MRS. QUINCY *busies herself about the room.*]

MR. ROWE. I don't know why anyone wants to put up with a poor, dispirited widow at cocktail parties, really.

CROFT. [*A bid for recognition.*] Mrs. Rowe?

MRS. ROWE. [*Turns swiftly.*] Gilson! I didn't notice you standing there.

CROFT. [*Flippantly.*] The unobtrusive male!

CONSTANCE. [*To* MRS. ROWE.] You've lost a bit of weight?

MRS. ROWE. [*Pleased.*] Have I really?

CONSTANCE. Dieting?

MRS. ROWE. Depressed spirits. I can't seem to locate my appetite. I suppose it's logical, after what I've been through.

CONSTANCE. I know, Reena, but you mustn't think of it this evening.

MRS. ROWE. But *how* can one forget?

CROFT. Cocktail?

MRS. ROWE. Oh, please!

CROFT. Martini?

MRS. ROWE. Very dry.

CROFT. Connie?

CONSTANCE. Not too dry.

[CROFT *goes into the kitchen.*]

MRS. ROWE. [*Sitting.*] Would you believe it, I had to *seek* the strength to make your party?

CONSTANCE. Even after I phoned you this noon?

MRS. ROWE. Do you know what I did, my dear? I dressed immediately and went straight over to the Palm Court, at the Plaza. I spent the entire afternoon there, in solemn meditation.

CONSTANCE. [*Offers a cigarette box.*] Time . . .

MRS. ROWE. [*With a deep sigh.*] Why on earth does it go so slowly for me? Thanks, my dear.

MRS. QUINCY. [*Offers a dish to* MRS. ROWE.] Peanuts?

CONSTANCE. [*Noting* MRS. ROWE'S *hesitation.*] They're synthetic. Oil-less. [MRS. ROWE *is convinced: she scoops up a handful of peanuts. The door chimes ring.* CONSTANCE *lowers her voice, confidingly.*] Gilley's grudgingly admitted that his guest's someone terribly special, so be prepared . . .

MRS. ROWE. [*Dramatically.*] Oh, my dear, how can I be prepared for anything except death?

[*The door is opened by* MRS. QUINCY, *and in come* JULIET PEDDLE *and* MALCOLM NEWCOMB. *Their ages, like their personalities, are difficult to determine, but* JULIET *has the vestiges of voluptuous beauty. Her hair is quite blond, and her wardrobe has the colorfulness of a World's Fair Midway.*]

CONSTANCE. [*Rushing over to them.*] Juliet! Malcolm!

[*There are kisses and embraces.* MRS. QUINCY *returns to the kitchen.*]

JULIET. We met in the elevator.

MALCOLM. Where's Pappy?

CONSTANCE. Mixing drinks.

MALCOLM. I'd better lend him a professional hand.

CONSTANCE. [*Taking hold of* MALCOLM's *arm.*] Before you do, I want you to meet Mrs. Benson Rowe. Juliet Peddle, Malcolm Newcomb.

MRS. ROWE. How do you do?

JULIET. Hi!

MALCOLM. Howdy! [*Anxious to get to the bar.*] Now!

CONSTANCE. Give Gilley your orders.

MALCOLM. [*To* JULIET.] Lambkin . . . ?

JULIET. The usual!

MALCOLM. I'll be swift as an arrow.

[*He hastens off into the kitchen.*]

JULIET. [*Looks around.*] Say, where'd you bury the "star attraction"?

CONSTANCE. I suspect Gilley's purposely asked him a bit late: to heighten the suspense.

MRS. ROWE. [*To* JULIET, *as she digs into the peanuts.*] So you and Mr. Newcomb are strangers?

JULIET. [*Sits.*] Strangers!

MRS. ROWE. I understood you to say that you'd just met in the elevator.

JULIET. Actually four years ago; on our way up to another party. So every year on our anniversary—y'know, sentimental and all—we meet again in an elevator, somewheres.

CONSTANCE. [*Attempts to explain to a somewhat baffled* MRS.

ROWE.] It's been . . . [*Turns to* JULIET.] May I tell Mrs. Rowe?

JULIET. Sure.

CONSTANCE. [*Sits next to* MRS. ROWE.] Rather complicated. Malcolm's married.

MRS. ROWE. [*Turns sharply, to* JULIET.] To you, of course.

JULIET. No. To Theresa.

[MRS. QUINCY *enters from the kitchen with a tray of cocktails and distributes them.*]

MRS. ROWE. [*Once she has regained her breath.*] Oh!

JULIET. It's working out okay, though. Where's Mr. Rowe? He here with you?

MRS. ROWE. My dear, he went down with his boat, last summer, off Mamaroneck.

CONSTANCE. They had such a lovely cabin cruiser. Forty-two feet.

MRS. ROWE. [*Dabbing at her eyes.*] He just couldn't make shore during that dreadful hurricane.

JULIET. Gosh, what a way to go!

MRS. QUINCY. [*Hands cocktail to* MRS. ROWE.] Extra dry, ma'am.

[*The door chimes ring.*]

MRS. ROWE. Thank you. Ever since, my life's been fruitless.

JULIET. [*Sips.*] I think fruit's overrated, anyway.

MRS. ROWE. [*Sips.*] Oh, this is heavenly! What brand of gin?

MRS. QUINCY. [*Hurries to the door.*] Brand A.

CONSTANCE. [*Quickly.*] Beefeater!

MRS. QUINCY. [*Muttering to herself.*] Better enjoy it while you can . . .

[*She opens the door and admits* JODY MC KENZIE, *a tailored, brisk woman of approximately forty.*]

CONSTANCE. [*Rises.*] Jody!

JODY. [*Crosses.*] I had one helluva time tearing away: spring inventory! [*Kisses* CONSTANCE.] How are you, Con?

CONSTANCE. Let me order you a drink.

JODY. God knows I need one.

CONSTANCE. Scotch and water?

JODY. Right.

CONSTANCE. Mrs. Quincy, Cutty Sark and water, please, for

Miss McKenzie! [MRS. QUINCY *goes off into the kitchen.* CON-
STANCE *turns to* JODY.] I believe you know Mrs. Benson Rowe?

MRS. ROWE. We met at the Wilson's Hyacinth tea.

JODY. First time I'd ever gotten a hangover on *tea.*

CONSTANCE. . . . And Juliet Peddle?

JULIET. Hi!

CONSTANCE. Well, now, Jody, how is the retail book business?

JODY. Stinks! Between the cut-rate shops and the recession . . .

MRS. ROWE. Recession? *I* haven't heard of any.

JODY. [*Sits.*] Ask me! But until there's a change of Admin-
istration . . .

CONSTANCE. Well, that's not likely for another two years.

JODY. Right! We're stuck.

MRS. ROWE. If the Democrats hadn't converted Washington
into a circus tent . . .

CONSTANCE. Reena, I always assumed you were a liberal . . .

MRS. ROWE. I am, my dear, when I agree with the point at
issue.

[CROFT *enters, carrying his own Martini, and a Scotch and water
for* JODY. *He is followed by* MALCOLM.]

CROFT. Jody, clench your tight little fist around this caramel
concoction!

JODY. [*Accepts the drink.*] Thanks, G. C.

CONSTANCE. Oh, Gilley, I don't believe Malcolm's been
introduced . . .

MALCOLM. [*Chortling.*] We'll catch up with each other.

CROFT. Jody, how are sales?

JODY. Unless you've got a "Sexualis suburbia" or a "How to"
you haven't got a chance today.

JULIET. [*Rather interested.*] A how-to what?

JODY. "How To Eat A Chinese Dinner With One Chop-
stick." *Anything!*

MALCOLM. Hey! I got one! Anybody know how to make a
Cannibal Martini? Well, you mix one-third vermouth, two-thirds
gin, stir, and drop into Martini small girl named Olive!

[JULIET *is bent over double with laughter; the others are not
quite so amused.*]

CONSTANCE. Malcolm!

MALCOLM. [*Blowing into* JULIET'S *ear.*] Woolly, woolly!

JULIET. [*Shrieks.*] Mal!

MALCOLM. Slide over to third, Lambkin!

[JULIET *moves a bit; he sits next to her.*]

CROFT. Man orders; woman obeys.

JODY. I'm doing whatever I can to refute that supposition.

CONSTANCE. [*Lightly.*] And just what measures have you taken, Jody?

JODY. I'm starting with the United Nations.

CROFT. [*Almost dropping his cocktail.*] United Nations?

JODY. I'm preparing a petition. If there were more female representation in the U.N., the world would be in a more tranquil state.

CONSTANCE. Good for you!

JODY. For centuries, the male has waged war. Strip him of war and you strip him of his bravado—and without his bravado . . .

JULIET. He'd sure be stripped.

MRS. ROWE. Mr. Rowe always maintained that a woman's place was in the home.

CROFT. Fortunately. Otherwise you might've been on that boat.

MRS. ROWE. I'm certain his last thought, as he went down, was not of his own safety, but of me in our lovely home, alone, without him.

[*And for punctuation, she drains her cocktail.*]

JULIET. [*Giggling.*] Aw, you been seein' too much TV!

MRS. ROWE. [*Drawing herself up to her full height.*] My husband, Miss Peddle, happened to be a gentleman, and *mine!*

JULIET. Okay, but I mean, let's look at it honest. If *you* were cuttin' loose into the next world . . .

MRS. ROWE. [*Rises indignantly.*] Excuse me.

[*She starts toward the bedroom.*]

CONSTANCE. [*Concerned.*] Want me to come with you, dear?

MRS. ROWE. [*Shaking her head; solemnly.*] Please . . . just a moment of meditation!

[*She disappears into the bedroom.*]

JULIET. Get that! After all, what'd I say?

JODY. I wouldn't take her too seriously.

CROFT. [*Taking charge.*] Come on now, girls, break it up! Better have a refill, before the main event.

JODY. Who *is* your mystery guest, G. C.? Con telephoned me . . .

CROFT. [*Buoyantly.*] Eight more minutes!

CONSTANCE. Where's he coming from, dear? Can't you even give us a hint?

CROFT. The roof . . . [*Hastily, checking himself.*] of the world!

JULIET. Siberia?

CROFT. The United Nations!

CONSTANCE. [*Delighted.*] Oh, Gilley, really?

JODY. My petition!

MALCOLM. [*His glass drained; he rises.*] C'mon, Pappy, we can't fly on one wing. I'll help you with the formula.

CROFT. No, no, you stay and enchant the girls. I'll summon you when I need you.

[*He exits into the kitchen.*]

CONSTANCE. [*Anxiously.*] Oh, dear, I do hope Reena's pulled herself together before he arrives.

JODY. [*Confidentially.*] Listen! From all I've heard from the Wilsons, Benson Rowe could easily have made that shore. He was an experienced sailor. But this was a legitimate opportunity to escape from her.

CONSTANCE. Jody!

JULIET. Couldn't he divorce the old biddy? I mean, wasn't that a bit much, goin' to the bottom?

JODY. A self-centered woman like her, granting him a divorce?

CONSTANCE. [*Indicating bedroom; cautiously.*] Sh!

[MRS. QUINCY *enters with a tray of canapés and passes them to the guests.*]

JULIET. Anybody can get a divorce. Mal can get one any time he wants. Right, hon?

MALCOLM. [*Uncomfortably.*] Sure All I have to do is mention it.

JULIET. See!

MALCOLM. [*Patting* JULIET *on the shoulder.*] But we don't want to spoil our happiness.

CROFT. [*Calls from the kitchen.*] Mal!

MALCOLM. [*Relieved to escape further embarrassing questioning, he happily retreats to the kitchen.*] Comin', Pappy!

CONSTANCE. [*After* MALCOLM *has disappeared.*] Juliet, are you really happy?

JULIET. Why, sure! I got a stone marten, full-length, and a co-op apartment. What else could a girl want?

CONSTANCE. [*Simply.*] A mate exclusively hers.

JODY. You put far too much emphasis on the beneficence of matrimony, Con!

JULIET. [*Insecurity in her voice.*] So what's happiness, anyway? Who knows real happiness? Or the truth?

[MRS. ROWE *re-enters.*]

CONSTANCE. Reena, we were just discussing happiness—from the female point of view.

JODY. Is there any other?

CONSTANCE. We didn't get very far, I'm afraid.

MRS. ROWE. [*With a telling glance at* JULIET.] Mr. Rowe worshiped me; that is my true and everlasting happiness.

JODY. [*To* MRS. ROWE, *with a biting sweetness.*] Certainly! Yours was an idyllic relationship. According to the Wilsons.

JULIET. [*As* MRS. ROWE *sits.*] Mrs. Rowe, I didn't mean to ruffle your feathers. All I tried to say was . . .

[*She is about to lapse into it again, when she is interrupted by* MALCOLM, *who returns with a large Martini pitcher. He conscientiously goes about the room refilling the empty cocktail glasses.*]

MALCOLM. Pappy doesn't want us to waste any time.

CROFT. [*Re-enters with a fresh drink for* JODY.] If Mohammed won't come to the bar, the bar will come to Mohammed!

JODY. [*Accepts drink.*] Thanks, G. C.

CROFT. A glass of *expensive* Scotch in your hand . . .

MRS. QUINCY. [*Turning sharply.*] We still on *A?*

CROFT. [*Drowning her out.*] . . . and your life's completely satisfactory.

JODY. [*Much too quickly.*] It always has been.

CROFT. No frustrations, no delusions?

JODY. None!

CROFT. [*With a wicked eye.*] Well . . . [*Raises his glass.*] One more cheer!

MRS. QUINCY. [*As* MRS. ROWE *takes a handful of canapés from the proffered tray.*] Glad you located your appetite, ma'am. [*The door chimes ring.*]

CROFT. [*Quickly, putting down his glass.*] This one's on *me*, Mrs. Quincy.

[*He hurries to the door.* CONSTANCE, *the anxious hostess, follows him.* MRS. QUINCY, *her chores momentarily completed, returns to the kitchen.*]

CONSTANCE. Oh, darling, is there any special protocol? [*With a grand flourish,* CROFT *opens the door and admits* ROY RADHAKAMAL. ROY *now is ornamented with a glistening white turban and a multicolored ribbon, which is pinned across his chest.*]

CROFT. [*Exuberantly.*] Shri Radhakamal!

ROY. [*With an unsteady glance at the letter of instructions in his hand.*] It was most—cordial—of you—to request my presence . . . [*With a swift jerk,* CROFT *extracts the letter from* ROY'S *hand. For a second,* ROY *is at a loss. All eyes in the room are now focused on this colorful guest.*]

CROFT. [*Waving the letter.*] Marvelous, these diplomats! A prepared speech of introduction! [*He quickly slips the letter into his pocket and places his arm around* ROY'S *shoulder.*]

CONSTANCE. [*To* ROY, *breathlessly.*] I'm Mrs. Croft!

CROFT. [*Makes the formal introduction.*] Shri Radhakamal, cultural attaché to his—er—nation's ministry; delegate *nulli secundus* to the United Nations! [*He signals* ROY *with a sharp tap on the arm.* ROY *picks up the cue, a bit slowly and with some diffidence, then takes* CONSTANCE'S *hand and kisses it.*]

JULIET. [*Cooing.*] Ooh! I'm next.

CROFT. [*Continues with the introductions.*] Miss Peddle!

[JULIET *thrusts her hand forward;* ROY *kisses it. By now, he is beginning to enjoy his diplomatic privilege.*]

JULIET. Tell me, what's a Shri?

CROFT. [*Without losing a minute.*] Mister!—In his native language.

JODY. And the feminine gender?

CROFT. *Shrew.* Miss McKenzie!

[ROY *is about to kiss* JODY's *hand, but instead, she takes hold of his and gives him a vigorous handshake.*]

JODY. I'm preparing a petition which may be of considerable interest . . .

CROFT. [*Snatching* ROY *away.*] Mrs. Benson Rowe!

ROY. [*He is about to kiss* MRS. ROWE's *hand, but momentarily is blinded by her ring.*] That is—genuine ring?

MRS. ROWE. A gift from my dear departed husband.

ROY. You are widow?

MRS. ROWE. Yes.

[ROY *kisses her hand with exceptional fervor.*]

CROFT. [*Separating* ROY *from* MRS. ROWE.] Malcolm Newcomb!

MALCOLM. Howdy, sir! [*He hands* ROY *a Martini.*] Might as well pipe in a li'l American oil!

CROFT. Well, these are our friends, Shri.

ROY. I am—most flattered—to be—in company with you. [*He bows slightly, then takes a swig of his cocktail.*]

MRS. ROWE. Is your country seen on the Grand Tour, Shri Radhakamal?

ROY. Grand—Tour?

MRS. ROWE. Mr. Rowe and I took it twice, before and after the war.

CROFT. Doubt it, Reena! They've been too overcrowded to accommodate tourists. But Shri Radhakamal tells me they're extending their borders . . .

JODY. Without war?

CROFT. They're filling in some sea. No one uses it much, anyway. Polluted!

CONSTANCE. [*Curiously.*] Gilley, where'd you meet Shri Radhakamal?

CROFT. Matter of fact—in a restaurant.

CONSTANCE. [*Approaches* ROY *with a tray of canapés.*] You never told me.

CROFT. [*Playfully.*] I don't ask who you've met at the hairdresser's, my love. [*Quickly, offering a cigarette.*] Shri?

CONSTANCE. [*Replaces tray.*] Just what are the duties of a cultural attaché, Shri Radhakamal?

ROY. [*Momentarily lost.*] Duties?

CONSTANCE. Yes, what do you perform?

CROFT. [*Intervening.*] I'm afraid Shri Radhakamal isn't really in a position to answer that, dear. He's working at a "top secret" level.

CONSTANCE. Culture, top secret?

CROFT. Well, this particular kind of culture, yes. Right, Shri?

ROY. [*With the assistance of his cocktail, he is gaining assurance.*] Oui!

CROFT. They may not understand each other at the U.N. but they all seem to understand French.

ROY. [*Enjoying his cocktail.*] Oui!

CROFT. Now, if none of you allows this to leak to the press: Shri Radhakamal's government is working on a sequel to the Dead Sea Scrolls!

CONSTANCE. How fascinating!

MRS. ROWE. I adored that book.

JODY. [*Efficiently.*] I appreciate the importance of such a project, Shri Radhakamal, but I have one of more personal concern. I deplore the uneven balance of male and female representation at the U.N. Just what are *your* views on the subject?

ROY. [*Thinks a moment.* CROFT *holds his breath.*] It is my —belief—that we *are* evenly balanced. One beautiful, lovely woman—equals—ten men.

[CROFT *breathes a sigh of relief.*]

CONSTANCE. [*Proudly.*] There, now!

MALCOLM. Say, that tribute calls for another round, fella! [ROY *happily extends his glass.* MALCOLM *is about to refill it from the Martini pitcher.*]

CROFT. Hold it! Shri Radhakamal's national customs prevent his having more than a *single* cocktail.

ROY. That custom—prevails—only on our native soil.

[*With a little bow, he turns his cocktail glass over to* MALCOLM, *who gleefully refills it.*]

MALCOLM. Where you located, pal?

CROFT. [*Before* ROY *has a chance to reply.*] They're sandwiched in between the Near East and the Middle East. You know that thin little strip of land?

MALCOLM. Me? Hell, I haven't looked at a map in years.

CONSTANCE. [*Starts toward the book shelves.*] Here, let me get one for you.

CROFT. [*Grabs hold of* CONSTANCE'S *arm and steers her in the opposite direction.*] I think Jody's ready for replenishing . . . [*With a curious look at her husband,* CONSTANCE *takes* JODY'S *glass and hastens off into the kitchen.* MALCOLM, *meanwhile, proceeds to replenish the Martinis wherever necessary.*]

JODY. [*To* ROY.] Just what is your country's population?

ROY. We breed so—rapidly—that it is—regrettable—we cannot take—official . . .

[*He is stuck for the proper word.*]

JODY. [*Helpfully.*] Census?

ROY. Yes, thank you, Miss . . .

JODY. McKenzie. Now, about my petition . . .

CROFT. [*Heartily.*] Shri Radhakamal's off duty now!

JULIET. [*Surveying* ROY.] Y'know something: you're even sexier than your picture.

MALCOLM. [*To* JULIET, *suspiciously.*] Where'd *you* see his picture?

JULIET. Where'd y'think? In the *Journal*, coupla days ago.

MALCOLM. [*Relieved.*] Oh. Yeah. [*To* ROY.] That the one where you were makin' some kind of speech, pal?

CROFT. [*Relishing all this.*] Something about antiquities!

JODY. I believe I read the text of it in the *Times*. Didn't someone smuggle them out of the country?

CROFT. Developed into an international incident! Now it's before the U.N. Darn moving speech, Shri! Heard there wasn't a solitary throat without a lump in the Unesco Council Room. [ROY *bows most graciously.* CROFT *quickly turns to* JULIET.] That's the cable address for United Nations Educational, Scientific and Cultural Organization.

JULIET. Some handle! No wonder they got a cable.

MRS. ROWE. [*To* ROY.] Will you write a book about it, like the Dead Sea Scrolls?

CROFT. [*Loftily.*] Shri Radhakamal is collaborating with me. [CONSTANCE *returns with* JODY'S *drink.*]

CONSTANCE. *You,* Gilley?

CROFT. Why not me, dearest?

CONSTANCE. You've never tackled anything but novels, fiction . . .

CROFT. [*Wryly.*] Well, this *is* in the nature of fiction, isn't it, Shri?

ROY. At home, we say: fiction and truth—are separated by— a pinhead.

CONSTANCE. [*Delightedly.*] Oh, Gilley, darling, you've held all this back from me.

JODY. When's the publication date, G. C.? I'll plan a window display.

CONSTANCE. [*With breathless anticipation.*] Promise me, in front of our friends, darling, that we'll invest a portion of the royalties from this noble book in a pilgrimage to Shri Radhakamal's native land.

CROFT. Now, hold it a minute, Connie . . .

[MRS. QUINCY *enters with a platter of hot little delicacies, passes among the guests with them, then returns to the kitchen.*]

MRS. ROWE. I'm cerain, Shri Radhakamal, I heard my late husband speak of you. He did a great deal of business with your nation, I believe.

CONSTANCE. Quite possibly! Mr. Rowe was always traveling: introducing Lily cups in the most remote corners of the world.

ROY. Oh, yes—yes—now I remember. He was fine man.

MRS. ROWE. See! I *knew* you'd met!

MALCOLM. [*To* ROY.] How's the pipeline?

[ROY *automatically extends his glass for refilling.*]

CROFT. [*Gesturing.*] Shri! You asked me to remind you of the time. It's six of five: time for departure.

CONSTANCE. [*Slightly horrified.*] Gilley!

ROY. [*Uninfluenced by* CROFT'S *signal.*] I am not due—next appointment—till seven.

CROFT. He specifically requested that I watch the time.

CONSTANCE. I know, but . . .

ROY. Time is of little—consequence—when one is in— presence—of such charming ladies. [*He takes* CONSTANCE'S *hand and kisses it.*]

CONSTANCE. [*Overwhelmed.*] Couldn't you postpone your seven o'clock appointment? You may use our phone . . .

CROFT. Connie! Stop interfering with the progress of the U.N.! [*Gesturing even more emphatically to* ROY.] You've got an emergency caucus tonight! If you don't punch in, you may be dismissed.

CONSTANCE. Nonsense, darling, his isn't a *menial* job!

ROY. [*Ignoring* CROFT'S *latest hint, glides over toward the piano.*] Ah! I see, Mrs. Croft, excellent polished piano.

CONSTANCE. Do you play?

CROFT. [*Pointedly.*] They don't have pianos in his . . .

ROY. [*Sits at piano.*] Correction, Mr. Croft. One of my ancestors—far back—he *invent* piano.

CONSTANCE. Do play something for us, please!

JULIET. [*Applauding.*] Go on!

[ROY *begins to play an unfamiliar piece.* JODY, *entranced, rises and wanders over to the piano.*]

CONSTANCE. What an enchanting piece!

JODY. [*To* ROY.] Isn't that your national anthem?

MRS. ROWE. Quite different from "The Star-Spangled Banner."

JULIET. Sure is livelier!

[ROY *now plays more rhythmically and with more abandon.*]

CONSTANCE. Darling, just *listen* to him!

CROFT. I hear him!

CONSTANCE. Oh, Gilley, how wonderful of you to've asked Shri Radhakamal! This *is* a memorable cocktail party.

CROFT. [*Ominously.*] It's going to get even more memorable in a few seconds.

[ROY *continues to play during the following conversation.*]

ROY. Miss McKenzie—will you do me—honor—by coming to dinner? We can therefore discuss your—petition—in privacy.

JODY. I have a more intriguing idea. Why not come to my apartment? It'll be a great treat for you. I'll fix an American meal. [*Starts to itemize.*] Barbecued chicken . . .

CROFT. [*Storms over to the piano.*] He's as familiar with barbecued chicken as he is with his own name!

CONSTANCE. Gilley!

JODY. [*Startled.*] G. C.!

CROFT. I mean, I don't think it's a very respectable policy, Jody. He's *married!*

JULIET. So where's the crime?

JODY. Oh, don't be such a Puritan!

CONSTANCE. Gilley, I'm amazed . . .

CROFT. [*Entreatingly.*] Now, listen to me! All of you!

JODY. [*Turns away from* CROFT.] Tomorrow, at six?

ROY. I will arrange it.

JODY. Forty-seven Barrow Street.

CROFT. [*Finally galvanized into action.*] WILL YOU LISTEN TO ME? [*He slams the piano lid down;* ROY *withdraws his hands just in time to escape injury. The others are startled.*] You're all making damn fools of yourselves!

CONSTANCE. [*Stricken.*] *We* are?

ROY. [*Rises, with serene dignity.*] In my country, it is— disrespectful—to interrupt—national anthem.

CROFT. [*His patience exhausted.*] It's no more your national anthem than it is mine. I signaled you to leave—*ten minutes ago.*

CONSTANCE. [*Thoroughly bewildered and embarrassed by this sudden turn of events.*] Gilley, are you all right?

MALCOLM. [*Picks up* CROFT's *cocktail glass.*] Here, Pappy, better take a chaser!

CROFT. I've had enough. You've all had enough. I hired this man to prove a point. The point's been well proven, *too well* proven.

CONSTANCE. What in the world are you talking about?

CROFT. Shri Radhakamal is plain Roy Radhakamal, an employee of Ralph's Rotisserie, Lexington Avenue.

CONSTANCE. You're being vindictive because Shri Radhakamal's monopolized our attention!

CROFT. Ho-ho! I was right! A cocktail party's the perfect arena to test people's credulity! [*To* ROY.] I'll give you your fee, and you can go! [*He rips into his wallet and extracts a bill.*] There!

ROY. [*Refuses; with diplomatic grace.*] I do not require payment—for my—presence.

CONSTANCE. [*Apologetically.*] You must forgive my husband, Shri Radhakamal! The first week in spring always seems to affect him . . .

CROFT. Look! I passed him off as an official of the U.N. *I* supplied the turban and the ribbon and the airs and the grace and all those damn bows. And you—all fell for it. Won't anyone believe me?

MRS. ROWE. Ridiculous! He knew Mr. Rowe very well.

ROY. [*With complete serenity.*] Since, Mr. Croft—I am the object of this—

JODY. Slander! That's all it is, slander!

ROY. [*Bows.*] I would like to—withdraw—peaceably—

CONSTANCE. [*Wretchedly.*] Oh, do please stay and have another cocktail!

ROY. I appreciate the—generosity, Mrs. Croft. But perhaps your husband is—correct. I have had enough. [*With a slight tilt, he crosses to door; then turns.*] I take my leave—with fond goodbyes—to all of you, who have made—party—so pleasant for me. If any of you so desire—you may reach me—care of—*The United Nations.* Good evening.

[*He bows and exits.*]

CROFT. [*After a moment.*] I know what you're all thinking.

CONSTANCE. [*Her fury mounting.*] I see what you meant by "memorable"!

MRS. ROWE. [*Rises.*] I question your manners, Gilson!

CONSTANCE. I question his *sanity!*

MRS. ROWE. [*Has gathered her things; turns to* CONSTANCE.] Goodnight, my dear. You have my sympathy.
[*She crosses majestically to the door and exits.*]

MALCOLM. Ball becomes brawl: old Chinese proverb. Ready, Lambkin?

JULIET. [*Rises.*] Y'know, I never thought much about that United Nations business, but after meetin' the Shri, I think I'm gonna take it in, some rainy afternoon.

CONSTANCE. I'm dreadfully sorry the party's turned out this way.

MALCOLM. C'mon, Jody. We'll give you a lift. 'Night, Con. Pappy.

JODY. [*Starts off.*] Better watch that bar stuff, G. C.!
[*They go.*]

CROFT. Gullible fools!

CONSTANCE. [*Enraged.*] Now, you . . . !

CROFT. [*Protesting.*] Wait, wait, dearest . . .

CONSTANCE. [*Sharply.*] Don't address me as "dearest"!

CROFT. I admit I'm partially at fault: tricking you all into believing he was with the U.N. *was* a low curve, but . . .

CONSTANCE. You can conserve your breath!

CROFT. I only intended to demonstrate . . .

CONSTANCE. You demonstrated, all right! You can be brutally cruel. A combination of gin and natural bitterness!

CROFT. I barely touched my cocktail.

CONSTANCE. You humiliated me. In front of my friends . . .

CROFT. You know as well as I do, they're not your friends. Just a bunch of guzzling gypsies, drifting from one party to another! [*Moves closer to her.*] Connie, can I help it if the thing got out of hand? [*He digs into his pocket.*] Here! Read my instructions!

CONSTANCE. [*Sobs.*] Get away from me!
[*She sweeps the letter out of his hand; it sails to the floor.*]

CROFT. What do I have to do to convince you?
[*He turns toward the door.*]

CONSTANCE. That's the awful part of it! I love you, even though I find it difficult to believe you. [CROFT *starts to exit.*] Where are *you* going?

CROFT. I'm going to treat myself to a barbecued chicken! Turban and all!

[*He slams the door and goes.* CONSTANCE *dabs at her eyes; as she does so, her glance is attracted to the letter on the floor. She reaches down, picks it up, reads it. When she emerges, her tear-misted eyes seem to take on a bright new sparkle.*]

CONSTANCE. *Me!* At my own cocktail party, too!

[*She finally bursts into laughter.*]

CURTAIN

THE HUNTED

By

Edward Senior

(*Published here for the first time*)

CAST

Time: The present.

Place: A three-hour drive from New York City.

THE HUNTED

The stage is divided to represent three locations:
(1) Left downstage: A place on the hillside above the town.
There is a tree stump at extreme left.
(2) Right downstage: In town, the fence separating the Cripps
and Farney yards.
(3) Upstage: Alongside a road in the hills above the town. A
shot is heard just before the curtain rises. At curtain, under
dim light, SARAH JANE *is sprawled motionless, downstage center.*
A child's picture book is alongside her. BRANT *is sitting with his*
back against the tree stump; he is sighting his rifle. He puts the
rifle down and crawls toward SARAH JANE. *He poises his hand, as*
if he wanted to touch the back of her head.

BRANT. [*Tensely.*]
    Red. red . . . !
It will be hibiscus, like the flower painted
By a Gauguin for the hair of some Tahitian girl.
[BRANT *touches the back of* SARAH JANE'S *head; he takes his hand*
away and glares at the blood on it; with a shiver of disgust he
wipes his hand on the ground; all at once he seems to go limp.
BRANT *crawls back to the tree stump; he sits, his back resting*
against the stump.]
    Let the hunters come tomorrow; they will be
A valueless purple [*Crying out.*] in the mud!
The hunters will come, Sarah Jane. Let them!
But the night comes first. And tomorrow
What will they learn? Nothing. Can't you hear them
Asking, "How did it happen?" How did it?
[*Laughing bitterly.*]
I can tell you, Sarah Jane, I can tell
Because I am an artist, not a hunter.
I was never a hunter, never wanted to be.
How much better to be an artist! More:
An artist for whom they hunt! Oh, they'll hunt

97

For us, but when they find us, Sarah Jane,
They'll be no wiser. For the story is entrusted
Only to me. Only I could tell them—and I won't.
At the end, an artist arranges everything
For *himself:* from the beginning to the end.
It makes the story his own. Just think . . .

[BRANT *rises and goes slowly right, to the upstage side of the fence.
He takes a handful of empty shotgun shells from his pocket.*]

Suppose I start this morning, with Mr. Gableman.
Mr. Gableman is a hunter, a very good one.
How well he hunted this morning, with my dogs!
And what an excellent shot he is! Imagine,
He never, never misses. Five lovely pheasants,
He brought down. But I? Nothing.

[SARAH JANE *begins to raise herself to a sitting position. The
lights come up.*]

I missed every time . . . I missed my wife.
He brought her down, too. Now Mr. Gableman has
Five pheasants *and* my elegant wife.
And *that* is quite a bag for one day.
Now, I—what did I bring back to you?
Nothing, Sarah Jane, but a handful
Of empty shotgun shells. To you the trophies,
Testimonials to my unremarkable marksmanship.

[SARAH JANE *seems to be looking at the picture book; but now she
notices* BRANT *and gets to her feet, carrying her picture book. She
comes toward the downstage side of the fence.* BRANT *holds the
empty shotgun shells out to her, over the fence.*]

I give you these empty prizes.

SARAH JANE. Yes, mister?

BRANT. Come here!

[BRANT *leans over the fence to stuff the empty shells in* SARAH
JANE'S *pocket. Then, taking her free hand in his, he draws her
gently against the fence while he removes a toy dog from his
pocket. He presses the toy into her hand.*] There!

SARAH JANE. Yes, mister?

BRANT. Look! A fine dog for your birthday. For you, Sarah
Jane. Take it!

[*He lets go her hand suddenly, almost guiltily. She stares at the dog.*]

SARAH JANE. Dog . . .

BRANT. To hunt with—on your birthday.

SARAH JANE. [*Excitedly.*] Fifteen. Mom says . . .

BRANT. A lovely girl for the age. Happy birthday!

SARAH JANE. [*Droning.*] Fifteen, four, two . . .

BRANT. Yes, yes, all of them. But most of all: fifteen. Congratulations!

[MRS. CRIPPS *enters along the downstage side of the fence.*]

SARAH JANE. [*Softly.*] Ride, mister?

MRS. CRIPPS [*Remonstrating.*] Now, Brant, don't encourage her!

BRANT. We're just having a friendly chat, Clara.

SARAH JANE. [*Louder.*] Ride, mister?

BRANT. [*With great ceremony.*] What? A ride? Well, I'd be honored to take you in my automobile—if . . .

MRS. CRIPPS. She doesn't need a ride this late in the day.

BRANT. [*Playfully.*] An extra-special birthday ride?

MRS. CRIPPS. [*Noticing the toy in* SARAH JANE's *hand.*] Oh, you've given her another present. A dog! You shouldn't, Brant. Every week end you spoil her. Then after you've gone, she's just impossible to handle.

SARAH JANE. [*Urgently.*] Ride, mister?

BRANT. Well, why not?

MRS. CRIPPS. [*Resigning.*] There! Now I'll have to let her go. If not, there'll be weeping and wailing.

BRANT. Yes, ride, Sarah Jane!

SARAH JANE. [*Delighted.*] Ride, ride!

MRS. CRIPPS. [*Trying to quiet* SARAH JANE.] You're to blame, Brant. You put her up to it.

BRANT. [*Extravagantly.*] I'm happy to oblige the little girl next door.

MRS. CRIPPS. [*Hesitating.*] But your wife, and that Mr. . . . ?

BRANT. [*Covering.*] Oh, my wife's ready to leave for the city. She's driving down with Mr. Gableman.

MRS. CRIPPS. [*Softly.*] I see.

BRANT. [*Pressed to be casual.*] You know—a party. One of

those big Saturday night New York affairs. I hate them. I'm keeping *this* week end for myself. And then early tomorrow, without a headache, I can do some more hunting.

MRS. CRIPPS. Well, Sarah Jane, you'll have to get ready for your ride.

SARAH JANE. Ride, ride!

[MRS. CRIPPS *and* SARAH JANE *exit along the fence, right.*]

BRANT. [*Calling after them.*] I'll have my car waiting in front.

[BRANT *stares after them, failing to notice that his wife and* MR. GABLEMAN *enter from upstage right.* MRS. FARNEY *is elegantly dressed; she wears a fur coat.* MR. GABLEMAN *has on a sport jacket; he carries a well-stuffed game sack in one hand, a small suitcase in the other; and a shotgun case is slung over his shoulder.*]

MRS. FARNEY. [*Fumbling in her purse.*] Now wherever is my key to the apartment? [*Without looking up.*] Brant, you'll be back in New York for supper tomorrow? [*Apparently having found the key, she shuts her purse, and looks at* BRANT'S *back.*] Well, Brant?

BRANT. [*Turning slowly; speaking mildly.*] All set to go, dear?

MRS. FARNEY. [*Irritated.*] Really, Brant, have you been bothering that idiot child again?

BRANT. [*With feigned indignation.*] Bothering? Why, I never bother Sarah Jane.

MRS. FARNEY. Can't you make an effort to stay away from that fence? You know how it annoys me.

MR. GABLEMAN. [*Boisterously kidding.*] Got yourself a sweetheart next door? A bright pretty little home-town girl?

BRANT. [*Returning in kind.*] A charmer! She lets *me* do all the talking.

MRS. FARNEY. Then please talk to her when I'm not around.

MR. GABLEMAN. Brant, I do believe you make your wife jealous!

MRS. FARNEY. [*To* GABLEMAN.] Jealous? It makes me ill. Come along.

BRANT. [*Still cheerful.*] I suppose one of these days I'll talk myself to death—both of us.

MRS. FARNEY. [*To* GABLEMAN.] Come along.

BRANT. [*Suddenly resigned.*] Well, Gableman, don't be late! Got your pheasants?

MR. GABLEMAN. [*Holding up the game sack.*] In the bag— all here.

MRS. FARNEY. [*Grudgingly accepting a perfunctory kiss from* BRANT.] All right, dear. Have a nice day tomorrow.

MR. GABLEMAN. Thanks for the hunting, Brant. Tomorrow keep your eye on the *birds.* And better luck!

[MR. GABLEMAN *and* MRS. FARNEY *go around the fence to exit right, extreme downstage.*]

BRANT. Good-bye. Yes, tomorrow—better luck. I hope.

[BRANT *stares after them, then scowls blackly and exits by the same route. The lights black out.* —— *When the lights come up,* MRS. CRIPPS *enters along the downstage side of the fence, a shawl around her shoulders. She peers anxiously into the distance; she glances several times at her wrist watch. The* FIRST TOWNSMAN *enters left, crosses extreme downstage, says,* "Good afternoon, Clara." MRS. CRIPPS *nods, and smiles vaguely in return. The* FIRST TOWNSMAN *exits. The* SECOND TOWNSMAN *and* THIRD TOWNS-MAN *cross the stage. They carry shotguns and gunny sacks—the day's bag of game.*]

SECOND TOWNSMAN. Hello, Mrs. Cripps.

MRS. CRIPPS. [*Absently.*] Oh, hello, boys.

THIRD TOWNSMAN. G'd afternoon.

MRS. CRIPPS. [*Echoing.*] Afternoon? It's evening. [*Suddenly awake to her manners, she smiles.*] Well, almost evening. Have a good day, boys?

THIRD TOWNSMAN. [*Indicating gunny sack.*] A couple of rabbits and a pheasant. We missed a few shots.

SECOND TOWNSMAN. It wasn't cold enough. For real good sport, give me a day with a bite to it. Tomorrow ought to be better.

MRS. CRIPPS. [*Pulling her shawl tighter.*] They say it's going to get colder. I can feel it coming.

THIRD TOWNSMAN. Wind's from the northwest.

MRS. CRIPPS. [*Her attention wandering.*] I hope Sarah Jane won't be chilly.

SECOND TOWNSMAN. Sarah Jane—why, how's she doing?

MRS. CRIPPS. [*Absently.*] Nice enough, thank you. [*Attentive again; a little sadly.*] It's her birthday, you know. She's fifteen today.

SECOND TOWNSMAN. [*Purposely vague.*] Is that so? well, now . . .

MRS. CRIPPS. [*Attempting cheeriness.*] She's out on a special birthday ride with Brant Farney. It gives her such a thrill to ride in his car.

SECOND TOWNSMAN. Now that's right: we did see them driving along.

THIRD TOWNSMAN. Yeah, in his Chrysler Imperial. Some swell buggy!

MRS. CRIPPS. [*Instantly curious.*] Where was that?

SECOND TOWNSMAN. [*To* THIRD.] On Hightown Road, wasn't it? We were coming in . . .

THIRD TOWNSMAN. Yeah, they were going out.

MRS. CRIPPS. [*Half to herself.*] It's almost time for Sarah Jane's supper.

SECOND TOWNSMAN. Too bad Farney don't have kids of his own.

MRS. CRIPPS. Whenever he's here from New York, he's mighty good to Sarah Jane.

SECOND TOWNSMAN. I'd say he ought to adopt one. That is, if his wife . . .

MRS. CRIPPS. [*Knowingly.*] Of course, his wife. . . . She doesn't seem very . . .

[*She shrugs.*]

SECOND TOWNSMAN. [*Ready to leave.*] Well, happy birthday to Sarah Jane!

MRS. CRIPPS. Thank you.

THIRD TOWNSMAN. G'bye, Mrs. Cripps.

MRS. CRIPPS. Good-bye, boys. Have a good supper.

THIRD TOWNSMAN. [*To* SECOND.] I'm starved.

[*The* TOWNSMEN *leave, and* MRS. CRIPPS *again peers anxiously into the distance, looks at her wrist watch, and reluctantly withdraws.*

The lights black out. Then the upstage light comes up dim.

BRANT'S *voice is heard from upstage right; he sounds short of breath, and at the same time, exuberant.*]

BRANT.

Let's stop, Sarah Jane, where we can see . . .

This place will do—for the moment.

[SARAH JANE *tugs ahead of* BRANT *from the extreme right to center of stage.* BRANT *has hold of her wrist. In his free hand, he carries a rifle. A blanket is draped over the rifle, almost concealing it.* SARAH JANE *still carries the toy dog in one hand, her picture book in the other.* BRANT *sits, and pulls* SARAH JANE *down to a sitting position on the ground beside him.*]

Look, the hillsides going down, down;

And away down there—far below: the town.

The same town as last week! And away up here

The same you and me as last week. So

You never even missed that week—did you?

But the town is older, the hills are browner,

The weather colder, and you have become fifteen.

SARAH JANE. [*Regarding* BRANT.] *Two, four, fifteen . . .*

BRANT.

Fifteen! And I? I do believe I have grown

Another grey hair.

[BRANT *touches his hand to his temple and* SARAH JANE *puts the hand in which she holds the toy dog to the same spot.* BRANT *pushes her hand away, and she giggles.*]

Oh, it's funny to you who can never get older.

You can laugh. You have always been young—

Always will be.

SARAH JANE. Go hunt? Hunt?

BRANT.

In another minute we'll run and we'll hunt.

Everything to please the little girl next door!

Oh, yes, big girl now! All of fifteen!

A delightful age, Sarah Jane. Big enough

To hunt . . . *to be hunted.*

Let me ask; how can you hunt if you are locked

In a dismal frame house? Or confined to a yard

Down there with a fence around you? And yet,
How much more confined, Sarah Jane, you would be
In my New York apartment. I mean my wife's
Apartment, now that it's going to be hers.
Up against those walls you wouldn't last long.
Pictures are made for walls; *they* go there.
Now, I have a Braque, a Matisse, a Modigliani—
Paintings I hunted extensively to find.
I thought I wanted them. But I don't.

SARAH JANE. Go hunt, mister?

BRANT.

Very well, a-hunting
We will go.

SARAH JANE. Dog, mister?

BRANT.

Dog?
Why, certainly.
Oh, where, oh, where has my little dog gone?
Oh, where, oh, where can he be?

[SARAH JANE *holds up the toy dog to* BRANT; *he touches it.*]

There it is! A great success, my singing!
But at hunting—will I fail again?
You see, Sarah Jane, I have new glasses,
Stronger ones than I had last week.

[BRANT *looks* SARAH JANE *straight in the eyes and taps his glasses.
She shrinks back, apparently frightened.*]

So the glasses make my eyes big—big
From your side? Great, rolling fish bowl eyes?
Don't be afraid, Sarah Jane. I'll look away.
I'll turn to the subject of hair.
You, for instance, have lovely amber-
Dropping hair. So the poet describes it.
While mine is brown—as mud! Well, mostly
Brown, all but the important part, which is
Grey and spreading. It's a matter of time;
Everything alive will spread or shrink.
Take chests, for example. Would you know
My chest has been shrinking? While yours—

Well, look at you!

[BRANT *flips back her coat and looks at her bosom. He chuckles,*
then turns away. SARAH JANE *takes no notice.*]

    SARAH JANE. [*Urgently.*] Dogs, mister?

    BRANT. [*Puzzled for an instant, he looks at the toy.*]

Dogs? But you have one. There!

Oh, I understand. You want to see

The dogs at Mr. Tandy's. No, not now!

The hunting dogs are tired. They have worked

Very hard today. We'll let them rest

A while at Mr. Tandy's—while we hunt.

The dog in your hand is quite enough for *us.*

[BRANT *gets up and pulls* SARAH JANE *to her feet.*]

    SARAH JANE. Run, mister . . . ?

    BRANT.

Yes, a little farther. Run now!

[*They run off, upstage left. The lights black out. A little out of*
breath, BRANT *and* SARAH JANE *re-enter from downstage left, as the*
lights come up dim. He forces her to a sitting position in the
same spot she occupied when the play started.]

Now! Far enough! Here you can watch

A bird, rabbits, anything that moves!

Be very still!

[*He crawls to the tree stump, left, and sits with his back resting*
against the stump. SARAH JANE *is facing right; she holds out the*
toy dog and points it. BRANT *is excited.*]

Don't move, Sarah Jane!

I'll make you see everything.

I can do it. Don't move!

[BRANT *uncovers the rifle; he raises it, aiming it at the back of*
SARAH JANE'S *head; he lowers the rifle, raises it again while he*
talks. The light grows dimmer.]

The fields, the birds, the town;

My father's old house next to yours;

My New York apartment, my office,

My bank account—and my elegant wife.

Oh, yes, Sarah Jane, I can show you . . .

[SARAH JANE *slowly sinks into the same sprawled position as at the*

opening. BRANT *puts rifle down, crawls to her and arranges her*
clothing and hair. He closes her eyelids.]
>   Just as though today were tomorrow! A story
>   Out of the future! It ends our adventure,
>   Completes our hunting. Finishes the picture?
>   Yes! So nothing can be changed.
>   How could I change you? That would spoil the picture.

[BRANT *crawls back to the stump and pulls the blanket around his*
shoulders. The lights slowly dim down and out.]
>   You will see! You will see like an artist!
>   You'll appreciate how eager they are
>   To find us. Those eager fools, they'll be
>   No *wiser.* They are just hunters; and we
>   Have become the hunted.
>   [*With a short, bitter laugh.*]
>   Imagine!
>   Can't you believe it's morning again? Almost?
>   Can't you see how the men blow on their hands?
>   It's cold, and their breath is like—well—
>   Like puffs of white dust. And they stamp
>   Their feet against the cold while they gather
>   Near a black sedan. The sedan is mine.

[*The lights come up, dim.* FIRST TOWNSMAN *and* SECOND TOWNS-
MAN *appear; they blow on their fingers, shift their feet; they carry*
rifles or shotguns.]
>   Farther back, more automobiles are parked
>   Almost bumper to bumper. And occasionally
>   A new arrival makes his way along the road
>   To stare at my sedan as though it were
>   The fallen leader of a column.

[MRS. FARNEY *and* MR. GABLEMAN *enter and exit upstage. The two*
TOWNSMEN *stare after them.*]
>   You see, Sarah Jane,
>   The hunt is getting ready to start.

[THIRD TOWNSMAN, *with his rifle, enters.*]
>   THIRD TOWNSMAN. Ain't it light enough now?
>   SECOND TOWNSMAN. Just about!
>   THIRD TOWNSMAN. Then who's holding us up?

FIRST TOWNSMAN. We're ready to go, but Tandy isn't here.

THIRD TOWNSMAN. Hell, we don't need . . . [*Pointing left.*] Say, is that Mrs. Farney? Look!

FIRST TOWNSMAN. Yeah, woman in the fur coat.

THIRD TOWNSMAN. [*Fascinated.*] Well, I'll be damned!

FIRST TOWNSMAN. Police tracked her down in New York.

SECOND TOWNSMAN. She got here in two hours. [*Thumbing.*] That sporting guy of hers did the driving.

THIRD TOWNSMAN. [*Still gaping.*] Two hours? Man, that's driving! So he's the guy . . .

SECOND TOWNSMAN. That's him all right. Gableman's the name—races autos, horses, sailboats. [*Laughingly to* FIRST TOWNS-MAN.] All kinds of sports!

FIRST TOWNSMAN. He was up here yesterday. Farney took him hunting.

THIRD TOWNSMAN. [*Shocked.*] Farney took him hunting? [*Sarcastic; loudly.*] Now that's what I call swank! Chumming up to his wife's boy friend! [*He spits.*]

FIRST TOWNSMAN. [*Warningly to* THIRD TOWNSMAN.] Not so loud . . .

SECOND TOWNSMAN. [*To* THIRD TOWNSMAN *half-mockingly.*] What did you expect of Farney? He don't divorce her, so he might as well act nice to her boy friend. [*Seriously.*] Anyway, she's got too much class for Farney.

FIRST TOWNSMAN. A nifty piece o' woman—I'll tell the world!

SECOND TOWNSMAN. I'd like to try her. Any night!

THIRD TOWNSMAN. [*The youthful critic.*] But she ain't no Hollywood queen.

SECOND TOWNSMAN. She's got a few miles on her—so what?

FIRST TOWNSMAN. Yeah, thirty-six or -seven, same as Farney. But she don't show it.

SECOND TOWNSMAN. You wonder what she wanted with Farney in the first place. Couldn't she do better?

FIRST TOWNSMAN. [*Pointing left.*] Well, she's doing better *now*. Look at that sporting guy.

THIRD TOWNSMAN. Yeah, sure . . . [*Suddenly baffled.*] And Farney just let 'em carry on right under his nose?

FIRST TOWNSMAN. [*With an older man's wisdom.*] Look, if you can't handle a woman, there's two things you can do about it. Get rid of her, or let her . . .

[A SHERIFF'S TROOPER *enters right.*]

TROOPER. Tandy's on his way with the dogs.

FIRST TOWNSMAN. We're waiting to go.

TROOPER. Did you see Mrs. Farney?

FIRST TOWNSMAN. [*Swinging gun.*] Right over there!

TROOPER. Oh, thanks.

[*He exits.*]

THIRD TOWNSMAN. [*Half to himself.*] Just thinking of that Farney guy—it makes me wanta throw up. [*Growing angry; to the others.*] Say, you know what happened last week at the garage? Farney drove his car in. A headlight wasn't working. I changed the bulb—that's all. And you know what he did? Suddenly he says to me, "You're John Miller's son, aren't you?" As if he wasn't sure I was! And then he says, "Here's a little something extra for your trouble." What does he hand me? A five-buck tip! Like he was King of England, and I was begging for charity!

SECOND TOWNSMAN. [*Winking at the* FIRST TOWNSMAN.] You thanked him, didn't you?

THIRD TOWNSMAN. I should have thrown it on the ground and spit on it.

FIRST TOWNSMAN. [*Musing.*] Crazy: passing out that kind of money for a tip.

THIRD TOWNSMAN. Why is it those sad sonofabitches always have money to throw away?

SECOND TOWNSMAN. I heard he just cashed in on another big job—fixing over one of those department stores in New York. Macy's or Gimbel's—one of those big ones.

FIRST TOWNSMAN. [*Sarcastic.*] *Artistic*—that's Farney.

SECOND TOWNSMAN. [*Amused.*] Guess he got the knack watching his old man paint houses. Damn good house painter, the old man was! But Farney? I just can't figure the crazy guy.

FIRST TOWNSMAN. Well, Farney always was—now, I don't

know about crazy—but a sad little bastard. You wonder how he got so far in New York.

THIRD TOWNSMAN. [*Still angry.*] Why didn't he keep to New York? Coming back here on week ends . . . [*Sarcastic.*] To relax! Or maybe for some hunting!

SECOND TOWNSMAN. [*Knowingly.*] And for Sarah Jane Cripps.

THIRD TOWNSMAN. [*Louder.*] Yeah, Sarah Jane. Jesus, what a kid to pick on! Why, goddammit, you'd think Mrs. Cripps would have known . . .

FIRST TOWNSMAN. [*Hushing the* THIRD TOWNSMAN.] Pipe down! What do you expect from a widow, in her situation? Clara Cripps and Brant Farney grew up here together. What would she think if Farney took her daughter for a ride? Damn nice of him. I thought so, myself.

THIRD TOWNSMAN. Yeah, damn nice! Now you know!

[*The* TROOPER *crosses backstage.*]

TROOPER. All right, men! Tandy's here with the dogs.

[*He exits. The* FIRST TOWNSMAN *exits after the* TROOPER. MRS. CRIPPS, MRS. FARNEY *and* MR. GABLEMAN *cross to extreme right, where they halt.*]

FIRST TOWNSMAN'S VOICE. Well, it's about time! [*Calling.*] Hey, Tandy, bring those dogs up!

THIRD TOWNSMAN. Plenty of light now!

TANDY'S VOICE. [*Complaining.*] Hell's fire! I don't get the idea. What do you want from these dogs? Mr. Farney paid me to train 'em for birds.

THIRD TOWNSMAN. [*Calling.*] They're Farney's dogs, ain't they? They oughta know him.

TANDY'S VOICE. Know him? They'll never forget him. Lord, how Mr. Farney disappointed 'em! Worst shot a dog could have worked under!

FIRST TOWNSMAN'S VOICE. Godawful! Farney shot like a blindman.

SECOND TOWNSMAN. [*Calling.*] Let's cut the gab and get moving!

TANDY'S VOICE. Well, I don't guarantee a thing from these dogs. They ain't trained for such work.

SECOND TOWNSMAN. [*Calling.*] Well, they can't hurt, any. We can watch how they move.

THIRD TOWNSMAN. [*To the* SECOND TOWNSMAN.] You think they'll point if they catch his scent?

SECOND TOWNSMAN. [*With a shrug.*] No telling.

FIRST TOWNSMAN'S VOICE. Put them in the car, for a sniff!

TROOPER'S VOICE. I hope they'll get the idea.

[*There is the click of a car door being opened.* MRS. FARNEY *and* MR. GABLEMAN *investigate.*]

MRS. FARNEY. Look! The car robe is gone.

MRS. CRIPPS. [*Whining.*] Gone? You're sure there was one?

MRS. FARNEY. Yes, certainly there was.

MR. GABLEMAN. He might have a rifle, too. A semiautomatic.

TROOPER. [*Coming over.*] What makes you think so?

MR. GABLEMAN. Well, after we drove in from our hunting, Mr. Farney took his shotgun into the house. But as I remember, a rifle was still lying on the car's back seat.

TANDY'S VOICE. Ain't no rifle there now.

MRS. CRIPPS. [*Moaning.*] Oh, Lord, what's he done to her?

MRS. FARNEY. [*To* GABLEMAN.] Brant and his infernal guns!

TROOPER. Look, Mr. Gableman, you'd better get Mrs. Farney out of here! And will you take Mrs. Cripps to her house? There's women there. They'll give you coffee.

SECOND TOWNSMAN. [*Leading* MRS. CRIPPS *off left, his arm around her.*] You can't do any good here, Mrs. Cripps. We'll find 'em quick, now it's light enough.

[*They exit.*]

TANDY'S VOICE. Shall I turn the dogs loose?

TROOPER. [*Exits right.*] Turn 'em loose. And be careful, men ! He's probably got a rifle.

[*The* THIRD TOWNSMAN *exits, right.* MR. GABLEMAN *starts to move; he takes* MRS. FARNEY'S *arm.*]

MR. GABLEMAN. It's only a question of time till they're found.

MRS. FARNEY. [*Bitterly.*] Yes, yes, I know. It was always a question of time for Brant. He never could wait. Every week end he had to rush back to this stupid little town. And as soon

as he was here, over he'd rush to that fence. Like yesterday! You
heard him? Talking over the fence—to that disgusting child.
Talking, talking; talking to himself, I'd call it.
[MR. GABLEMAN *and* MRS. FARNEY *exit. The lights go out, then
up on* BRANT *and* SARAH JANE.]

> BRANT. [*Casually.*]
> So that's what Mrs. Farney would call it:
> Talking to myself. How funny.
> [*He ponders.*] . . . But
> More amusing, Sarah Jane: Mrs. Farney is angry,
> And—I really do hope—a little frightened.
> As yet she does not realize that people are sure
> To consider her a martyr. She is the one
> They'll feel sorry for. Not me. So it goes.
> And in a little while she will actually enjoy
> Discussing me—and you. Frank discussions
> With intimate friends! With Mr. Gableman, for example.
> She'll repeat and repeat. She'll tell about the men
> And the dogs—how they came to find us.
> The dogs are unnecessary; but they do lend a touch
> Of artistry: Hounding me out with my own dogs!
> Well, Sarah Jane, soon enough they'll find us;
> And when they do, then they'll start asking:
> "How did it happen?"

[*Setting down the rifle, and pulling the cover from his shoulders,*
BRANT *crawls to* SARAH JANE.]

> We know how it happened,
> You and I.

[BRANT *"composes"* SARAH JANE *again. He poises his hand as
though he would touch her head, then draws his hand back as
though sickened, and cries out.*]

> Don't reproach me, Sarah Jane!
> Nothing is spoiled.

[BRANT *crawls back again to the stump, and collapses.*]

> I'm an artist, not a hunter!
> [*Calming.*]
> I'm the artist who was made to watch and wait.
> I had to put up with the elegant Mrs. Farney.

I had to watch her while she changed. Those arms
And bosoms reaching everywhere—swelling
Out of silken evening gowns! Not to forget
[*With a trace of hysterical laughter.*]
Those bloated, adolescent, sweaters!
God, how inartistic! *Why* did I wait?
Waiting ruins everything.

[BRANT *removes his glasses, stuffs them in a pocket, then picks up the rifle and slowly turns its muzzle toward him, while he slides his hand to the trigger.*]

Shall I wait, Sarah Jane, for the hunters?
And the dogs? They're all coming toward us.
Only a question of time! They'll find us.
Well, let them come and let them ask:
"How did it happen?" They'll never find out.
The beginning is too close to the end.

[BRANT *takes the rifle muzzle into his mouth.*]

CURTAIN, *and then a shot.*

BLOBO'S BOY

By
Albert J. Zuckerman

(Published here for the first time)

For Muriel

CAST

SHIRLEY RILSKY
VOICE OF ANNOUNCER
THOMAS F. QUINN
MORRIS RILSKY
GEORGE RILSKY
MILTIE RILSKY
VOICE OF MESSENGER
VOICE OF SENATOR
MICKEY DONOHUE

TIME: The present.

PLACE: New York City.

BLOBO'S BOY

It is early evening. On two-thirds of the right-hand side of the stage is the Rilsky living room, Central Park West, New York. The room has been furnished by a decorator in the latest Japanese-modern style, not at all in keeping with the people who live in it. The lights are lit in the living-room portion of the stage. SHIRLEY, *a carefully groomed and dieted bleached blonde in her middle forties, in elegant lounging clothes, glances nervously at her watch and then strides toward the television set. She is ready to turn it on when the phone rings. She hesitates momentarily, turns it on, and then crosses to answer the phone.*

SHIRLEY. Hello! . . . No, I'm sorry, I'm not giving out any interviews. Look, mister, I'm all tied up now. I'm sorry.
[*She slams down the phone, dashes back to the television set and turns it up. Lights dim in the living room, and we see a televised Senate hearing. There is pantomimed action during the announcer's speech.*]
VOICE OF ANNOUNCER. [*Offstage.*] And now tomorrow's headlines! Tempers flared and flash-bulbs popped today on Capitol Hill, ladies and gentlemen, as the Senate Committee continued its investigation on underworld influences in New York City politics. Star witness was again Morris "Blobo" Rilsky, reputedly a former bootlegger who went on to become a kingpin in the labor and protection rackets. Rilsky, however, has never served a day behind bars. He and his lawyer, Mickey Donohue, kept the hearing room in a constant state of turmoil and agitation. WLQF has kinescoped for you some of the highlights of this afternoon's spirited testimony. A hot-tempered Blobo almost came to blows with his interrogator, Thomas F. Quinn, the Committee Counsel.
QUINN. Mr. Rilsky, is it or is it not true that you, shall we say, campaigned in behalf of Mr. Frank Grimes when he was running for Mayor of New York in 1936?
MORRIS. I refuse to answer on the grounds that I don't want to have to incriminate myself.

QUINN. Mr. Rilsky, I fail to see how any answer you might give to that question could in any way serve to incriminate you.

MORRIS. Aw right. I don't remember.

QUINN. Perhaps this will refresh your memory. I read from *The New York Times* of October 29, 1936. "At the close of the rally, an open one-ton truck appeared. Morris Rilsky, a well-known East Side figure, came out on the rear of the truck and distributed one-pound salamis, inscribed with 'I love Frank Grimes' to all comers." Now do you remember?

MORRIS. [*Rises out of his chair in anger and answers, shaking his fist.*] So what's wrong with that? They're better than them crummy buttons you people give out. You can't eat buttons.

QUINN. [QUINN *rises in righteous indignation while* MICKEY DONOHUE *reseats* MORRIS *and whispers in his ear.*] Mr. Rilsky, may I remind you that this is a hearing of the United States Senate!

MORRIS. Wait a second! I withdraw that statement. I wasn't no more interested in that campaign than any other public-spirited citizen.

[QUINN *pantomimes conferring with a Senator, while* MICKEY DONOHUE *is busy whispering to* MORRIS.]

VOICE OF ANNOUNCER. [*Offstage.*] Then there was a lull while Committee Counsel Quinn consulted with the committee members—while Rilsky's lawyer, Donohue, made strenuous efforts to restore him to a state of calm. Quinn resumed by first warning Rilsky that he could be found in contempt of Congress, and then continued the questioning.

QUINN. Could you tell us the present whereabouts of one Mr. Stanley Beltenheim, the gentleman you succeeded in 1936 as First Vice President of Local 402 of the National Butchers Guild?

MORRIS. That was twenty years ago.

QUINN. Did you know that, after a long disappearance, Beltenheim was recently discovered in a New York institution for the mentally ill?

MORRIS. No.

QUINN. Registered under a different name?

MORRIS. Excuse me, no.

QUINN. Mr. Rilsky, is it or is it not true that in 1936, when you were *elected* to high office in the National Butchers Guild, you had never previously worked as a butcher? And I mean to use the term in its purely literal sense. And that after your election the Guild contributed $10,000 to Mr. Grimes's campaign?

MORRIS. I didn't get all that. You wanna say again?

QUINN. [*Whispers mockingly to* SENATOR.] He didn't get it. [*To* MORRIS *in a deliberate and mocking manner.*] Were you ever a butcher before your election as an official of the butchers' union [MORRIS *tries to answer, but is stopped by* QUINN, *who holds up his hand as he continues.*] and I use the word butcher in the sense of one who slaughters, cuts or sells *animal* flesh and . . .

MORRIS. [*Rising from his chair.*] There is insinuations in a question like that. I do not think it is the right thing for someone so high up like the Congress to ask it like that. [MORRIS *pushes his lawyer,* DONOHUE, *who has risen in an attempt to reseat him, back into his chair.*] I got a clean record.

VOICE OF ANNOUNCER. [*The Voice comes in over the hubbub, and pounding of a gavel.*] At this point Mr. Donohue again forced Mr. Morris "Blobo" Rilsky to his seat, and then requested a recess, claiming his client was suffering from a blood pressure attack. To our surprise, his request was granted, and the hearings will be resumed Monday morning. Earthquakes in the Sahara, ladies and gentlemen. Desert oases untroubled for thousands of years today experienced . . .

[SHIRLEY *snaps off the television. She pours herself a drink and downs it. The door chimes ring. She exits.*]

VOICE OF MESSENGER. [*Offstage.*] Mr. and Mrs. Morris Rilsky?

SHIRLEY. Yes.

MESSENGER. Telegram.

SHIRLEY. I'll take it. [*She returns, tearing it open, and is surprised and then furious as she reads it. For a moment she is bewildered, and then, determined, strides to the telephone and dials.*] Hello, Mr. Hanley, please . . . This is Shirley Rilsky . . . Well, thanks a lot . . . No, I don't want to wait till tomorrow and talk to him in the office. I wan't to talk to him now.

Look, I'm pretty keyed up, so you better put him on . . .
Max? Listen, I just got a wire from that fabulous dump in
Palm Beach we was supposed to go to next week. All of a sudden they're full, and they're canceling our reservations . . . Skip
it, will you? Max, after twenty years in the travel business, you
know as well as I do why they're so full all of a sudden. It
don't become the worst dump in the world after last week it was
the best . . . No, I don't want to go to Acapulco. Just listen for
a minute and get down what I'm telling you! You tell the manager or whoever you know in that stinking outfit that I'd better
get a wire from them by noon tomorrow saying they'd be honored
to have us in their crummy joint, and that that last wire was a—
an unfortunate mistake, or I'll sue them in and out of every court
in the country for defamation of character. Everybody and his
brother knew we were going down there . . . I don't care
whether I have a case or not. I'll keep them in court for ten
years. Noon, Max! Good-bye! [*She hangs up.*] I wouldn't go to
that dump in a million years.
[*She recovers her composure as she hears someone enter.*]
   MORRIS. [*Offstage.*] You home?
   SHIRLEY. In the living room, Morris. [*She helps him off with
his coat, as he enters.*] Hello.
   MORRIS. Miltie here yet?
   SHIRLEY. Miltie?
   MORRIS. I only got one kid brother, you know. I got a tele-
gram at the hearings that he was gonna come up here to New
York.
   SHIRLEY. I thought we all agreed he was going to stay in
Miami. I hope they don't let him off the plane.
   MORRIS. Look, all I asked you: was Miltie *here* yet? You
don't have to fall in love with him . . . Now, what have you
got to eat?
   SHIRLEY. I wasn't expecting you. Five minutes ago I was
watching you on the television. I guess that was a replay, though,
wasn't it?
   MORRIS. [*Starting to exit.*] I'm goin' down McCleary's for
a steak. I'll see you later.
   SHIRLEY. [*Stopping him as he tries to take back his coat from
her.*] Morris!

MORRIS. You wanna come?

SHIRLEY. There's stuff to eat. I just wasn't expectin' you, that's all. I even got steaks.

MORRIS. Why didn't you say so?

SHIRLEY. I'm sorry. I'll put one on for you right now. In ten minutes it'll be ready.

[*She goes toward the pantry.*]

MORRIS. Never mind.

SHIRLEY. You feelin' all right?

MORRIS. So I'm not hungry no more. That mean I'm sick?

SHIRLEY. They were pretty rough on you, weren't they?

MORRIS. What're you talkin' about?

SHIRLEY. Morris, I already had enough without your trying to take it all out on me.

MORRIS. [*As* SHIRLEY *starts to exit.*] What's a matter with you? Where you goin'?

SHIRLEY. I'm expectin' your son, and he might be hungry when he gets here.

MORRIS. George comin' home?

SHIRLEY. Yeah, and I don't know what to make of it. He called around four and said he was coming. I wasn't expectin' him till Thanksgiving.

MORRIS. He musta made a top grade in some exam, so they give him a week end pass.

SHIRLEY. I didn't like the way he sounded on the phone.

MORRIS. Stop it, will you! That kid—he's on top of the world.

SHIRLEY. Sure. Like you and me. Just like *we're* on top.

MORRIS. Never mind. Lousy two-bit politicians! They ain't got nothin' on me, and they couldn't do nothin' if they had.

SHIRLEY. Look, you're home. Relax!

MORRIS. Only thing they care about's gettin' their fat pusses on the front page. Makin' a commotion over twenty years ago. Lotta good it'll do 'em. Bunch o' windbags! I'd take any one of 'em and show 'em who's who. I mean it.

SHIRLEY. Morris, we've got to get out of this. I'm *worried*.

MORRIS. I told you they haven't got nothin' on me.

SHIRLEY. That's not everything. It took eleven years before people in this building would say "Hello" to me. And now—

You think you can take all of *them* and show them who's who, too?

MORRIS. Anybody gives you a hard time, you tell me.

SHIRLEY. I almost wish we could try and ask for help from Joe Pironi.

MORRIS. He'd do what he could, but you know that we can't.

SHIRLEY. I know. And our vacation next week! Palm Beach. We never been to Palm Beach.

MORRIS. So what about it?

SHIRLEY. Nothing. My father, he should rest in peace; he knew, Morris. He knew . . .

MORRIS. Poor shmoe. What'd *he* ever know? Couldn't even tell when the kids were stealing all the penny candy right from under his nose.

SHIRLEY. Everybody loved him, everybody in the neighborhood. "Peace and quiet," he'd say; and I'd say, "What in God's name would I want that for?" Excitement, that's what I wanted. That's what you were to me. I'd see you come walkin' in that candy store in one o' them sharp suits, and the blood would dance right through my skin every time. Well, we're not kids no more, and I'm tired. I want some peace.

MORRIS. So you think I'm crazy about all this hullabaloo? [SHIRLEY *again starts to exit.*] Where you goin'?

SHIRLEY. I already told you. [*She hears a door slam, and exits hastily offstage.*] George, let me look at you!

GEORGE. Hi, Mom.

SHIRLEY. How was the trip?

GEORGE. Okay, Mom. [SHIRLEY *and* GEORGE *enter. He wears the uniform of a Naval Academy Midshipman.*]

SHIRLEY. We'll have to get an oil painting of you in that uniform. But you're thinner. You haven't been eating right.

MORRIS. Hiya, Admiral! You look okay, kid; don't let your mother worry you. [*He unloosens* GEORGE's *tie and top shirt button.*] Let's untie the monkey suit. You're makin' me choke, just lookin' at you.

SHIRLEY. I wasn't expecting you for another ten days.

MORRIS. Yeah, wha'd'you come out low man on demerits, and win yourself a week end?

GEORGE. Well, you see . . .

SHIRLEY. George, are you feeling all right? I—I just don't like the way you look.

MORRIS. Stop pickin' on him! He's *gotta* be healthy.

SHIRLEY. Can you stay the whole week end?

GEORGE. Sure. Sure, I can.

MORRIS. Great! That's great. Well, it's good to see you, kid. Uh, how come you're surprisin' us like this?

GEORGE. You see it's—it's kinda complicated.

MORRIS. Come on. You musta shined them buttons so bright, it hurt their eyes lookin' at 'em.

[MORRIS *laughs, covering his concern with an air of bravado, while* SHIRLEY *is openly worried.* GEORGE *notices his mother and realizes that he must reassure her.*]

GEORGE. Sure. How'd you know? It was something almost just like that. I never thought you knew that much about the Navy.

SHIRLEY. You hungry? I'll fix you something.

GEORGE. I'm okay, Mom. You don't have to.

SHIRLEY. You sure you feel all right?

MORRIS. Can't you leave him alone?

SHIRLEY. A chicken sandwich on toast, the way you like it, and some chocolate cake?

MORRIS. You deaf? He said he's not hungry.

SHIRLEY. And a milk shake! I've got some cherry vanilla ice cream in the freezer.

GEORGE. Sure, Mom. That sounds fine.

SHIRLEY. Maybe some tomato soup, too? Get something hot in you!

GEORGE. That's a lot of chow for a guy that's not hungry.

SHIRLEY. My baby! I don't get many chances to fatten you up these days.

MORRIS. Baby!

SHIRLEY. [*As she exits.*] If I live to be a hundred, and you're an old man of seventy-five, you'll still be my baby.

MORRIS. [*To* GEORGE.] Don't mind your ma. She ain't normal today.

GEORGE. [*After a short pause.*] I guess you're right.

MORRIS. [*Laughingly, and in an expanding manner.*] Sure. She ain't used to me bein' a celebrity. You know, I'd sue every one of them lousy politicians for slander, but they got immunity kinda: they're Congressmen. Immunity! I never heard of nothing so crazy.

GEORGE. [*A short pause.*] Those are the breaks, I guess.

MORRIS. It's how you play it, kid. Nothin' don't just happen. I shoulda never gone near that City Hall crowd. Now the Hudson Street mob is in, they're tryin' to make it hot for *my* old bunch.

GEORGE. I guess you're right.

MORRIS. What's a matter with you?

GEORGE. Nothing.

MORRIS. You know why they're doin' this, don't you? They're not after *me*. I'm just a spade they're usin' to shovel dirt on Grimes and everybody else that's not on their side.

GEORGE. What's the difference?

MORRIS. What do you mean, what's the difference? Whose kid *are* you?

GEORGE. I'm sorry. Forget it.

MORRIS. I don't get it, George. The front pages of all them papers, the newsreels, TV, that's nothin'?

GEORGE. So what am I supposed to do: ask for your autograph?

MORRIS. Wh'd'you say?

GEORGE. Nothing. Forget it.

MORRIS. Them brass buttons goin' to your head? I don't know what they been teachin' you down there, but I don't like it. [GEORGE *starts to leave, but is caught by* MORRIS.] You get what I'm tellin' you?

GEORGE. Yes.

MORRIS. [*Somewhat pacified, releases him.*] Okay. [GEORGE *again starts to exit.*] So where you goin'?

GEORGE. You won't have to look at it any more, okay?

MORRIS. No. I don't know what you're talkin' about, but it's not okay.

GEORGE. The brass buttons. I'm taking them off. For good.

MORRIS. Your uniform?

GEORGE. My monkey suit.

MORRIS. What happened?

GEORGE. Nothing happened.

MORRIS. WHAT HAPPENED?

GEORGE. Don't you ever believe me? I just decided I didn't like it any more, and left. Okay?

MORRIS. George, I'm not puttin' no heat on you. I just want you should tell me, that's all. Six weeks ago, when we was down there, you were crazy for all that stuff.

GEORGE. Right, I was crazy. Marching to eat, marching to classes, marching to play ball, saluting all the time! So I got sick of it, that's all. THAT'S ALL.

MORRIS. Yeah, but you knew all that before you went there.

GEORGE. So I changed my mind. What's the big deal? You never liked anything about the whole idea, anyway.

MORRIS. You're leveling with me?

GEORGE. Sure, I am.

MORRIS. It's important, 'cause I don't want nothin' should happen on account of . . .

GEORGE. What do you want me to tell you? You tell me what, and I'll tell it to you. Okay?

MORRIS. Son, you know I never saw nothin' in that deal. *You* wanted it. That was good enough. You *don't* want it. That's even better. We square? [GEORGE *shrugs in a sort of negative affirmation.*] Now you're talkin'. Well, we gotta start thinkin' about somethin' else for you.

GEORGE. I'll find something.

MORRIS. Listen, it's gotta be a lot better than just something. We'll go down to Miami, you and me. I'll get you started with Miltie in the club. Girls, big timers; there's a life for you.

GEORGE. [*Seeing his mother enter with a tray.*] Gee, Mom, that was fast.

SHIRLEY. Morris, what's happened? [*He doesn't answer. She turns to* GEORGE.] George?

MORRIS. [*Indicating that he'd prefer to be left alone.*] Me and George, we're havin' a little talk, father and son.

SHIRLEY. What is going on?

GEORGE. Nothing, Mom.

SHIRLEY. You're my baby, George. Even if I didn't hear what your father said, all I have to do is look at you to know something's not right. I want to help you, but how can I if you don't tell me . . .

MORRIS. Nothing's the matter. Don't you understand English?

SHIRLEY. Morris, for God's sake!

MORRIS. Okay: he quit your fancy pantsy Naval Academy. That's all. How'd you ever expect my kid to go for all that baloney?

SHIRLEY. Is that what you told your father?

GEORGE. Yes, Mom.

SHIRLEY. It's not true, though. Is it, darling?

MORRIS. Will you stop it already?

SHIRLEY. Morris, you've got to tell me . . .

MORRIS. What is the commotion? He went to the school. Now he quit. It's only a school. Okay? Now if you don't mind . . .

SHIRLEY. Morris, if you can't see how screwy this is, you're gettin' blind. George, you've been sailing boats in that Central Park Lake, dreaming about the Naval Academy since you started public school, always building models, the Sea Scouts, then studying for that exam. You don't just leave that! Something happened. We all know it, and we can't just make believe it didn't.

MORRIS. Will you please . . .

SHIRLEY. [Motioning to MORRIS to shut up.] George, you can tell us. We're not the best in the world, but we're your parents. We'll love you, no matter what. We want to help you, darling, and you have to let us.

GEORGE. Mom . . .

SHIRLEY. Yes, my sweet?

GEORGE. [Going to his mother for comfort.] I didn't want to leave.

MORRIS. What do you mean?

SHIRLEY. My poor baby.

MORRIS. What's the big idea? You tell your old man a story —you better damn well tell it straight.

SHIRLEY. He must have gone through enough without you . . .

MORRIS. [*Trying to pull* GEORGE *away from* SHIRLEY, *while she tries to protect him.*] Talk! What happened?

SHIRLEY. Morris, please! Not like this. Not now.

MORRIS. [*Pulling* GEORGE *away and shaking him.*] You gonna talk, or am I gonna have to . . .

GEORGE. [*Breaking away.*] You! *That's* what happened.

MORRIS. Never mind me!

GEORGE. Don't I wish I could!

MORRIS. [*Grabbing* GEORGE *menacingly.*] Spill it! And don't get fresh.

GEORGE. [*Taunting him, hysterically.*] Don't hit me, Blobo! *I* won't squeal. I'll pay all the protection you want.

MORRIS. Shut up!

GEORGE. Tonight's the night, Blobo! We knock off the night watchman, and pull a fast hoist on the mid-terms. What do you say, Blobo?

MORRIS. I said to shut up!

SHIRLEY. [*Trying to calm him.*] My baby, what did they do to you?

GEORGE. In the middle of the night, they came into my room, every guy on the deck. They dragged me into the head, and they pushed my face in the urinal, and they . . .

SHIRLEY. [*Trying to hold him, but he breaks away.*] Oh, George.

GEORGE. [*In tears.*] But they didn't even have to. I already felt like I was contaminating the uniform from the inside.

SHIRLEY. Darling, you mus'n't ever feel like that.

GEORGE. Every time I heard them call my name in class, it'd be the voice of that Committee Counsel, and I'd want to hide.

MORRIS. Now you listen to me!

GEORGE. I couldn't stand listening to my own name: your name, Rilsky. No matter who said it, I'd want to disappear right into the ground, if I could. Now will you leave me alone?

MORRIS. [*Grabbing hold of* GEORGE.] There's a coupla things we're gonna get straight right away.

GEORGE. [*Breaks away, and screams as he exits.*] I wish I never *had* a father.

[MORRIS, *shaken, starts after him.* SHIRLEY *restrains him.*]

SHIRLEY. Morris, let him alone.

MORRIS. He don't mean that. He can't, can he?

SHIRLEY. No. Of course he doesn't.

MORRIS. I done everything for that kid, Shirl. What else have I got?

SHIRLEY. I know, Morris.

MORRIS. Why'd he say it then?

SHIRLEY. When they're upset, everybody says things they don't mean.

MORRIS. I don't care what those politicians, or any of them crum bums say—but my own boy!

SHIRLEY. You're his father. He didn't ask to be born.

MORRIS. Maybe not, but . . .

SHIRLEY. He doesn't owe us. We owe him. He didn't get himself into this mess.

MORRIS. Runs away, my kid!

SHIRLEY. Wha'd'you want him to do?

MORRIS. I just never, I just never thought my own kid could . . .

SHIRLEY. But this is his dream—all shot to hell. Can't you see that?

MORRIS. And he's how old? Eighteen. Nine, that's all I was when my ma, she should rest in peace, one morning I woke up and she was ice cold right next to me in the bed; the old man gone in the Russian Army; and I had to scrounge and steal and beg enough to eat for me and Miltie . . .

SHIRLEY. Me, big Morris! Me me me me! Can't you think about anyone else, even your own son?

MORRIS. I got over having dreams fast enough. Where'd it get us, Shirl? The day he was born I told you I'd quit the rackets, and I did. You know how many propositions I turned down since then. Good ones. By now I coulda been callin' the shots right across the country. For him: so he could have an old man that was legit. For him. And did he have one thing to say—feelin' sorry about that rotten mess in Washington?

SHIRLEY. He wants to love you, but . . .

MORRIS. So what am I? A small-time night-club operator with one son who wishes I was dead. And it's my fault, all my fault. That's what you're gonna tell me, ain't it?

SHIRLEY. We've got to help him, Morris. The hearings'll straighten out sooner or later, but we're more than halfway. George's just startin' out. He's got to go back. If he doesn't . . .

MORRIS. He can do whatever he pleases. I got bigger worries . . .

SHIRLEY. He's only a boy.

MORRIS. . . . And you do too. I'm goin' out.

SHIRLEY. For God's sake, he's your son.

MORRIS. So what am I supposed to do?

SHIRLEY. You've got to help him.

MORRIS. He quit on his own, didn't he?

SHIRLEY. You mean on *your* own . . .

MORRIS. Okay, you got your digs in? I had enough. I'll see you later.

SHIRLEY. Morris, if you walk out now, there's a night-spot in Miami and a packing house here in New York. You might see 'em again from the outside, but they're in my name, and I'd never let you see the inside of 'em again, and you'd never see me again, either.

MORRIS. Are you crazy? You don't even know what you're sayin'.

SHIRLEY. I know what I'm sayin'. Morris, I want this more than anything I've ever wanted: that kid's got to have a chance.

MORRIS. He's had a thousand for every one you or me ever had. Now, don't make me mad. I wouldn't wanna do nothin' . . .

SHIRLEY. So I'm supposed to be scared? What do you think it is about you that means something in this house? Your golden personality? Your dough? No, it's bein' a father, a big strong father to a certain kid, and that kid needs him now, and I'm not going to let you run out on him.

MORRIS. Run out? You go around promising the moon, and you want me to hand it over. Well, I don't have the moon, and neither do you, and neither does anybody. Now, you better get off your horse! You ain't the queen of East Broadway no more, yourself.

SHIRLEY. If he gives up now when he's eighteen, what kind o' life's he gonna have? I don't care if he's a Navy officer or a Fuller Brush man, but inside himself he's gotta think he's okay. If we let him run away, he never will. And you've gotta do it, Morris! He'd never take it from a woman. He's gotta stand up, no matter what they do to him, or to us.

MORRIS. No one's doin' nothin' to us.

SHIRLEY. If we don't help him now, we couldn't face him again.

MORRIS. He's the one that's gotta face up.

SHIRLEY. Yes, Morris, yes; but you've got to show him, explain to him.

MORRIS. *I've* got to?

SHIRLEY. You, Morris.

MORRIS. I don't know: has he got it in him?

SHIRLEY. He's our boy; mine and yours.

MORRIS. Yeah, you're right.

SHIRLEY. [*Throwing herself into his arms.*] Morris!

MORRIS. Okay, okay.

SHIRLEY. He'll go, won't he?

MORRIS. We'll see. Leave me alone. [SHIRLEY *remains standing behind him.*] Leave me alone! [SHIRLEY *exits tiredly.* MORRIS *is perplexed, goes to call* GEORGE, *then changes his mind and strides to the telephone.*] Get me the Commandant of the Naval Academy in Annapolis, Maryland, person to person . . . No, I don't know his number; that's what they're payin' you for. Hello, Annapolis? . . . Of course he's not in his office this time of day. So get him out of bed! Tell him it's—it's the Commander of the Brooklyn Navy Yard, Admiral McGillicudy! . . . Hello, this is Morris Rilsky . . . Because I wanted to make sure I got you, that's all . . . Morris Rilsky. My boy's one of your midshipmen . . . So you got thirty-two hundred midshipmen. I only got one boy . . . Rilsky, R-I-L-S-K-Y, like in hearings . . . Yeah, my boy, George. He came home today AWOL. Some of your kids been makin' life a little hard for him . . . No, I'm not blamin' you. I'm not blamin' nobody. I just want to make sure it's okay for him to come back . . . I realize it's serious . . . Resign? And what if he don't . . . A court-martial, huh? . . . So it's maybe a court-martial. Commandant, listen to me, that kid's so Navy blue, sometimes I think he's got salt water in him instead of blood. You people treat him right and you won't get nobody'll do a better job for you, and I'm not sayin' that just because he's my boy, either . . . Say, that's okay . . . I mean, well, thanks! Listen, I'll try and get him back there in a hurry. You're okay, Commander. Good-bye. [*He hangs up.*] George! George, come on in here! [*After a moment,* GEORGE *appears.*] Come in! Sit down, George!

GEORGE. Yes?

MORRIS. Look, uh . . .

GEORGE. I'm sorry. Okay?

MORRIS. That's not what I called you in here for. If I got started, *I* could do some apologizin', too. George, your ma and me want you should go back right away.

GEORGE. To Annapolis?

MORRIS. Right.

GEORGE. Don't you understand? I can't.

MORRIS. Shut up! Never mind: you wanna say something, go ahead and say it. Okay, this is the first time things gone bad on you, ain't it? Really bad, I mean? Well, it is, ain't it?

GEORGE. I guess so.

MORRIS. Up till now me and your ma, we done pretty good for you. The Thunderbird, cashmere suits, whatever you wanted. You wanted Annapolis; we seen to it you got there. You think my parents, or your ma's, ever did any of that stuff for us?

GEORGE. I'm grateful. But I'm your son. It just won't work.

MORRIS. Why not? You think your old man's not as good as the next guy? You never been outa kindergarten. I never gave you that spiel about the birds and the bees that kids are supposed to get from their fathers, did I? The facts of life, I suppose you think you know them.

GEORGE. Yes. I'm afraid I do.

MORRIS. So I'm no angel! I never said I was. George, when I got off that boat in 1921, I was sixteen, I had two quarters in my pocket, and I didn't speak a word of English. The best job I could get paid four bucks a week, nights, cleaning out elevators in an office building. Maybe I'd be janitor now if I'd stuck it. But I got tired eating beans all the time, and cleaning other people's mess. The liquor business was a good business then. Illegal, sure, but the same judge that was throwing guys in the clink, that come into his court, was buying plenty of the stuff from me at home. All your hoity-toity buddies at the Naval Academy—all their fathers were buying it when I was selling it, and it was just as illegal . . . Only I made some money out of it and they didn't. That's the only real bitch they got.

GEORGE. I know. I understand that, but . . .

MORRIS. You don't understand. You don't like to hear your own name, you said. It makes you feel dirty. Well, you're gonna live with that name for a long time, so you better understand it. I worked hard for what I got, and what you got.

GEORGE. I don't want any of it.

MORRIS. You don't, huh? So act like it. Stand up on your own two feet! . . . You get knocked down, you don't whine, you don't quit, you get back up.

GEORGE. Just like that! Sending me back there is going to straighten everything out. People don't bother *you*. You don't give a damn what anybody says. But me? If you have me around, you'll know our lives are a mess. All the time you'll know, and that's the one thing you don't want.

MORRIS. You finished?

GEORGE. Yes. Before I ever began.

MORRIS. Son, I'm sorry about what happened to you down there. But it woulda been my fault, too, if I never got nowhere and you was just one more East Side bum of a kid like I was. Where'd you get all your fancy ideas? Kids on the East Side don't have them, because they cost. I paid for 'em, with sweat and boot licking, but I ain't sorry. You're better than them. There's some ways you're better than me, 'cause I wanted you to be. You got that: because I wanted you to be. But there's one big way you ain't yet. Guts! You grow up where it's tough, and you learn to fight back without even thinkin' about . . . You want to go back there, don't you?

GEORGE. Maybe. Yes, if I could be someone else.

MORRIS. You know what that means you're sayin', don't you? If you can't be yourself there, you can't be yourself no place else, either. You're throwin' in the towel right after your first big bout. Everybody loses, some time; but that don't mean you give up.

GEORGE. I guess I lost before I ever got in the ring.

MORRIS. Kid, if you give up now, you're dead. Listen! First time I went in the liquor business, it took a week, and some rough-housers come down at night, smashed every penny's worth of the stuff I had, and beat up the guy I had watching it. So where'd I be now if I chickened out then, like I was supposed to? You think it was easy? Every cent I'd saved and borrowed, money from my kid sisters, Uncle Jake, my Chinese laundryman, was in that smashed pile of stinking glass. I begged and borrowed all over again. The second time, I didn't have so much. I hid it better, watched it myself. Then when they found out, they knew I was in that business for real, and I stayed. You see what I'm talkin' about?

GEORGE. Sure. Only the Naval Academy's not a bootleggers' club, and I'm not you.

MORRIS. Who are you, then? Chew on that! You don't know, and you never will if you don't go back and look 'em all in the eye. Then they'll know and you'll know.

GEORGE. I do know, though, and you do, too, and I wish to hell I didn't.

MORRIS. [MILTIE, *a younger looking version of* MORRIS, *but on the surface jovial and bouncy, has entered.*] Miltie, I didn't hear you come in.

MILTIE. Natchurly, yellin' to knock the roof off! Wha'd'-you expect? Hiya, kid! How's the boy?

GEORGE. Hello, Uncle Miltie.

MILTIE. You're lookin' good, kid. Lookin' good— Wha's a matter, the old guy givin' you a hard time?

GEORGE. Nice to see you again.

MORRIS. [*As* GEORGE *starts to exit.*] George, stick around!

MILTIE. Hey, hey, hey—let him go. Wha's the big idea? George, when I finish with the old man, you and me got a lot to catch up on.

MORRIS. Look, Miltie, a hundred per cent sure why you come up here, I'm not, but if it's what I think it is, it's not gonna hurt him none to hear about it. He's gettin' pretty big.

MILTIE. You're the boss, but . . .

MORRIS. What's on your mind? [*To* GEORGE *as he again starts to exit.*] Stay, I said!

MILTIE. Morris, them hearings, why're you lettin' 'em ruin us? The height of the season, and the club's empty! Another coupla days o' them hearings, and you couldn't get a customer in there if you had the Gold Star mother of the year doin' the strip. I'm worried. The State's even talkin' about revokin' the license.

MORRIS. Seein' as you just flew all the way up here from Miami at my expense, I guess I'm supposed to ask you if you got any bright ideas.

MILTIE. Twenty questions, that's a wonderful game; but this ain't no time for it.

MORRIS. You came up here to tell me what to do, didn't you? So tell me.

MILTIE. Are you kidding? One good reason!— Just give me one good reason why you're letting them. I don't get it, and nobody else does, either.

MORRIS. I'm waiting . . .

MILTIE. For crying out loud! Joe Pironi, he's still a Congressman, ain't he?

MORRIS. So?

MILTIE. *You* got that guy the nomination, didn't you? He wouldn't be nothin' if it wasn't for you. So you gonna let 'em roll all over us, when all he's gotta do is stick up his little finger?

MORRIS. Right.

MILTIE. I don't get it, Morris. What's the story?

MORRIS. No story. He's an old friend of mine.

MILTIE. So I should go to the dogs, and you, too, because Joe Pironi's your friend? Some friend!

GEORGE. Could he really stop the hearings?

MILTIE. [*Snapping his fingers.*] Like that!

GEORGE. Could he?

MILTIE. He knows damn well he could.

MORRIS. . . . Joe Pironi wants to stick his neck out, that's his business.

MILTIE. Do you owe that guy somethin', or don't he owe *you?*

MORRIS. We're square.

MILTIE. How? A nothing, and you make him a big shot, a Congressman. He never even got you no refund on your income tax.

MORRIS. Miltie, I'll play this one the way I see it.

MILTIE. Call him up! For crying out loud, you want I should call him?

MORRIS. [*Menacingly, as* MILTIE *heads for the phone.*] Look, next time I want you should be makin' my telephone calls for me, I'll tell you about it. Okay?

MILTIE. Okay, Morris, if that's the way you feel, okay. But when you get that profit and loss statement, don't you give me that business about what kind of a joker I am.

GEORGE. Pironi's the one who appointed me to the Naval Academy, isn't he?

MORRIS. Somebody had to.

GEORGE. Is that why you're not asking him to try and get you out of the hearings? On account of what he did for me? You mean, you and Mom might not be going through any of this, maybe, if it wasn't for me. Would you . . . ?

MORRIS. Maybe . . . You think I should ask him?

GEORGE. Well—I mean—I don't know.

MORRIS. Who do you think it would help?

GEORGE. You, Mom, Miltie, all of us, I guess.

MORRIS. How about Joe Pironi? If that ever gets around, and this kind of stuff usually does, he'd be layin' himself wide open . . .

GEORGE. But how about you?

MORRIS. I'm figurin' on sticking it out the best I can.

GEORGE. But you could be put away in . . . Anything could happen.

MORRIS. Son—you need help, you don't ask a friend to stick out his neck to give it to you. You take your own chances. You fight back, and you don't run away.

GEORGE. It's awful hard.

MORRIS. Yeah, it is. Awful hard.

GEORGE. About what I said, Dad, I'm sorry.

MORRIS. Sure, I know.

GEORGE. I am.

MORRIS. Okay, but *that's* not gonna really help nothin', is it?

GEORGE. I know . . . When do you think I should go?

MORRIS. Now, right now! Grab your coat, and Miltie'll take you down the station.

GEORGE. Will you?

MILTIE. Sure, kid.

GEORGE. Okay. Let's shove off.

MILTIE. [*To* MORRIS *as* GEORGE *exits.*] What in hell was that all about?

MORRIS. Drive him to the station, Miltie! [MILTIE *shrugs and exits.* MORRIS *stands near the door, waves to* GEORGE *as they leave. He stretches himself out on the couch.* SHIRLEY *enters and sits beside him.*] He's going back.

SHIRLEY. I know. What happened about Pironi?

MORRIS. Nothing.

SHIRLEY. You're not asking him, are you?

MORRIS. No, I can't. If it came out about Pironi, George wouldn't catch it from the kids only. Him and Joe would be in the papers instead of me.

SHIRLEY. You did a good job.

MORRIS. No, you were the one knew what he had to do. He shouldn't have had it so rough, Shirl. He's a nice kid.

SHIRLEY. But you weren't?

MORRIS. I don't know. No, I wasn't.

SHIRLEY. I'd argue with you, but we got enough to worry about with those hearings.

MORRIS. [*Resting his head on her breast.*] Shirl, what should I do?

CURTAIN

HEAVEN IS A LONG TIME TO WAIT

A Play on the Emotions

By

E. P. Conkle

(Published here for the first time)

CAST

PETRIYA
VELINKA
ANOKA
MATHIAS

TIME: Past, present, and future.

PLACE: In the hearts of children.

HEAVEN IS A LONG TIME TO WAIT

We see what was once the living room in an old farmhouse. It is now entirely vacant. There is only a fireplace with a few dying embers. There is only a window with no curtains, which looks out into the coming evening where there is wind, and sleet, and snow. There are four small bundles of rags near the fireplace. Voices of people come from offstage. A cow moos somewhere in the storm. Then silence. The door to the other room opens, and what seems to be a conglomerate bundle of rags is shoved into the room. Gradually they separate into separate entities, and we see that they are the children PETRIYA, ANOKA, VELINKA, *and* MATHIAS. PETRIYA *is the elder sister;* ANOKA *and* VELINKA *are girls of the same age, twins;* MATHIAS *is the little brother.*

PETRIYA. [*Motioning toward the fireplace.*] Here, little Mathias, over here!

VELINKA. [*Patting his hand.*] Do not cry, little Mathias!

MATHIAS. [*Wiping his eyes.*] I am not crying; I am really very angry.

VELINKA. It will be all right . . .

ANOKA. What is a *"welfare society"*?

VELINKA. [*To* ANOKA.] Come over here by the fire, what there is of it, and settle down.

PETRIYA. The fire has almost gone out, but we can keep ourselves warm.

[VELINKA *and* MATHIAS *huddle around* PETRIYA *on the floor.*]

VELINKA. We will have to keep us all warm now. Isn't that so, Petriya?

PETRIYA. Yes, it is so. If they will allow us . . .

VELINKA. Won't they allow us?

ANOKA. [*Who stands apart, deep in thought.*] Yes, what is a *"charity case"*?

MATHIAS. Why are they all in there? Should I go back in, and put them out?

PETRIYA. No, little Mathias. It would do no good.

[ANOKA *goes to the door, to listen to the voices in the other room.*]

ANOKA. I should like to know what they are talking of, now that we have left.

MATHIAS. I should like to have them see what Father would have done!

ANOKA. Or Mother.

VELINKA. [*Crying a little.*] If they were only alive again!

PETRIYA. Mother was lying in her bed upstairs only a week ago.

ANOKA. Don't cry, Velinka. We wouldn't want her to be here again—with things like this.

VELINKA. Shall we be taken where we cannot see her grave at all?

MATHIAS. We shall not be taken anywhere, if I can help it. I shall fight them, like Father did in war.

ANOKA. They are now talking strange things of us.

PETRIYA. I cannot help thinking about poor Mother, alone upstairs there—on her beautiful bed—and dying.

VELINKA. In spite of all our prayers.

ANOKA. Father fought for freedom in the old country, didn't he, Petriya?

PETRIYA. So he used to tell us.

MATHIAS. And over here, for this one, also!

VELINKA. [*With wonder.*] Where is—the old country?

ANOKA. Oh, it is somewhere out yonder . . .

MATHIAS. If I had me a bright gun, I should go in there and shoot them all, I should.

PETRIYA. You would be kind and gentle like Father, little Mathias.

MATHIAS. But I should do something!

VELINKA. Perhaps the old country was a happier land.

PETRIYA. It has been quite happy here at times, until now.

ANOKA. Until the thing "Mortgage" came, and Mother worked hard to pay it, and lost all our money from Father's war.

PETRIYA. Mother loved it here, and Father . . .

MATHIAS. Nevertheless, I shall not let them take us!

ANOKA. This is our proper home, isn't it?

PETRIYA. What do they say, Anoka?

ANOKA. They speak of how the farm is all run down . . .

PETRIYA. How little do they know of that!

ANOKA. And how the mortgage has not been paid in full, nor the medicine bills for Mother.

PETRIYA. Do they speak of how hard poor Mother worked to pay things?

VELINKA. And buy us all what to eat?

MATHIAS. I shall go in and tell them in a little while.

PETRIYA. Sit, little Mathias!

VELINKA. I am afraid of them.

MATHIAS. I am not!

ANOKA. [*Listening.*] Now, it is how everything in the house has been sold away . . .

VELINKA. They do not know how it once looked, do they, Petriya?

ANOKA. Father's beautiful walnut chest over there, with the deeply inscribed angels.

VELINKA. The lovely, deep velvet curtains of blue . . .

ANOKA. And Mother's little what-not in the corner, all full of lovely dishes . . .

MATHIAS. And the wicker basket of nuggets Father brought from off somewhere far . . .

PETRIYA. From Bechuanaland, and Tanganyika.

MATHIAS. Yes, from Bech—from far off there!

VELINKA. The rug! The thick, gray rug—so your bare feet would sink into it almost to the very ankles!

PETRIYA. And always a bright fire in the hearth when it was cold like this now.

ANOKA. Mother's little rocking chair rocking busily . . .

VELINKA. Squeak, squeak . . .

ANOKA. As she told us little stories.

PETRIYA. All—gone!

VELINKA. And grandmother's parlor, as we looked out the window in the evening, where the fire of the fireplace seemed to be burning merrily upon the center table.

PETRIYA. When Mother had to sell things one by one, it broke her heart.

ANOKA. Only she didn't sell them; she said she *"let them go."*

VELINKA. Yes, Anoka. And they went very fast, too.

ANOKA. It was so sad.

PETRIYA. We are almost alone.

ANOKA. We *are* alone, the four of us.

VELINKA. But for dear old Jet, the cow.

ANOKA. Dear old Jet, the cow, will go tomorrow, they say.

VELINKA. Out of the barn, and gone away . . .

PETRIYA. No more shall we drive her with our little sticks to the meadow Patagonia.

VELINKA. They will not kill her to eat her, will they?

PETRIYA. Not for a while. She gives down too much milk for that.

ANOKA. Too much fine cream.

MATHIAS. I wonder if they have fed her yet, tonight?

ANOKA. They are saying Mrs. Henk really suffered a stroke here yesterday.

MATHIAS. I shall strike *them.*

ANOKA. . . . And that she could never come back to live with us again, even if they would let her.

VELINKA. Something is going to happen.

ANOKA. We do not know what, yet.

VELINKA. Perhaps we shall know soon.

PETRIYA. Let us be as happy as we can here, while we can.

MATHIAS. Whether we are happy, we must be brave.

VELINKA. The fire is quite gone now.

PETRIYA. It will soon be out.

[*Silence. The sound of the storm comes in. The children huddle closer. The voices become louder.* ANOKA *listens.*]

VELINKA. [*As she huddles closer to* PETRIYA.] Brrr, it is cold in here, even like outdoors.

ANOKA. There is snow and sleet, I'm sure.

PETRIYA. What are they saying now?

ANOKA. They are eating all the food left. Mr. Hooper is gobbling up the last of Mother's fruit cake we were saving till Eastertide.

MATHIAS. I shall gobble him up when I get a chance, I bet!

ANOKA. The skinny lady is putting the can of chili beans into her big purse. She says she doesn't think they should be left here to freeze in the empty house, till someone else moves in, in the spring.

VELINKA. Someone else—move in here—where we belong?

ANOKA. [*Crying.*] The empty house—no more nice parties here for us.

VELINKA. [*Tears.*] And then the spring—the meadow Patagonia without us, nor Jet, the cow!

MATHIAS. Perhaps we shall never get the little red pony Mother promised us.

PETRIYA. We cannot know all these things yet, little Mathias.

ANOKA. Then why do we not all sing?

MATHIAS. [*Improvising a tune, as he marches about with a mock rifle on his shoulder.*] Tramp, tramp, tramp, the soldiers are marching to glorious war.

VELINKA. Let us not sing of war at a time like this.

MATHIAS. What better time is there? What is better than war? Did not Father give his life in war? Are they not . . .

ANOKA. Shshsh!

MATHIAS. [*Booming.*] Tramp, tramp, tramp . . .

PETRIYA. [*Whispering loudly.*] Be still, little Mathias! Let us hear what . . .

ANOKA. They are talking about us again, and something of what they call "separation."

VELINKA. [*With fear.*] Sep-a-ration?

[*The girls move closer to the door. The twins stand closest,* PETRIYA *a little away. Little* MATHIAS *still marches around the room making war sounds.*]

ANOKA. [*Breathless.*] They say no one will take all four of the children . . .

MATHIAS. [*Stopping his marching.*] Separ-a-tion? What does that mean, Petriya?

[*He moves over to the girls.*]

VELINKA. Separate us? Oh, no!

ANOKA. Listen! They are saying many different people want orphans.

PETRIYA. . . . That it is best for us, they think . . .

ANOKA. Also, it is against their rules to give four orphans to one family.

VELINKA. Why are we being *given* to anyone?

MATHIAS. Us—living apart the rest of our lives?

[*They huddle together, moving away from the door in horror and fear and tears.*]

VELINKA. No more to play together merrily as we often do?

ANOKA. Never to see one another again?

MATHIAS. Perhaps forever?

VELINKA. [*Breaking down, sobbing.*] Oh, no, no, no!

ANOKA. They must not do that!

VELINKA. They will not, will they?

MATHIAS. They cannot!

PETRIYA. Perhaps it will not be so.

VELINKA. But it seems that they have decided.

ANOKA. Listen! You are to go alone, Petriya. Velinka and I are to go together, since we are twins. And little Mathias is to go to someone by himself.

MATHIAS. Never fear, I shall not let them! I shall go to war with them!

VELINKA. But we shall all be unhappy, living apart.

ANOKA. Yes, but they have voted and decided.

MATHIAS. They never asked us about it.

PETRIYA. No, when we were in there, they only looked at us. They would not let us open our mouths.

ANOKA. In all our tatters, too.

PETRIYA. But they are clean.

VELINKA. And we love one another.

ANOKA. And get along without too many quarrels.

VELINKA. Oh, Petriya, cannot you do something?

ANOKA. Little Mathias, all alone!

VELINKA. None of us to blow his little nose when it runs.

ANOKA. Or wash him, or patch his shirts.

VELINKA. Or keep his little pants buttoned up properly.

MATHIAS. [*Bravely.*] Do not cry over that, nor me. It is you girls who need crying about. It is you who need me to fetch in the firewood.

VELINKA. Why can we not all of us stay here by ourselves?

ANOKA. We could care for ourselves with a little help from God.

MATHIAS. Old Mrs. Henk wasn't much help when she was here, anyway.

ANOKA. Mother was ill, too. It was we who kept her alive in her last days.

MATHIAS. No one else came in to help us, then.

ANOKA. Not a single one of those out there.

VELINKA. We were all alone.

ANOKA. Indeed, Petriya could cook the food for us.

VELINKA. Anoka and I could do the dishes willingly after every meal.

MATHIAS. I could cut the firewood with the big axe all winter.

PETRIYA. Where would we get the food?

ANOKA. From the meadow Patagonia, perhaps.

VELINKA. We could eat brown hay like Jet, the cow, if we could stay together, and had to.

ANOKA. Should we go in and ask them if we can stay?

PETRIYA. It would do little good.

VELINKA. They are bigger than we are.

ANOKA. There are more of them.

PETRIYA. They are older than we, also.

ANOKA. Then let us kill ourselves here, while they talk.

MATHIAS. Let us kill them!

PETRIYA. Who amongst us would go in and kill them?
[*Silence, no one moves.*]

VELINKA. I could not kill. Nor you, Anoka. Nor . . .

ANOKA. Nor could I kill Petriya.

PETRIYA. Nor could we kill each, himself.

ANOKA. We have nothing to jab with.

MATHIAS. I could kill myself by striking my heart, thus . . .
[MATHIAS *starts beating his breast. The girls rush to stop him, frightened.*]

VELINKA. Do not do it, little Mathias!

MATHIAS. Well, I could.

PETRIYA. Let us talk no more of killing.

ANOKA. Perhaps we could then talk of running away?

VELINKA. Yes. The door is unlocked and the far road begins just past the barn.

MATHIAS. Let us wrap our outer wraps on, and run away.

VELINKA. Then we shall all be together.

ANOKA. Then we can go where there are no *committees* and no *institutions*.

VELINKA. And no orphans.

ANOKA. I once heard of a land where children are always all cared for first.

VELINKA. Let us go there—all of us!

[*She moves to the outer door, as do* ANOKA *and* MATHIAS.]

ANOKA. Come, Petriya! Petriya will come if we start first.

[*They open the door. Wind, cold, sleet, and snow; and bitter darkness.*]

MATHIAS. [*A bit taken aback.*] I see it has grown dark outside.

VELINKA. It is evening, but there are no twilight stars outside.

ANOKA. The snow and sleet are blowing bad.

PETRIYA. I think we could not find the road beyond the barn, even to start out.

MATHIAS. I could go first and clear away the wild beasts, if I had a club.

PETRIYA. Perhaps we should all get into worser things than we are now in, little ones.

ANOKA. [*Pulling back from the door a little.*] It is all black except the snow, and it is white and very cold.

VELINKA. Close the door against it, Anoka.

ANOKA. I am tired, besides.

[*She closes the outside door.*]

PETRIYA. It has been a very busy day for all of us.

VELINKA. What can we do?

MATHIAS. I wish *I* had something to eat.

ANOKA. We have had no supper, have we?

VELINKA. They have not thought about us eating, I suppose.

ANOKA. They have all been too busy about our futures and our souls.

VELINKA. They have already eaten all our food.

PETRIYA. It will all be over soon, and they will come in.

VELINKA. [*Crying.*] Let us hide ourselves from them.

PETRIYA. When they come, we shall all know . . .

ANOKA. Do not cry, Velinka.

MATHIAS. That is not brave.

VELINKA. But it is *me,* and I am not brave, and I cannot help it.

ANOKA. Shall we never see one another again?

PETRIYA. We shall meet in Heaven. Perhaps we should all be glad and smile, for that.

VELINKA. Heaven is such a long time to wait.

ANOKA. When will they be done in there with us?

PETRIYA. There is no telling.

VELINKA. I am so tired . . . so, so tired in my arms.

[*The cow's "moo" is heard.*]

ANOKA. That is Jet, the cow.

PETRIYA. No one has given her her evening meal.

ANOKA. She is alone, and lonesome out there in her stall.

VELINKA. Should we go out and give her a wisp of straw, even . . . [*No one moves;* VELINKA *looks down onto the hearth.*] The little marsh-bug, who makes his home on the hearth, will get cold winter-long.

MATHIAS. How do we know he is a marsh-bug?

ANOKA. We do not know. We just call him that, for a name.

VELINKA. I think he will be happier than we.

PETRIYA. We must trust.

ANOKA. And hope.

MATHIAS. [*Yawning and dropping to the floor.*] I shall fight, also, when I wake up.

VELINKA. [*She sits beside him.*] I am sleepy, also, as well as tired.

ANOKA. [*She drops to the floor.*] We are all so bad off, yet we cannot but sleep a little.

VELINKA. We are not too old, you must remember.

ANOKA. Yes, we are just young people.

MATHIAS. I am not as angry and fearful as I should be.

ANOKA. We shall not know where we are, even when we get there, shall we?

PETRIYA. [*Dropping to her knees beside him.*] Let us wrap our wraps around us and be ready.

[*She wraps them in their rags.*]

VELINKA. We must be kind.

PETRIYA. I am sure God will be good to us, even though others are not.

ANOKA. As we have all tried to be good to Him.

VELINKA. I should like to cry a bit.

[*She does so, then stops.*]

ANOKA. [*Listening, from where she sits.*] They have stopped talking.

PETRIYA. Soon the doorknob will turn.

ANOKA. And they will come in, to tell us what we already know.

VELINKA. And lead us all apart . . .

ANOKA. Petriya to one place. Velinka and I shall be together, but . . .

VELINKA. Little Mathias alone, by himself . . .

MATHIAS. I shall strike them, [*He raises his little fist.*] clear to the last!

PETRIYA. Yes, little one. Yes, little lambs. Yes. Yes . . . s.

[*All but* PETRIYA, *sleep.* PETRIYA *cries softly to herself, and puts her arms around them all as they sleep huddled together, a troubled and restless sleep.*]

CURTAIN

EASY MONEY

By

Helen Poverman

(Published here for the first time)

CAST

JOEY MANSINI
PA MANSINI
ANGIE
JIM
VOICE OF CHILD

TIME: Summer.

PLACE: An industrial city in New England.

EASY MONEY

The scene is a modest living room of a five-room flat on the second floor of a two-family house. It is a working-class neighborhood. On the right wall are two large windows which look out to the street. Rear, right, is a door leading to the porch, which is off the living room. On the porch, there are many plants in pots and dishes of all shapes and sizes. Rear, left, is a door leading to the front hall. Left, center, is the door to the kitchen. The furniture is the overstuffed, old-fashioned kind, worn, but in passable condition. It consists of a sofa and a couple of chairs, a table with a telephone on it, near the sofa, and a couple of smaller tables. There are many family photographs around the room, and a number of doodads.

It is about one o'clock on a hot summer's day. The windows and the door to the porch are open. The sunlight is streaming in. The room looks as though it has all been vacuumed and dusted about ten minutes before. On the table near the sofa, there is a bunch of fresh flowers, which have been stuck into a glass jar without any effort at artistic arrangement.

JOEY MANSINI enters through the hall door. He is a clean-cut, fine looking young man of twenty-eight. His manner is free and easy. JOEY is a "Good guy," easygoing; never wants to hurt anyone, just wants to enjoy life. The easy way: that's for JOEY. He is dressed in working clothes. Although it is a very hot day and he is perspiring profusely, there is a buoyancy in his step, in his manner, instead of the dragging gait which usually goes along with a sweltering day. His manner, as he comes through the door, is that of the small boy with a wonderful idea.

JOEY. [Bursts through the hall door, at the same time calling out.] Hi, ya, Pa! [As he gets no response.] Pa, hey, Pa, where are you? [He opens the door to the kitchen, and sticks his head in.] Pa? [As he gets no response, he goes out to the porch and looks around. Then he opens the hall door and calls downstairs.] Hey, Angie, where's Pa?

ANGIE. He went to the store to get some things for supper. He'll be right back. Hey, how come you're home?

JOEY. See you later, Sis. [*He closes the hall door and goes into the kitchen. He comes back into the living room with a can of beer in his hand. He sets the beer down on the table. He strips off his shirt, wipes the perspiration from his face and body, and tosses the shirt down on the chair. He takes off his shoes and socks. He notices flowers on the table, smells them, and then thinks out loud.*] Good old Pa! [*He stretches out on the sofa and drinks beer, with obvious enjoyment and complete relaxation.*] Boy, oh boy, oh boy . . . [PA *enters through the hall door. He is about sixty-seven years old, and looks all his age. He is of medium height and sturdy build. He looks like a work-worn man who has lived life with its ups and downs. His manner expresses warmth, dignity, and pride. His face is red and perspired from the heat. He is tired, and drags in an armful of groceries. He doesn't notice* JOEY *at first, but starts toward the kitchen.*] Hi, Pa!

PA. [*Startled by* JOEY'S *voice, comes back into the room and sets the bundles down.*] Joey, whatsa matta you home? You sick? You get hurt?

JOEY. Never felt better, Pa. Why you luggin' so many bundles in all this heat?

PA. We gotta eat, Joey. [*With disbelief in his voice.*] You no get laid off?

JOEY. Hell, no! They can use twice as many guys at the factory. Come on, Pa, have a cold beer and get cooled off. [*Stretching.*] Boy, this is livin'!

PA. Whatsa matta you home now? It's a one o'clock, only.

JOEY. [*Teasing.*] Aw, Poppa, you don't sound glad to have me home.

PA. Eh, you make joke. You know how glad I am to hava you home. [*Wistfully.*] Since Mama gone, what I do widouta you? Somet'ing wrong, you home now, Joey? Whatsa matta?

JOEY. Nothin'. Everything's swell. Oh, we're gonna live it up this summer, you and me. We'll go to the beach every day. [*He swings around on the sofa and sits up.*] Hey, we'll even get to a ball game. You'll like that, eh?

PA. You talk like crazy wit da heat. You getta million dolla someplace?

JOEY. [*Enjoying himself.*] Who needs a million? Sit down and relax; then we can talk. Nothin' wrong. Nothin' could be better . . .

PA. Is so hot? First I put everyt'ing in ice box. [*Picking up the bundles and starting toward the kitchen.*] I come right away. [*He exits to the kitchen.* JOEY *lights a cigarette, stretches, smokes, and seems to be thoroughly relaxed. In the kitchen, we hear the refrigerator door, opening and closing.*]

PA. [*From the kitchen.*] I gonna make veal with peppers for supper. You like dat, eh Joey?

JOEY. Swell! It's too hot to eat, but you make me hungry. I swear it, Pa: you're even a better cook than Ma was, and that's goin' some.

PA. [*Enters from the kitchen, with a can of beer in his hand, beaming.*] You like, eh? [*Chuckles.*] Papa is pretty good cook— is good for somet'ing. Maybe I fix some mushrooms. I know you like . . .

JOEY. Sounds good!

PA. [*Looking around.*] You see my glasses somaplace?

JOEY. Pa, you're wearing them.

PA. Eh? Dat's right. [*He sits down on a chair near the sofa.*] Now, whata you gotta tell you' Pa?

JOEY. [*Uncertain how to begin, yet cocky.*] Well—I made up my mind. I'm gonna take the summer off. No work for me for the next six weeks! I'm gonna enjoy myself. Both of us—just enjoy ourselves.

PA. How you mean? You no quit you job? [*With considerable concern.*] Maybe you sick? You no feel so good, and you not tell me nutting?

JOEY. Hell, I'm not sick. Why do I have to wait until I get sick? [*Beginning to get uncomfortable under* PA'S *scrutiny.*]

PA. I no 'stand you. You say you no sick, you no fired. How you "take off" like you say, da summer?

JOEY. It's simple: just not work.

PA. No work? What you' boss say?

JOEY. What can he say?

PA. I aska you question. You no answer. You make more question. Talka how you mean!

JOEY. I'm tired of workin'; I want to take it easy a while. [*Smiling at the thought.*] While the rest of the guys are sweatin' it out this summer, you and me'll be fishin'. We'll rent us a little rowboat. You always like that. Catch 'em and cook 'em! Pa, I bet you never really had a vacation.

PA. I no 'stand how you talk.

JOEY. [*Emphatically.*] Just enjoy myself this summer! Enjoy *our*selves. Is there a law against it?

PA. Is no law. You gotta so much money?

JOEY. How much do I need?

PA. Is not just today. You twenty-eight years— Now is time you settle down. Dis no way for you to live.

JOEY. Oh, Pa, let's not start on that again.

PA. [*Ignoring him.*] Is time you marry and have kids.

JOEY. Marry? You think I'm nuts? I got a good home. What the hell do I want to get married for?

PA. Home is not enough. You needa start you' own family. You needa woman.

JOEY. [*With a grand gesture.*] Dames! Haw!—They're a dime a dozen. Take 'em out to a joint dancing on Saturday night, and you're a swell guy! Love 'em and leave 'em; no problems that way.

PA. Is no good. You needa wife. You needa kids.

JOEY. Kids? Yeh, I like kids. I got plenty of nieces and nephews to fool around with. Take 'em to a ball game or the movies; give 'em a treat, and Uncle Joey is a swell guy. No stayin' up all night with bellyaches; no doctor bills; no headaches; no responsibilities. No, siree, not for me! I like things the way they are.

PA. [*Shaking his head.*] You maka mistake.

JOEY. [*As though explaining to a child.*] Listen, Pa, the more money I make, the more the government gets back. It's not like in the old days: every cent you made went into your own pocket.

PA. Is okay today. Everybody still live better.

JOEY. Anyhow, as far as the buck is concerned, I'm just as well off if I don't make the full six weeks' pay.

PA. Whata you figure?

JOEY. I'll collect unemployment insurance. By the time the government gets through deductin' from my pay, I'm just as well off at the end of the year if I loaf six weeks and collect my unemployment insurance.

PA. Dey needa you at factory, huh?

JOEY. Sure, they do.

PA. Well, how you collect insurance?

JOEY. [*Getting more uncomfortable under* PA's *questions, rises, goes over to the window and looks out, his back to* PA.] Look, Pa, there are always angles—ways you can work it and get away with it. Listen to the other guys! I've been a sap long enough.

PA. What you do is crooked—is not right.

JOEY. [*Turning around angrily.*] Right? Right? What's right? Does everything have to be the hard way to make it right? So you worked hard; you did everything right. What you got to show for it? Did you get any fun out of life?

PA. [*Reflecting, and then as though probing something deep inside him.*] Fun? What you call fun? Everyt'ing is easy is fun, huh? Dat for *you* make everyt'ing right? I tella you dis: I look in de glass; I no 'shamed when I see my face. I looka my kids, Tommy, Frankie, Tony, Angie. Dey alla nice, good. Dey married. Dey gotta family. Is good. Whena you alla small, me worka hard; Mama worka hard. I no maka too mucha money. What we got, my Maria and me, we giva you. We no ask nutting from nobody. We no taka nutting . . .

JOEY. [*Turning to look out of the window again and speaking under his breath.*] For Christ sake!

PA. [*Continues.*] Fun? Fun? I no 'stand fun lika you talk fun. What I do make me feel good inside, ina here!

[*He bangs his fist against his heart. During this last speech, he has risen from his seat, and comes over to* JOEY.]

JOEY. [*Resentful.*] So—what's all that got to do with time off this summer? To hear you talk, a guy would think I was robbin' a bank.

PA. [*Growing angrier as he talks.*] What you do is not right.
Boss need you. You needa job. You needa money. You wanna
money, but you wanna *easy money. Easy money.* Dat's it—*easy
money.*

[PA and JOEY *are now glaring at each other.*]

JOEY. So what? From the little shmoe to the big-time
politician, everybody wants easy money.

PA. [*Steadily growing angrier.*] Is not right!

JOEY. Here we go about rights again! All I know is, if you
don't take what's easy pickins, you're a sap.

PA. Sap, huh?

JOEY. [*Reconciliatory in manner.*] Listen, Papa: nobody
really loses anything on the deal. Maybe the government gets a
few bucks less, but that's all. The boss doesn't really lose anything, and I don't really lose anything.

PA. [*Thinking, shaking his head.*] Is no wonder government
has to take so mucha money from honest people' pay.

JOEY. [*Belligerently.*] Now maybe you want to make over
the whole government. All because I want a few lousy weeks
this summer. You want it like old times, huh? No unions, no
social security, no old age pensions, no unemployment insurance?

PA. All dese is good. Is right in right place. Man sick—
no can work—kids needa eat. Is good he have insurance and no
need charity. But you—is different.

JOEY. I've been workin' since I'm out of the army, pretty
steady. I haven't pulled any punches. The guys all call me a
sap. I'm single. I have no worries. It's just you and me. That's
fine by me. Now you are raisin' a big stink over nothing. Christ,
Papa, I came home feeling good—damn good! We could have
ourselves a time this summer. It's great to have high ideas, when
they pay off.

PA. And you tink you' big ideas "Pay off" like you say?
Hah—Like hell! Give you big head. Give you big head; swell
up. Full of nutting, like balloon. Then *Pfft,* blow up and what
you got? Nutting. Sure, you put it over. You betcha, you put
it over. Not on de boss, not on de government. You beega fool!
— You put it over on you'self.

JOEY. [*With a sweeping upward gesture.*] Big, big thoughts! I don't follow you.

PA. I know you no follow me. Dat's de trouble. You tink I old-fashion. I no canna make you see what you do for you'-self—make you strong, strong ina heart, ina mind. You needa work, and sava how you can. Stand on you' owna feet. If you tink like dis— [*Voice imitates that of a small boy.*] Whena I sick, de govement taka care o'me. Whena I no work, de govement taka care o'me. Whena I too ole, de govement taka care a me . . . [*Natural voice.*] Is okay when you small boy, you tink like dis—Papa taka care o'me. Is right. Now, whena you beega man, you keep tink lika small boy, make you lika mush inside.

JOEY. That's pretty talk. Real pretty. But loafin' all summer still looks good to me. I can't see nothin' wrong with it. If I'm smart enough to figure out how to do it and get away with it, good for me. It's too damn hot to argue now. I've made up my mind, and I'm gonna enjoy myself, beginning right now. So lay off, will ya, Pa?

[*He comes back to the sofa and stretches out.*]

PA. [*His anger has reached the point of exasperation.*] You no listen to me? You do whatcha wanna, huh?

JOEY. You'll see: we'll have a good time.

PA. [*Thrashes around, like someone who is bound down and will break his fetters.*] You wanna keep you' way? Keep! You find out, you'self. You no listen to me, huh? I know what I gotta do. [*With great vehemence.*] I won't taka one cent froma you, no more, no more!

JOEY. [*Disturbed by* PA's *wrath, sits up again, pleading.*] But, Pa . . .

PA. [*Banging his fist down on the table.*] Quiet, Joey! Not one penny! I know what I gotta do.

JOEY. Please, Pa, take it easy! Don't get so excited. Please!

PA. [*Paying no attention.*] You forget, huh, I sell half million dollar ina defense bonds ina war time. I sweat plenty. I maka much money for dis country. I proud, and now whata you t'ink you make me do? You taka money froma govement! I taka money froma you? No. No. No.

JOEY. But, Pa . . .

PA. I know what I gotta do.

[*Starts frantically hunting around the room. His movements are erratic and seem to express his anger and restlessness rather than purpose.*]

JOEY. Aw, Pa, calm down, will ya?

PA. [*Still moving around the room.*] Calma down! You say calma down! Justa lika dat!

JOEY. It's so damn hot. With your blood pressure, you shouldn't get so excited.

PA. Excited, huh! You t'ink I no reason get excited, huh? [*Still hunting, but more purposefully now: he goes through some magazines and newspapers, which are neatly stacked on a table.*] Musta be here somaplace!

JOEY. What are you lookin' for, anyhow?

PA. Wait, wait! Me showa you. [*He pulls out another newspaper and looks through it.*] Musta be here somaplace. [*He hunts some more.*] Here, here! Dis isa what I looka for. [*He triumphantly slaps his hand against the paper.*] Dis isa what I want. See, see, whata say here . . .

[*Bringing the paper over to* JOEY.]

JOEY. [*Looking at the paper.*] Where? Where? What is it? What are you trying to show me?

PA. [*Talking louder and more excitedly.*] Righta here. Biga piece ina paper, all ona one side. See whata say? Mena wanted.

JOEY. [*On the defensive.*] So—what about it?

PA. [*With pride and assurance, looking at* JOEY *and letting it sink in.*] Dat's where I getta job.

JOEY. [*Shocked.*] Get a job? You?

PA. Datsa what I need. Datsa what I gonna do.

JOEY. [*Recovering.*] Pa, where could you get a job?

PA. [*Really convincing himself.*] You see? Justa say, "Mena wanted." No aska how old, nutting. Justa say, "Mena wanted" an calla S. ana O. Brass Factory. I call. I call. I getta job. You see. Whena day needa men, anybody getta job.

JOEY. Quit kidding yourself.

PA. [*Going to the phone.*] I no kid.

JOEY. [*Shaking his head.*] It's no use, Pa. [PA *spreads out the paper near the phone and dials.* JOEY *watches him. He starts to go toward* PA, *but stops himself.*] Hang up, Pa! It's no use. Hang up!

PA. [*Talking into the phone.*] Hello. Isa S. and O. Factory? You hava ad ina paper. You looka for men to work. Yeh, yeh, yeh. [*Nods head enthusiastically.*] I no 'fraid to work. Me no lika kids today. Me no watcha clock . . . Isa lifting heavy cables? Dat's okay. Sure, I canna do. I no lika some man ina my years . . . Sure, sure, me strong. Me wanna work. No. No, I never do heavy lifting before. [*Long pause.*] Mebbe you have nudder job? Isa beega factory? Mebbe isa somet'ing not so much lifting? You say, I try ina state employment office—dey hava more dana one kind job, huh? Isa number CO-8-5320. Tanka you very much. [*He hangs up the phone.*] Datsa good idee! I call in employment office. Datsa how I getta job. [*He picks up the phone and starts to dial again.*]

JOEY. [*Has been watching his* PA's *movements with tension, and then relief.*] Pa, please hang up! It's no use. You gotta face facts.

[*But* PA *stays at the phone.* JOEY's *tension mounts.*

PA. [*On phone.*] Isa state employment office? I look for a job. Mebbe you hava somet'ing for me? Me no fussy, and me no 'fraid to work. You hava job? Yeh, yeh. Sure. Sure, I cana come see you today. Drive a truck? Datsa okay. I cana drive. You say isa beega trailer truck. Experience? No—isa no good, huh? [*Dejected.*] Cook? You no need aska me no more. Me very good cook! [*With great enthusiasm.*] Cana maka soup, meat, everyt'ing. I ever cook ina restaurant? No, but me good. Can maka da besta veal scaloppine and lasagna. Oh, ma, ma mia!— Youa taste! Isa somet'ing. I maka wonderful eggplant Parmesan! I tella you. I make ana bringa you some today. You see . . . Isa best you ever eat . . . Isa no good, huh? Must be short-order cook, fast wita lot experience! [*Dejected.*] Mebbe you look see whata else you have? . . . Yeh. Yeh. [*He perks up.*] Datsa fine! Datsa besta job you coulda find! Sit atta bench ana work all day. Datsa what I like: worka wita my hands. Me good workman. You want? Sure, I cana do job. Isa easy for me—put on little piece ona lock. You say: must hava very sharp eyes, huh? [*Long pause.*] No, I no canna do. Trute is my eyes isa . . . Mebba you hava nudder job for me? Somet'ing I canna do? Me no waste time ona job. Me no lose a day froma work. Somet'ing else, please, you see. Notta now, huh? Tanka you very much. You very nice. I calla you again.

[*He slowly puts down the receiver, discouraged.*]

JOEY. Just forget it, Pa, and cool off.

PA. [*Ignoring him; putting his head back and thinking.*] I remember coupla days ago, Jim tella bout job somaplace. Yeh, I calla Jim.

JOEY. Please, Pa, give it up; please, Pa.

PA. [*With renewed hope, dials.*] Hello, Jim. Isa me. You remember couple days ago, you tella me bouta shop where dey needa man? Yeh, dey needa man. Where isa place? . . . I aska for myself . . . Yeh, yeh, me. *Me* wanna job . . . Sure I canna work. I sita home too long, isa no good . . . I no crazy. No crazy at all. [*His face falls.*] Dey no keepa man dere after sixty-five years, huh? You sure? You know sure, huh? . . . Tank you. [*He hangs up the phone.*] Isa no use.

JOEY. That's what I've been trying to tell you.

PA. [*Sits down in despair.*] Me wanna or me no wanna, me gotta stay home lika ole shoe. No good for nutting. I gotta no use to nobody—no more.

JOEY. [*Moved.*] Pa, don't feel bad about it! I'm glad you didn't get a job. I want to take care of you. I want to do everything I can for you, give you anything you need. All of us kids feel that way about you, Pa. You know it.

PA. Yeh, yeh, I know. Me like, or me no like: me gotta swallow how you do, what you do.

JOEY. Be sensible! Take it easy. Anyhow, even if you had a job, with taxes and all, it wouldn't be worth it.

PA. You no 'stand me. To me, would be worth it.

JOEY. Your working days are over. So relax and take it easy.

PA. [*Slowly, as though trying to impress it all on his mind.*] Dat's how is. I too old. My eyes not so good no more. I no canna fix shoes no more. Oney job I canna find isa heavy work, isa too hard. I no canna do. Dat's how is.

[*He nods his head, and straightens out the papers.* JOEY *is stretched out on the sofa, and drinks his neglected beer. We hear someone running up the back stairs.* ANGIE *bursts in through the kitchen door. She is in her late thirties. She is an intense, nervous kind of person, on the lean and jumpy side. She is wearing a summer house-dress, with an apron over it.*]

ANGIE. Pa, you came home loaded down with bundles. I saw you. Do you have to drag so much in all this heat? Hey, Joey, how come you're home? [*Behind* PA'S *back,* JOEY *motions with his hands for* ANGIE *to drop the subject. She wipes perspiration from her face with her apron.*] Is it hot! Baby won't go to sleep. [*She goes over to the hall door and listens, and then comes back into the room.*] Papa, you're awful flushed. You feel all right?

PA. Sure, sure, just is so hot . . .

ANGIE. [*Very concerned.*] Maybe you better lie down and take a rest this afternoon.

PA. [*Irritated, yet with affection.*] Stoppa worryin' so much! Alla time you worry, worry, worry.

ANGIE. [*Patting him on the cheek affectionately.*] Papa, we all love you. Frankie called to say he was working late tonight, but that he will stop by on his way home.

PA. [*Responding to* ANGIE.] Dat's good. Yeh, I gotta good kids.

ANGIE. Talking about kids, I don't know what I'm going to do with my Tommy.

PA. Whatsa matta wit Tommy?

ANGIE. You know, he's going to be sixteen in September. He wants to quit school. I want him to finish high school.

PA. So he finish!

ANGIE. What can I do? I talk, talk, talk. Just like to a wall! He's got an answer. He says, "Ma, you know my teacher, Mr. Haley: he went four years to college; four years. So now the fellows in the factory are makin' more than he is."

PA. [*Nodding his head.*] Tommy isa smart ina school.

ANGIE. Sure, he is.

PA. You maka him finish! Isa good t'ing to learn. Whena man old, he no canna worka with his hands sometime; he still canna work hisa head. You maka him mind!

ANGIE. Make him?

PA. Tom want him finish? [ANGIE *nods.*] Isa no question. Fadder isa head o' family.

ANGIE. But, Pa, it's not that easy any more. You gotta explain things to kids. You gotta *reason* with them. You gotta eat your heart out and knock your brains out to make 'em see what you're talking about. When we were kids, there were no "ifs, ands, or buts." Papa said so, and that was it!

[*We hear a baby crying from downstairs, followed by a child's voice.*]

VOICE OF CHILD. Hey, Ma, the baby's crying.

ANGIE. [*Calling down from the hall door.*] Turn her over, and be quiet.

VOICE OF CHILD. Ma, can we have some soda?

ANGIE. Have some soda and be quiet, you hear!

[*She comes back into the room.*]

JOEY. Got any cigarettes?

ANGIE. Yeh, plenty, downstairs.

JOEY. I sure could use one. Tell me where they are.

ANGIE. I'll get them. I want to go down and look in on the kids anyhow . . . Be back later, Pa. [*She starts toward the hall as* JIM *is entering.*] Hello, Jim. Pa's home.

[*She exits through the hall door.* JIM *enters. He is about the same age as* PA. *He tends to be fat and jovial.*]

JIM. Hey, Pa! Hey, Joey.

PA. [*Obviously glad to see him.*] Come in, come in, Jim!

JIM. Boy, isa hot! Phew! Isa sona ma gun hot day! Phew!

JOEY. How about a cold beer?

JIM. Yeh, I like, but no lika me. [*To* PA.] I tella you I come today ana bringa seeds ana plants. I helpa you—we fixa yard little bit, eh?

PA. [*Not very enthusiastic.*] Yeh, yeh.

JIM. Hey, whatsa mat'? You no wanna? I bringa special plants froma yard: biga, biga tomatoes, lika you never see.

PA. You gooda friend, Jim.

JIM. You no wanna work ina yard, hah?

JOEY. Lay off! It's too damn hot.

PA. Olda man lika us, what else we canna do?— Diga ina yard. [*Sighs.*] Watch t'ings grow up. We growa down.

JIM. Humph! We not so old, nota lika dat, nota lika you talk. Whatsa mat' for you today? You no feel good? . . . Den what is alla talk abouta job whena you calla me?

PA. Isa just idee I have.

JIM. Isa some idee!

PA. [*In utter weariness.*] Jim, you know, I gotta no sense, no sense, no sense atall. Whata you t'ink? I looka for job—no sense. Who wanna me? Ima sixty-seven years ole. Ima ole. Ima tired. Ima worn out. Ima good for nutting. Who wanna me ona job?

JIM. Ha! To hell wita job. Why you talk lika fool? Whata for you needa job? Whata you get ina you' head make you talk wita no sense? You worka hard all you' life. You taka care you' kids. Now you' kids taka care you. Now is time you rest. Work ina garden little bit. Sit ina sun little bit. Play wita kids. You' time to work isa finish. Where you getta such idee to work?

PA. Oney job he have: lifting cables. Isa hard job, too hard for me. I no canna lift alla day. I no canna do such heavy job.

JIM. Why you looka for job? Joey isa good boy. Isa good to you alla time.

PA. Yeh, Joey isa good boy. Alla time he wasa honest. Gooda heart. Alla time, he wasa good to Mama ana me.

JIM. [*To* JOEY.] Say, whatsa mat' you no work today? My Tommy work today. You no sick? Maybe you getta vacation, huh? [PA *nods uncertainly.* JOEY *rises, and stamps out.*] Everybody getta plenty vacation, now. [*Laughs.*] Not lika in old days, huh?

PA. Nobody wan' work today. Easy money—is ina air, is ina way people t'ink. You know, Jim, isa lika poison, slow poison. Make people weak, and dey no see what happen to dem. [*Musing.*] Easy job, easy money, govement taka care. Maka man lika baby.

JIM. Nobody wan' work today. Is not like when we young, eh, John?

PA. You remember, Jim, whena we come to dis country. We

wanna so much to work. Alla we want is de chance to work, to save little bit money. I strong lika bull; I worka froma first t'ing ina de morning until late in de night. All time, I wanna save little bit money so I hava my owna place—start my little business.

JIM. Sure, I remember. I remember how first day you open shop. You calla me so excited. [*Laughs.*] It wasa no bigga den a closet. I remember, howa one time, I so proud wenna beega car come up wita begga shot driving. He aska me if I know where isa dis John, da fella who maka da special shoes. I tella him: sure, me know. Me show him, disa John is besta friend. And den I remember how you work ana save until you buy dis house.

PA. Dat's when I strong lika bull.

JIM. Isa different now.

PA. Yeh, isa different now. I maka mistake: get mad atta Joey. Isa not Joey: *easy money* is ina air today, lika sickness. He catch it, but he good boy.

JIM. Alla young kids isa same.

PA. Yeh, yeh. Everybody wanna fun. Everybody sing, "Enjoy you'self."

JOEY. [*Coming back through the door.*] That's right. Enjoy yourself! That's how the song goes. [*Sings with gusto.*] "Enjoy yourself, enjoy yourself. It's later than you think." It's a good idea after all, huh, Pa?

JIM. [*Shaking his head and speaking to* PA.] You know, John, you no canna change world. You no canna change times.

PA. [*Nodding his head solemnly.*] You right; yeh, you right. [*Long pause.*] I t'ink—since world begin, isa good time, isa bad time. If man get lika mush inside, whata happen whena time isa not so good and money isa not so easy? Eh, Jim? Where de govement get all de money den? Eh?

JIM. Isa beeg question. [*Suddenly starting up, remembering.*] Say, I leave a plants ona porch downstairs. Isa so hot dey dry out. I put ina water, an I wait outside, John.
[*He goes to the hall door.*]

PA. I coma down in a few minutes.

[JIM *exits.* PA *and* JOEY *face each other.*]

JOEY. [*A bit uncertain just how to begin.*] Say, Pa . . . I, uh . . .

PA. Yeh, Joey.

JOEY. Well, I've been thinkin' about how you wanted to get a job . . .

PA. Yeh, Joey.

JOEY. Your eyes are not so good, huh?

PA. Datsa right. Not so good no more.

JOEY. You have trouble doing close work, huh, Papa? Gee, that makes it tough.

PA. Isa nutting new.

JOEY. You wanted that job so bad, didn't you?

PA. Yeh, would be fine. Not too hard: sittin' ana workin' wita hands. I lika. . . .

JOEY. You could go to work every day, and get your pay every week. And you could have had the job, if it weren't for your eyes.

PA. [*Nodding, with a sigh.*] But dat's how is, Joey.

JOEY. And you wanted that job so bad! You would have had the income you wanted every week, to feel—well, independent—something that was coming just to you.

PA. Dat's right.

[ANGIE *has entered through the kitchen. Seeing them both in conversation, she sits down quietly.*]

JOEY. It's just your eyes; you could have had a job, a good job.

PA. Yeh, so whata you tella me now?

JOEY. Just say your eyes are a little worse than they are . . .

PA. Whata for?

JOEY. Because of your eyes, you couldn't get that job.

PA. Yeh, datsa right.

JOEY. You still could get a little money for yourself.

PA. What you say?

JOEY. You really are entitled to it.

PA. I no 'stand you.

ANGIE. Joey, what are you talking about?

JOEY. He could get an allowance from the government. [*To*

PA.] It's coming to you, you know. It isn't your fault you can't take such a good job. You want to work; you're no loafer.

PA. Me wanna work. Me no lazy.

JOEY. All you have to do is say your eyes are a little worse than they are. That's all.

PA. [*Uncertainly.*] But dat's not tella da trute.

JOEY. Oh, it would just be stretchin' things a little bit.

PA. [*Thinking.*] You say, "stretchin' t'ings little bit," huh? Den I tella lie.

JOEY. It wouldn't be a lie. You would only be exaggerating some, telling things a little bigger than they are. You know what I mean, Pa?

PA. [*Studying* JOEY.] Yeh, yeh, I t'ink I 'stand you now.

JOEY. There's nothing to it, really.

PA. Nutting to it, huh? You wanna me tella beega story 'bout my eyes, so I getta money froma govement.

JOEY. But what's wrong with it? You yourself reminded me how you went out and sold half a million dollars worth of bonds during the war. That's a lot more than plenty of other guys did. Why shouldn't you get a little something, if you can?

PA. I getta money froma govement for doin' nutting? Justa tella lie, datsa okay? Huh? [*Exploding.*] So now, I canna be *liar, cheat.* LIAR, CHEAT, huh? Isa bad nuff you wanna do what is not right you'self. Now you wanna make *me* liar, cheat. You canna pusha, pusha man justa so far ana dat's all!

ANGIE. [*Tries to calm him.*] Pa, Joey doesn't want you to be a liar or a cheat. He doesn't mean anything like that. He's a good boy. He wants you happy. He wants it easy for you.

JOEY. Pa, I'm only thinking of you. If you had a job or any income, I couldn't deduct you as a dependent, and the government would take more out of my pay. I wouldn't gain anything; I'm only thinking of you.

[*Meanwhile,* PA *is stamping around the room, almost beside himself with rage.* ANGIE *is following him around, trying to talk to him. She tugs on his sleeve, as she tries to hold him with her hands as well as with her words.*]

ANGIE. Pa, now Pa, you didn't always get along with your Pa. After all, you came to this country because—because you saw things different from your father. You told me yourself, how he wanted you to stay, but you were young, and you had your own ideas and . . . That's the way it is, Papa. Young people and older people just can't always see everything the same way. You're smart; you know that. Remember how you told me, one time, how the young people lean way over on one side, and the old, way over on the other. Then you said how everything gets straightened out someplace in the middle? Remember, Papa, remember how you told me . . . ?

PA. [*Trying to pull away, but* ANGIE *is holding on to his sleeve.*] Let me go!

JOEY. [*Contrite and disturbed.*] Honest, I didn't mean anything. I'm just shootin' my mouth off. Forget it, Pa.

PA. Forget it? No. I canna getta job. Is lifting, sure, but I gotta take dat job. Must be dat way!

JOEY. Papa, please . . . What for? Like Jim said: You can't change the world.

PA. Me, justa myself, I no canna change whole world. Dat's right. I no canna change how my owna son t'ink. I no canna change how *I* t'ink. I no *wanna* change how I t'ink. Ina my way, I gotta live how I believe, how I t'ink. If no, me no man, me dish rag. Ina my way, I gotta live how I believe. Dat oney way man can be a man. I gonna taka dat job.

[*He exits through the hall and slams the door.*]

CURTAIN

A TOUCH OF MARBLE

By

Dan S. Potter

(Published here for the first time)

CAST

A *Touch of Marble* was originally produced at Studio 1, New Haven, Connecticut, on November 14 and 15, 1958, with the following cast:

HELEN .... Janie Herndon
PHIL .... Jim Flannery
HONEY .... Helen Yalof
MISS CARROLL .... Marianne Loosemore
AUNT MARGARET .... Genie Zust
ROGER .... Dale Cornelius

Director .... Roy Levin

TIME: Now, and the past.

PLACE: A Hotel room in a city.

A TOUCH OF MARBLE

SCENE 1

A soft, drowsy, bronze light filters through the faded, cheap lace curtains framing the single window of a dingy hotel room. A tall, nervous woman in her mid-thirties enters the room from the outside hall. She comes into the room hesitantly, like a stranger, frightened and tensed, ready to fly away like a bird at sudden noise, somewhat overawed by the sudden reality of the four enclosing walls. She is followed by a blond, young sailor, whose white uniform almost floods the room. This, coupled with his obvious physical magnetism, makes him a rather brilliant figure, in sharp contrast to the older-looking woman. He begins to move a duffle bag from the middle of the floor.

PHIL. I'm not very neat.

HELEN. There's something timid about being neat. I hate being timid. I was scared to death, walking through that lobby. It was like—like I was a statue, alone in a big, bare room, and everybody staring at me. [*She laughs nervously, her voice high and cool, then continues speaking with a girlish softness in her voice.*] I was afraid someone would recognize me.

PHIL. It's a big city.

HELEN. I've always felt like a stranger here—in the city.

PHIL. Cigarette?

HELEN. I don't smoke—or drink. There's an old joke about the girl who went out on a date, and first she turned down cigarettes, then liquor. But then, when her boy friend began to look unhappy, she said: "Well, you don't have to smoke and drink to have a good time!"

PHIL. Yeah . . .

HELEN. I've never been in a hotel room—with a man.

PHIL. Oh? Well . . .

HELEN. You must think I'm really *bad*.

PHIL. Why, no, I—you don't *feel* bad, do you?

HELEN. It's just that—it's November, you know. [*She looks out the window.*] November's such a lonely time. I sat in the park all afternoon, watching the leaves—faded like the pages of old books people forgot to read. Sometimes I feel like an old book. [*She laughs nervously.*] Oh, there I go again! Self-pity's such a terrible thing, isn't it? And then you came—so white and clean—and you know what I thought? I thought: if I could touch you, if I could move my hands along your body, I could feel that whiteness in my hands, and I wouldn't feel . . .

PHIL. [*Moving toward her.*] Helen . . .

HELEN. No, we mustn't hurry. Why, we've got—we've got all night.

PHIL. Sure! I don't have to be back till Monday at eight. We've got the whole week end.

HELEN. There's something sad about this little room. You can almost hear old, dusty whispers—and nothing can hide the stains . . .

PHIL. I wish I could've afforded something nicer.

HELEN. How old are you?

PHIL. Nineteen.

HELEN. Nineteen? He was nineteen . . .

PHIL. He?

HELEN. Someone I knew a long time ago: a sailor. It was during the war; I met him in the park, just like I met you. It's funny, isn't it, the way history repeats itself? I liked him very much, but he went away . . .

PHIL. Oh! [*He starts removing his shoes.*] Might as well get comfortable.

HELEN. Before you came, there was an old man in the park, picking up papers, with a nail on the end of a stick. I tried to talk to him. I always talk to people. I asked him about the pigeons. When I go to the park, I always feed them. They're so gentle and soft—but so easily frightened. So I asked about the pigeons, but he didn't answer. He just laughed and went away. Later he came back, and he had a dead one. He said he walked up behind it, and stuck the nail through its back. Blood was dripping off his fingers—and he laughed.

PHIL. Is that why you'd been crying?

HELEN. I suppose . . .

PHIL. There *are* people like that—cruel people. You can't do anything about it.

HELEN. No . . .

PHIL. Best thing to do is not to think about things like that!

HELEN. I'm so silly. I'm probably ruining all the fun for you.

PHIL. No, you aren't.

HELEN. Why did you stop? Why did you stop to talk to an old schoolteacher like me?

PHIL. Well, I don't know. I mean: well, I liked you. I liked the way you looked. I guess I thought you were lonesome, like me, kind of a stranger . . .

HELEN. A stranger?

PHIL. You weren't like the girls—well, the ones you usually run across. You're different.

HELEN. I hope not too different.

PHIL. [*Somewhat anxiously.*] Helen . . .

HELEN. I want you to understand: this never happened before. I've always been afraid. I was sitting there on the park bench, like every other week end for so long, and, well, it's almost winter. No one's ever ready for winter. But when I saw you, I didn't think of winter any more.

PHIL. It's all right. I understand.

[*Through the opened window comes the sound of music played on a piano. It is relatively simple music, and lushly romantic, suggestive of strong but youthful melancholy.*]

HELEN. Do you hear that?

PHIL. Comes from that building next door. Must be a piano studio. They woke me up this morning.

HELEN. I know that song . . .

PHIL. Kind of sad! Want me to get some jazz on the radio?

HELEN. No. No. I remember that song. I had a girl friend; we were roommates at a girls' school. She was very good at the piano. She was very good at everything. She used to play that song . . .

PHIL. [*Approaching.*] Helen . . .

HELEN. Are you sure that . . . I'm awfully nervous. Could I—could we have a drink?

PHIL. I thought you didn't drink.

HELEN. Not *usually*. But why don't you get a bottle of whiskey—a small one. And while you're gone, I'll order ice, and we'll have a little party here, and afterwards [*With mock assurance.*] we'll take a cold shower—not enough to be sober, but just enough to enjoy getting warm . . .

PHIL. Sounds great.

HELEN. I think I read that in a book somewhere . . .

PHIL. I'll be right back.

HELEN. Phil, I'm sorry.

PHIL. For what?

HELEN. To be so square!

PHIL. [*With a wave of his arm.*] Aww . . . [*He exits.*]

SCENE 2

The piano music swells. HELEN *takes pins out of her hair and lets it fall across her shoulders, and removes her jacket and glasses, revealing a dress of a girl in her teens. She twirls around girlishly, suddenly stops, catching a glimpse of herself in the mirror of the dresser. As if extremely conscious of the music, she turns around and goes to the window, raises the shade and the window higher. Music floods the room, and is suddenly overridden by her nervously delicate, slightly hysterical girlish laughter. The lights dim. Then* HELEN's *laughter merges with that of* HONEY, *offstage.*

HELEN. Honey? Honey Johnson, is that you?

[HONEY *enters: a thin but beautiful girl in a black dance costume with red sash. She carries a mirror into which she frequently stares.*]

HONEY. I'm practicing for our recital, Helen. Isn't it funny?

HELEN. Why is it funny?

HONEY. Such a sad song! I don't know why I laugh. I really don't.

HELEN. Come here, Honey, please . . .

HONEY. Look, Helen! It's my dance costume. I'm a raven —a beautiful raven who's been hurt. A cruel little boy has hurt me. See! [*Indicating the sash.*] This is blood; it's symbolic. At the end of the dance, I die. Isn't it sad, Helen?

HELEN. Yes. Honey, listen! I took that part in the play . . . [HONEY *stares.*] I didn't want to, since you were trying out for it, but . . .

HONEY. Oh, that! I've got more interests than that silly old play! Do you think I'm pretty, Helen?

HELEN. You're very pretty. Honey, I really didn't want the part . . .

HONEY. I don't *care* about the play! You know I'm the best *dancer* at Miss Carroll's. And I'm the best in Miss Prentice's gym class. And I write beautiful poetry for my English class . . .

HELEN. And you're my very best friend, Honey. My very best . . .

HONEY. I'm prettier than you. Aren't I, Helen?

HELEN. Yes.

HONEY. But I'm not as happy as you.

HELEN. You should be, Honey! You should be very happy. You're pretty, and you're good at everything.

HONEY. I'll never be happy; I know it. Never!

HELEN. Oh, yes, you will, Honey.

[HELEN *embraces her;* HONEY *shrinks back violently.*]

HONEY. Why did you touch me?

HELEN. Because I like you.

HONEY. Nobody likes me. And I know why. And I don't want anyone to touch me. You're like the others: jealous . . .

HELEN. No.

HONEY. You're jealous; but I don't care. I'll never care about anything. I don't care how many silly plays you're in!

HELEN. Oh, Honey . . .

[*She lays her hand on the girl's arm.*]

HONEY. *Don't touch me!* I'll tell Miss Carroll. I'll tell her you "touched" me! You know what will happen then.

HELEN. But I didn't mean . . .

HONEY. I don't care! I don't care what you meant. I don't care about anything. You know why? I'm a fallen leaf, that's why. [*Liking the melodrama.*] I'm a fallen leaf—and if I'm left alone, the wind will blow me around high in the air—and I'll be safe—away from everyone. But if you touch me, I'll crumble—all to pieces. [HONEY *laughs and dances around, and then comes back to* HELEN *angrily.*] Why did you take the part in the play? *Why?* You knew I wanted it. You knew . . .

HELEN. Honey . . .

HONEY. You hate me, that's why. You're jealous, like the others.

HELEN. That's not true.

HONEY. *It is!*

HELEN. I didn't want the part; they made me take it. Miss Prentice said I was shy, and it would do me good. She made me take it.

HONEY. That's a lie.

HELEN. I wouldn't lie to you, Honey.

HONEY. You would! You're jealous of me, because I'm so pretty. That's it, isn't it?

HELEN. No, Honey, please . . .

HONEY. It *is* true. You took the part, and you—*you* said you were my friend.

HELEN. I *am* your friend, your very best friend. [*She puts an arm around her.*]

HONEY. [*Hysterically.*] No, don't touch me! I told you not to touch me. I'll tell Miss Carroll . . . [*Running toward the back, yelling.*] Miss Carroll! Miss Carroll! I'll tell them all: I'll tell them you put your hands on me! [*She runs off.*] Miss Carroll! Miss Carroll!

[*There is a long scream, followed by a crash of glass, then darkness.*]

SCENE 3

HELEN *is collapsed on the bed.* MISS CARROLL, *a large, brisk administrator enters.*

MISS CARROLL. I'm so sorry, Helen. We should have known . . .

HELEN. Miss Carroll, it was my fault . . .

MISS CARROLL. We must try to forget it! It's been an ordeal for all of us—especially you, Helen. But you musn't blame yourself for Honey's death.

HELEN. I did touch her, but . . .

MISS CARROLL. Now, Helen, I know how you must feel; but you'll get over it. And there's no reason for you to leave. You weren't responsible for . . .

HELEN. I caused her . . .

MISS CARROLL. My dear, you're very tense!— I'm having some medicine sent to you. I want you to promise to take it, and you must promise not to run away.

HELEN. I can't stay here. Not now.

MISS CARROLL. Helen, I don't know how much you knew about Honey. We were concerned about her, and we had sent her to our psychiatrist. He said she . . . Helen, it wasn't your fault at all: she was very disturbed. You musn't blame yourself, or . . .

HELEN. Miss Carroll, please help me! I feel so guilty.

MISS CARROLL. What is it, Helen? I *want* to help you.

HELEN. My hands—I'm afraid!

MISS CARROLL. You'll get over it after a while. Come here, my dear . . .

HELEN. I can't.

MISS CARROLL. You musn't be frightened of people, Helen . . . [*The lights begin to fade.*] You musn't be frightened . . .

HELEN. I can't forget.

SCENE 4

There is a momentary blackout in which MISS CARROLL *is replaced by the* AUNT, *who stands coldly and resolutely before* HELEN.

AUNT. You *must;* do you understand? Helen, you've got to get hold of yourself! You can't be afraid of people all your life. You're even afraid of me. Why, Helen?

HELEN. Aunt Margaret, I . . .

AUNT. If you'd come to me, Helen, just once and . . . [*A long pause.* HELEN *makes no response.*] You must put the memory out of your mind, or it will destroy you. Do you hear?— Destroy you, just as that reckless girl destroyed herself.

HELEN. I've tried. I've tried. If I hadn't touched her . . .

AUNT. Helen, this is painful for me, but I know girls sometimes get crushes . . .

HELEN. It wasn't that! She was the best friend I ever had. I wanted to be nice to her—show her I liked her. But she was so afraid, and I . . .

AUNT. Helen, I won't have you brooding—being morbid and hating yourself! There's no sense in moping and taking on. I want you to finish school. I know you haven't had it easy: your mother dying when you were a baby, then your father. But that girl, Helen, was *doomed.* There was nothing anybody could do for her.

HELEN. Why? Why did she do it?

AUNT. There *are* people like that, and there's nothing anybody can do . . . You must *forget;* you can't live your life with fear and guilt. That way, every moment can be torture. You've got to build your life as you go, Helen, step by step. God knows, we all have our troubles.

HELEN. What if something makes me remember? This *pain* . . .

AUNT. Pain? You don't know what pain is.
[*She becomes self-absorbed.*]

HELEN. A fallen leaf . . .

AUNT. What?

HELEN. That's what she called herself: a fallen leaf.

AUNT. [*Shaking her violently.*] Now, you listen to me! I'm sick and tired of your despair and self-pity.

HELEN. Please . . .

AUNT. If there was nothing between you and that girl, then there's no reason for all this. I know it was a shock—but you haven't tried to forget. You haven't tried!

HELEN. I have. You don't understand.

AUNT. Listen to me! Do *you* understand what it is to be fifty and live in a dark, empty house? To go to a stuffy classroom day after day, and smile at rows and rows of other people's beautiful children? Pain, you say? Do you have a pain that stays in your stomach twenty-four hours a day and won't stop—won't ever stop? You're young, Helen. You still have time: time for children, your own good life. [*She begins shaking* HELEN.] I won't let you destroy yourself, do you hear? I won't let you do it! I won't; I won't. [*The* AUNT *suddenly turns away and crosses the room. After a long pause, she turns back to* HELEN.] You must promise never to mention that girl again, as long as I live.

HELEN. All right, Aunt Margaret.

AUNT. I'm going down to help the Red Cross. I think you could at least . . . Why don't you take a walk in the park, Helen? Maybe you'll meet someone . . . [*Realizes what she has said.*] A walk in the park would do you good, instead of hiding from people.

HELEN. I'm not hiding.

[*The lights fade out.*]

SCENE 5

HELEN *repeats:* I'm not hiding. *The lights come up again, and the following scene takes place in the park. A young sailor,* ROGER, *approaches* HELEN, *whose back is turned.*

ROGER. Who are you hiding from?

HELEN. What?

ROGER. The big, bad wolf?

HELEN. The big—I was just . . . I come here all the time.

ROGER. Good for you! People are dying, I get drafted, and you play games in the park.

HELEN. I was—thinking.

ROGER. Then think about me! Don't you feel sorry for me?

HELEN. Why, no.

ROGER. Why not?

HELEN. You look very strong and happy. Why should I feel sorry for you?

ROGER. I don't know. I just think somebody should . . .

HELEN. If there's something wrong, if you're in trouble . . .

ROGER. There's nothing wrong, except war and bombs and rackets and crimes—and maybe the Russians—and a few other misfits . . .

HELEN. What else?

ROGER. Aw, nothing! I don't have time to brood; this is my first liberty in two months.

HELEN. Oh!

ROGER. Two can stroll as cheap as one, can't they?

HELEN. Well, I . . .

ROGER. Why the frown? Your mother warn you about sailors?

HELEN. My mother's dead.

ROGER. Oh.

HELEN. I live with my aunt. She says she won't retire—from teaching school—until I finish college. It's like I was taking her place . . . She has it all planned.

ROGER. Sounds like fun.

HELEN. Am I boring you? I don't want to keep you—I mean, if you have something you'd rather do.

ROGER. I can always get drunk, unless something turns up.

HELEN. Maybe you'd better—get drunk. I'm not very interesting.

ROGER. I'll decide that. Okay?

HELEN. Okay.

ROGER. I'm Roger. What's your name?

HELEN. Helen.

ROGER. Helen. I like that. Well, Miss Helen, what are you looking for in this great big park?

HELEN. Me? Oh—should I be looking for something?

ROGER. Most people are.

HELEN. Well, I guess I'm looking for something then. I don't know what, though.

ROGER. Do you know what I'm looking for?

HELEN. No.

ROGER. No idea?

HELEN. It must be something nice. You look so white and clean. You look like—like you shouldn't be touched—you're so white.

ROGER. Yeah? I'm not *that* white.

HELEN. I don't think anybody could look like you—so white—and not be very nice.

[HELEN *moves away, walks idly off by herself, as the lights dim. When they come up, it is dusk. A street lamp glows.*]

ROGER. I was thinking about what you said about me being *nice.* You don't know much about—well—people, do you?

HELEN. No. I guess I don't.

ROGER. You learn a lot when you live with them like I do. You get too close. They're animals. They move, they act, they smell like animals. You've just got to be a better animal.

HELEN. Do you really feel that way?

ROGER. Sure.

HELEN. You sound so old! And you aren't as old as I am.

ROGER. I don't feel old. I feel young as that moon, and I want to have a good time. What about you?

HELEN. Yes, I suppose I want to have a good time.

[HELEN *walks away as before.*]

ROGER. You know, this is the third time I've been here, and all you do is turn around in circles. Don't you get dizzy?

HELEN. No.

ROGER. Don't you get tired of *not* doing anything?

HELEN. We talk a lot.

ROGER. We sure do.

HELEN. I know all about you: I know you're going overseas and . . .

ROGER. I don't know anything about *you*. I can't get close enough. I haven't even touched you.

HELEN. No, you haven't.

ROGER. I don't know why in hell I come back here.

HELEN. I'm not very exciting.

ROGER. You could be, Helen.

[*He moves to her; embraces her.*]

HELEN. Please . . .

ROGER. What is it?

HELEN. [*Breaks away.*] I'm sorry.

ROGER. You must like me: you keep asking me back. I don't get it.

HELEN. I like you very much.

ROGER. What are you afraid of?

HELEN. Whenever I think of putting my hands near you, I . . .

ROGER. Helen, I don't want you to think, well—that you're a pick-up or something. I know how we met; but you gotta meet some way. I like you. You make me feel good. I've never felt like this since I was a kid. You're so soft-looking, like a little bird. And the way you look at me . . . But I don't come in very often, and I sort of want to do something besides talk.

HELEN. There are—other girls.

ROGER. Sometimes I go out with other girls, after I leave you.

HELEN. You do?

ROGER. Helen, I want you to know: I don't care for those other girls. I don't even like them. I do like you.

[*In the distance, a clock strikes hollowly.*]

HELEN. I've got to go, Roger.

ROGER. Now?

HELEN. Yes. My aunt worries.

ROGER. For God's sake!

HELEN. Will you come Saturday? Will you meet me here?

ROGER. Look, Helen: we're going to sail any day. I may not even be in this country Saturday.

HELEN. You don't really want to come back, do you?

ROGER. Sure; I'll be here.

HELEN. You're sure?

ROGER. Yes.

[*He looks disappointed, scuffs the ground with his feet, and begins walking off. He turns back to look after her as the scene slowly fades out to blackness.*]

HELEN. [*Speaking in the darkness.*] You promised, Roger. You promised! And I had something special to tell you. I was going to be different . . .

SCENE 6

The lights come up bright in the dingy hotel room. PHIL *enters with the bottle in a paper bag.*

HELEN. [*Startled.*] Roger?

PHIL. What?

HELEN. I thought . . .

PHIL. I was someone else.

HELEN. Yes, for a moment.

PHIL. Well, I got a bottle.

HELEN. You surprised me, coming in like that. Do you like surprises? Life's no fun without surprises, do you think?

PHIL. I never thought about it.

HELEN. While I waited, I—I got to thinking about things— people I've known. About the boy in the Navy I told you about! And when you came in, I . . .

PHIL. Sorry, wrong guy!

HELEN. No reason to be sorry; it isn't your fault. He just didn't come back. Vanished.

PHIL. You want a drink?

HELEN. Isn't it strange?— I almost feel like I know you.

PHIL. You do!

HELEN. You meet girls in parks and maybe under street lights and you take them home, don't you? That's what Roger did. Maybe he met someone in another park somewhere. Maybe he died.

PHIL. You want a drink now?

HELEN. He's the only one, ever! Isn't it silly?

PHIL. You never married or anything?

HELEN. Oh, no. I'll be an old maid. Can't you tell?

PHIL. I think you're—attractive.

HELEN. Oh— While you were gone, I took my hair down. I just felt like it—letting my hair down. [*She laughs self-consciously.*] It makes me feel much younger.

PHIL. You aren't old, Helen.

HELEN. I *feel* old. I'm thirty-four.

PHIL. That isn't old. It's just right.

HELEN. Just right for what?

PHIL. Why, to enjoy yourself.

HELEN. You're very handsome. You make me feel very strange. Roger was like that: so white and clean-looking. I wanted to touch him—touch his lips and his arms. Do you like to be—touched?

PHIL. Yes, I do. [*He is about to embrace her.*]

HELEN. [*Turns toward him, instictively responding, then turns away.*] No . . .

PHIL. What . . . ?

HELEN. It isn't your— I want so much to put my hands against your face. But I know if I tried—like the old man in the park, running a nail through the little bird. I've always felt like that little bird.

PHIL. Something's happened to you, hasn't it? Something bad.

HELEN. No, not really. That's what's so funny. Nothing's ever really happened *to me*.

PHIL. Look, why not have a drink?

HELEN. [*At the window.*] It's still the same, isn't it?

PHIL. What, Helen?

HELEN. All the world outside. And us—I'm still me—and it's almost winter and the leaves have fallen . . .

PHIL. Do you live alone?

HELEN. Yes.

PHIL. Maybe you'd rather go . . .

HELEN. I live in a dark, empty house. You wouldn't like it there. It's so late—and cold. Are you cold?

PHIL. No.

HELEN. No, you're very warm. I can feel you now—warm like the sun on a little clear pool. But I'm so cold. My breasts are cold—and smooth like marble—like the breasts of a statue you shrink to touch. [*He moves toward her.*] You musn't . . . [*She picks up a leaf from the window sill.*] I guess the wind blew it here from the park. It was all alone, and the wind brought it here. [*She carefully folds his fingers around it, and then, with great effort, slowly moves her fingers up and presses them against his lips. There is something both tremendously moving and pathetic about her final attitude, as if she knew well and perversely enjoyed her lost, fragile role.*] Don't speak!— It isn't your fault. If you touch me, I'll crumble—into little pieces.

[*She exits slowly through the door.* PHIL *watches her, speechless, then looks at his closed fist, opens it, and watches the bits of leaf float gently down. He gazes once more at the door through which she disappeared, shakes his head. The same music as in* SCENE 1 *begins again. He lights a cigarette; takes a couple of puffs, then viciously puts his heel on it and crumples it into the faded carpet.*]

CURTAIN

TWO SIDES OF DARKNESS

By

Edwin R. Procunier

(Published here for the first time)

CAST

Two Sides of Darkness was originally produced by the Studio Club of the London Little Theatre in February, 1959, with the following cast:

CHORUS .... Mary Moore, Pat Walker, Marion Wood
LYSANDER .... Terry Russell
MELENA .... Pamela Russell
SON .... Ian May
BERT .... Paul Eck
JENNY .... Doreen Sneddon
FATHER .... Bob Leatham

Director .... Mary Brown

TIME AND PLACE: The scene alternates between the Greece of Agamemnon's time and present-day Canada.

TWO SIDES OF DARKNESS

The stage is divided into three parts, but only one section is lighted at a time. Center, upstage, is the area of the CHORUS. *The curtains open on a darkened stage. Still in darkness, three old* WOMEN, *who, when revealed, are seen to be dressed in the flowing garments reminiscent of Greece, begin to speak.*

CHORUS.
>When did time begin for us,
>For us, the children of men?
>When did the foul maw
>Of an immemorial past,
>Silent in a length of days,
>Spew forth the children of men?
>When did the fair beauty
>Of walking on feet, back straight
>And shining in the sun, hands
>To grasp and examine
>The fruits of a calmer earth,
>Begin?

[A center "spot" has gradually revealed the three WOMEN. *Left and right stage remain in darkness or gloom.]*

FIRST WOMAN.
>Was it with the Achaeans
>Coming out of the mist of the North,
>Bringing the still hidden seeds
>Of long, slow growth—growth
>To an opulent reaping,
>Garnered to a candid and classic
>Harvest—from the rich luxuriance
>Of multitudinous thought?

SECOND WOMAN.
>Or was it, for some, the flower
>Of Aaron's rod, the cry of beauty
>In Babylonia when even the humble slave

187

Was chainless? Or was it the thunder
And wrath of the Law-giver,
Condensed to the *rule* of law?

THIRD WOMAN.

Did it come with the savage,
Virile hordes charging over the Steppes,
The Wastes—with the rumble of hoofs
In the tone of their voices:
Germanic—Germanic—
Clashing at first, then blended, subdued
With those of the weary eagles of Rome?

[*When speaking individually, the* WOMEN *appear to be in discussion. The lines in* CHORUS *are addressed more obviously to the audience. They continue slowly.*]

CHORUS.

When did time begin for us,
For us, the children of men?
We cannot say, for we seem
Always to have been.
Can the old remember with clarity
The days of their youth?
Can even the young remember with eyes undimmed
The days of their childhood?
When did time begin for us,
And when will all things cease?
Again we cannot say, for time itself
Is timeless—a moment that,
Like a pebble upon the beach,
Sinks back with the ceaseless
Ebb, the unending flow,
To be again hurled upon the beach.

[*The center "spot" begins to fade midway in this last speech. When it is almost extinguished, a right "spot" lights the next scene. The setting is suggestive of ancient Greece—a rural scene with possibly a tree or two, and a broken pillar lying on its side. A young woman,* MELENA, *in Greek costume is revealed, sitting upon a stone, stage left of this scene. A moment passes, during which she sighs deeply. She faces left. Presently a young man in shepherd garb enters from the right.*]

LYSANDER. [*Coming toward her, and pretending that he has just seen her.*] Hello!

MELENA. [*Turning shyly.*] Hello.

LYSANDER. So you've come out again today?

MELENA. As you see—yes.

LYSANDER. And how are the affairs of the great city of Mycenae?

MELENA. My father says that all is well, or nearly well, or nearly as well as affairs can be. And is the countryside quiet?

LYSANDER. *My* father does not trouble himself to ask. But I can tell you that, except for the occasional fall of a ripe olive or the bleat of a lamb newly born, it is quiet.

MELENA. How peaceful that seems! And how I should like to live here!

LYSANDER. [*Eagerly.*] Would you?

MELENA. [*Realizing with embarrassment what she has revealed.*] Why—yes. Away from the crowds, the rattle of carts, the crying of merchants . . .

LYSANDER. [*Disappointed.*] Oh! Is that all?

MELENA. Perhaps.

LYSANDER. [*After a pause.*] Er—how are the great king Agamemnon, and his wife Clytemnestra, and their two daughters, and Orestes?

MELENA. [*Smiling at his attempt.*] I don't have a great deal to do with them. I'm not royal blood. You would know as well as I.

LYSANDER. I tend sheep, not royal families.

MELENA. [*Softly.*] Then why aren't you tending them now?

LYSANDER. I—well—I am. Or rather, I'm looking for one that strayed. Yes, that's it, one that strayed.

MELENA. Does one always stray—over here?

LYSANDER. What do you mean?

MELENA. That's what you said the last time I spoke to you. A strange shepherd boy, who can't keep his sheep together on one hillside!

LYSANDER. [*Hurt.*] Boy!

MELENA. Young man, then. Did I hurt your pride? My mother tells me that young men of tender age are easily wounded, and that I should be more careful of my speech—now that I'm older.

LYSANDER. Your mother! Why should my pride be hurt by the words of a—a wisp of a girl?

MELENA. A wisp of a girl!

LYSANDER. [*Laughing.*] There, now you're angry. Young woman, then! My father tells me that our rough-and-tumble days are gone. I think sometimes that I'm sorry for that, and sometimes I don't feel sorry at all. Do you?

MELENA. Growing up does seem to mean that you can't play the games you used to play. But I don't think I mind.

LYSANDER. [*After a pause, and then softly.*] Why do you come out here every day?

MELENA. [*Surprised.*] I—I don't come out here *every* day. How do you know I come out here every day?

LYSANDER. Because I see you. Sometimes I'm too busy to—to look for lost sheep, but still I see you.

MELENA. Well, I like to watch the caravans moving up the valley to Euboea and Boetia and Arcadia. And I like to see the country. In any case, why should *you* ask me that?

LYSANDER. [*Ignoring the question.*] Is that all?

MELENA. Perhaps. Why do you come over *here* looking for your lost sheep? You never find them.

LYSANDER. Why? Because I expect to find them.

MELENA. Is that all?

LYSANDER. [*Smiling.*] Perhaps. No, perhaps. I'm lonely, perhaps. I like to look at you, hear you speak, see you smile. [*On this last speech,* MELENA *rises and turns right to face* LYSANDER.]

MELENA. Perhaps I come to see the caravans and the valley. Perhaps, too, I like to see you leap the rocks, and hear your songs sounding among the hills.

LYSANDER. Sometimes, when I go to the city, I look at the women. I used to enjoy that before you came. Now . . .

MELENA. And now?

LYSANDER. Now I look only for you.

MELENA. I'm not sure that you should say that.

LYSANDER. But it's true, and what's true must be the right thing to say, mustn't it?

MELENA. Yes, I think so.

LYSANDER. Sometimes, in the city, do you look for me?

MELENA. I— Turn away from me for a moment! [LYSANDER turns; MELENA speaks softly.] Yes. Yes, I look for you.

[There is a blackout, stage right, and then the lights come up slowly, stage left, to reveal a bus stop outside an office building on a modern city street. Impatiently, JENNY, a young woman, waits at the stop. Presently a young man, BERT, comes on the stage from the entrance left. For a moment, he stands beside her, whistling impatiently.]

BERT. Is that thing ever going to come?

JENNY. [Turning to face him.] I—I beg your pardon?

BERT. The bus? Is it ever going to come?

JENNY. I think so. It hasn't missed yet.

BERT. It's slow—very slow. A car could get you home much quicker.

JENNY. [Turning away from him.] Not always.

BERT. [After a pause.] Do you like working there?

JENNY. [Turning back to him.] How do you know where I work?

BERT. Because I watch you come at five to nine, and I see you wait for the bus every day.

JENNY. Oh!

BERT. You didn't answer my question.

JENNY. It's a job. I like it well enough.

BERT. [After another slight pause.] The weather's mild for this time of year.

JENNY. Yes.

BERT. I'm not much good at conversation.

JENNY. Neither am I.

BERT. Sometimes I get all mixed up, especially . . .

JENNY. Especially?

BERT. Nothing.

JENNY. Do you like your job?

BERT. Yes. I like it fine, like to use my hands. I don't think I've got much brains.

JENNY. I haven't, either.

BERT. Oh, I'm sure you have!

JENNY. Why?

BERT. [*Flustered.*] Well, I—I don't know . . .

JENNY. One of the girls in the office says you fixed her car for her.

BERT. I work just across the street.

JENNY. I know.

BERT. You do?

JENNY. I've—I've seen you there.

BERT. [*Summoning his courage.*] Would you—would you like a ride home?

JENNY. [*Smiling.*] That's why I'm at the bus stop.

BERT. My car's parked just around the corner . . .

JENNY. Then why are you waiting for a bus?

BERT. To talk to you.

JENNY. Oh!

BERT. Where do you live?

JENNY. North Road.

BERT. That's near my home on Maple Street.

JENNY. But Maple is in the south end.

BERT. It's not far from North Road, just the same. It's a small city . . . Will you come with me?

JENNY. [*After a pause.*] Well—all right.

[*As they leave together, the light fades, and the center "spot" reveals again the three old* WOMEN.]

CHORUS.

    Delicate, sweet, and fragrant
    Is the first touch of love.

FIRST WOMAN.

    Like the rose gently unfolding
    Beside the pool in the garden.

SECOND WOMAN.

    Like the green sway of palms
    In the parched sands of the desert.

THIRD WOMAN.

Like the unclouding of snow
On the mountain in early morning.

CHORUS.

Delicate, sweet, and tender
Is the first touch of love.
Those who are young look forward,
Look forward—unwarned, unthinking—
To the time of the unfolding . . .
But we who are old look back,
Far back, far back,
To a time before burial,
To a time before death:
Before the smile ceased to be,
Before the voice sickened and whimpered,
Before the hand became gnarled and cold.
And sometimes
We do not remember . . .
For the earth is old and we are old,
And we are the children of men;
And the time when the world began
Is not known to us.
But sometimes—sometimes,
We do remember!
Like the searing pain of the knife
Which cut for causes forgotten.

FIRST WOMAN.

Remember the time of parting . . .

SECOND WOMAN.

Remember the times of sorrow . . .

THIRD WOMAN.

And the breaking of nations.

CHORUS.

The coming to be of things
Which we did not know!

[*The center "spot" fades, and the light comes up on the scene right.* LYSANDER, *dressed in armor such as the Greeks wore, comes in, hand in hand with* MELENA, *who is obviously with child.*]

MELENA. Why did you bring me out here, Lysander?

LYSANDER. It was probably silly of me, but I wanted to say "Good-bye" where—where we met.

MELENA. "Good-bye!" One year we've been married, one short year, and you have to say "Good-bye!"

LYSANDER. It can't be helped.

MELENA. How senseless it seems.

LYSANDER. To us, perhaps; but it has to be. You know that.

MELENA. I only know that you're leaving. The other, I wish I understood—what everyone else seems to understand. But I don't.

LYSANDER. But I've explained it to you.

MELENA. It's foolish of me, Lysander, but I want to hear again. Perhaps this time I'll understand. Why do you have to go?

LYSANDER. [Protesting.] Melena!

MELENA. No, I mean it. I want to know.

LYSANDER. You torture yourself; but it's really very simple. Sometimes, I think too simple. [MELENA seats herself upon the stone. LYSANDER stands, his foot resting against the broken pillar.] As you know, one of the Trojan princes, Paris, Priam's son, came here on a diplomatic mission. I don't mean here exactly; I mean to Sparta. And he took the wife of King Menelaus back to Troy with him. Menelaus objected—that part, at least, is reasonable enough—and so he's organized a war to get her back.

MELENA. From what I've heard, she probably went of her own choice.

LYSANDER. [Smiling.] And from what I've heard of Menelaus, she probably hadn't your reasons for staying. In any case, we don't know much. Paris is supposed to be a very beautiful young man—even Aphrodite wanted him.

MELENA. Aphrodite is welcome to all beautiful young men.

LYSANDER. [Laughing.] Even your husband?

MELENA. No, not my husband, but all others. Do you think she's worth it, Lysander? . . . Helen of Sparta, I mean. Worth fighting for?

LYSANDER. Men say so. Our own king, Agamemnon, is leading the army. After all, he's the older brother of Menelaus, and Sparta *is* our ally. They say a thousand ships will set out from Aulis when the wind turns. Think of it, a thousand ships! [*He moves downstage right.*]

MELENA. I didn't know there were that many in the world . . . But it seems small reason for all the shedding of blood.

LYSANDER. [*Turning to face her.*] And what has reason to do with it? One excuse is as good as another. In any case, the old men of Mycenae, those who handle the business affairs, explain it another way.

MELENA. Oh? How?

LYSANDER. They say that Troy's become too powerful, that this is the chance we've been waiting for . . .

MELENA. But Troy's so far away! I never even heard of it before last month.

LYSANDER. It's on the grain route to the Euxine Sea. The Trojan ships have been interfering with our trade.

MELENA. Do you believe that?

LYSANDER. I don't know. It seems to be true. All I know is that Mycenae's at war, that I have to leave. There isn't much more to know than that, is there?

MELENA. And so men must die for a few ships of grain?

LYSANDER. Yes.

MELENA. Husbands and fathers?

LYSANDER. [*Hesitantly.*] And more than men, if the rumors in the market place are true.

MELENA. What do you mean? What rumors?

LYSANDER. I heard in the city that Colchis, the priest, has had Agamemnon order the sacrifice of one of his daughters.

MELENA. [*Standing, horrified.*] The sacrifice of his own child?

LYSANDER. Yes.

MELENA. His own daughter! But why, Lysander, why?

LYSANDER. To give us good winds to Troy.

MELENA. [*With great hesitation.*] What—what would *you* do?

LYSANDER. What do you mean?

MELENA. If you had a child, a daughter, and you were asked to do the same thing . . .

LYSANDER. I'm not a king. I don't know.

MELENA. You don't know? Couldn't you be sure, even of yourself? [*Turning from him.*] His own daughter! How mad can this world become!

LYSANDER. [*After a pause.*] Melena?

MELENA. Yes?

LYSANDER. I'm going—now.

MELENA. [*Turning back to him.*] Lys . . .

LYSANDER. No, don't turn until I've gone! Take care of yourself—and the child—when the time comes.

MELENA. [*Still turned away.*] The child! How can I bear a child while you're away fighting? Perhaps even being killed . . .

LYSANDER. You must!

MELENA. [*Turning.*] Lys . . .

LYSANDER. No! We can't change the world—even if we want to. Good-bye.

MELENA. [*Sobbing as he leaves, right.*] Good-bye, Lysander. Good-bye.

[*The light fades quickly, and stage left becomes bright. The scene is the same as before, except for a large poster on the bus, advertising war bonds.* BERT, *in the uniform of a common soldier, enters with* JENNY.]

JENNY. But I want to go to the station with you.

BERT. No, Jenny, I don't like saying "Good-bye" in places like that—with everyone standing around.

JENNY. I wouldn't see them.

BERT. But *I* would. They'd be just like us, multiplied by a thousand. We've said what we have to say.

JENNY. Yes, we've said what we have to say. [*After a pause.*] Did you see your mother?

BERT. No. She locked herself in her room, and wouldn't come out. I had to call to her through the door. She left me a present, a going-away present, on the hall table. See! A wrist watch.

JENNY. A wrist watch?

BERT. [*Mirthlessly.*] My old one never did run right. The label inside here says it's guaranteed against rust, water, heat, and moderate fall-outs. Can't you see a battlefield with nothing making a sound except thousands of fall-out-proof watches ticking time away?

JENNY. Oh, Bert, how can you make a joke about it?

BERT. [*Harshly.*] You think I'm joking?

JENNY. Oh, I don't know. Since this war started—if I only understood . . .

BERT. Understood?

JENNY. Yes. Why must you go? I don't see why you should go. What have *you* done?

BERT. It's simple enough, or at least it seems simple enough. We made a treaty with them, and they've been attacked. So now we have to fight.

JENNY. But I never even heard of them before!

BERT. Neither did I; not even when I used to collect stamps. I thought I knew the world in those days.

JENNY. Does it all make sense to you? You're a man. Does it all make sense?

BERT. No.

JENNY. I'm frightened, Bert.

BERT. So am I. I know I'm not supposed to be, but I am. I'd rather work at cars in the garage. [*Looking at his new watch.*] It's almost train-time, and I have to report.

JENNY. Bert?

BERT. No, you stay here! Take the bus back! And, Jenny . . .

JENNY. Yes?

BERT. [*Trying to be humorous, but failing miserably.*] Don't let any smart-aleck garage mechanic talk you into his car this time!

JENNY. Oh, Bert!

[*They kiss hurriedly, desperately.* BERT *leaves, left. As the light dims,* JENNY *stands alone. The "spot" comes up again on the three* WOMEN.]

CHORUS.

Today the lover, tomorrow the warrior;

In a short time fulfilling
The two instincts of man.
So we would be led to think,
Since both have always been.

FIRST WOMAN.

But let us in the strict, detached,
And nice tradition of the Chorus
Pause to examine this state of affairs.

SECOND WOMAN.

Let us pause.

[*The three* WOMEN *form a more obvious group, as though chatting in the natural way of gossips.*]

THIRD WOMAN.

Love is a necessary, almost necessary state,
If we are to bring forth a new generation.

FIRST WOMAN.

This is as it has been said,
And it were best not to question too closely.

SECOND WOMAN.

The lover might be a tiller of soil,
In hope of a good harvest—
Though the harvest is not always as planned.

THIRD WOMAN.

He might be thought a dreamer of dreams—
Though he may not rise refreshed from them.

FIRST WOMAN.

He might be the deliberate planner
Of a social fabric—
Though the purpose is sometimes obscured,
As it were, by what is surely
Irrelevant, transient
But not altogether unpleasant
Sensation.

CHORUS.

In all truth, this we have observed,
Though for us time past is time past.
Still, as the children of men,
We have seen these things.

For in some ways time is changeless.
The seemingly pulsing,
Implacable, onward rush
Has brought two sides of darkness.
The fever-pulse of the lover is dark,
But the darkness can be sweet.
His wanting is often greed;
Yet a greed that's shared
Is only greed
To one who stands without.
[*The lines which follow are spoken rapidly and with much force,
building to a climax.*]

FIRST WOMAN.

But the shrieks and groans,

SECOND WOMAN.

The retching and writhing,

THIRD WOMAN.

And afterwards the pain
Of lost emptiness
Of war,

CHORUS.

Are such that we, being simple,
Being really, in age, children,
Do not understand.
This
Is the second side of darkness.

FIRST WOMAN.

What is the madness of the chariot?

SECOND WOMAN.

What the fierce glint of the lance?

THIRD WOMAN.

What the gun, the bomb, the deprivation,
Desolation, ache of the heart?

CHORUS.

Being both old *and* young,
We do not understand.

THIRD WOMAN.

Somewhere in the nature of things,

It began.

FIRST WOMAN.

In some moment primeval and lost.

SECOND WOMAN.

Too ancient for such little wisdom
As we have been granted.

CHORUS.

Yet let us not desert the race of men.
Let us say that here
There is nobility, courage, virtue,
A way to defend, a faith to uphold;
Though in this are passages
Of deepest obscurity,
And we see the smile of the Sphinx
And the wink of the maid of Apollo.
For we do not always see the way,
And the lamp of faith has been known
To cast lurid shadows.

FIRST WOMAN.

Let us say there is a way . . .

SECOND WOMAN.

Let us say there is a lamp . . .

THIRD WOMAN.

Let us say these sides of darkness

CHORUS.

Are often dark
Because we do not choose to see.
But the darkness is no less dark,
Though we have created symbols
To beguile the children of men.

FIRST WOMAN. [*After a pause.*]

And so another war ends.

SECOND WOMAN.

This surely the last!

THIRD WOMAN.

But a war without beginning

CHORUS.

SHALL HAVE NO ENDING.

[*The center "spot" fades on this last speech, and we return to the Grecian scene, right. The stage is at first bare. Presently a haggard* MELENA *enters left with her* SON.]

SON. Do you think the rumor was true, Mother?

MELENA. I've heard many rumors; in ten years of war, there have been thousands. Which one is this, my son?

SON. The one in the market place this morning: that the ships have come back from Troy, that my father and Agamemnon are coming down the valley!

MELENA. [*Wearily sitting upon a stone.*] I don't know.

SON. The old men said that Queen Clytemnestra was preparing the palace to welcome the king.

MELENA. No doubt.

SON. [*After a pause.*] Mother?

MELENA. Yes?

SON. Mother, what's a paramour?

MELENA. [*Startled.*] A what?

SON. A paramour. The men say that Aegisthus is the queen's paramour. Is he a kind of servant in the house?

MELENA. [*Smiling in spite of her feeling.*] Yes, you might call him a kind of servant.

SON. Why don't we have one? Can't we afford him?

MELENA. No, we can't afford one.

SON. They say the king will reward him when he returns.

MELENA. He very probably will.

SON. Why did they laugh when they said it?

MELENA. You'll understand later.

SON. Later! Everything's later! How I'd like to see a thousand ships! I heard they've landed at Aulis. That's in Boetia.

MELENA. [*Smiling.*] Yes, I know.

SON. And now they must be marching down the valley to Mycenae, mustn't they?

MELENA. If the rumor's true.

SON. Then it has to be true, and we'll see them, the whole army coming back from Troy!

MELENA. [*With dread.*] Those who come back, we'll see.

SON. I hope my father is in the front rank.

MELENA. Yes, he will be in the front rank.

SON. [*Pausing.*] Mother?

MELENA. Yes?

SON. Why do we come here every day?

MELENA. Don't you like it in the country?

SON. Oh, yes, I like it. Do you know what I want to be when I grow up?

MELENA. [*Wearily.*] A soldier, I suppose.

SON. Oh, no, Mother. A shepherd!

MELENA. [*Almost in tears, softly.*] Lysander, Lysander!

SON. What's wrong? Why are you crying?

MELENA. Nothing. I'm only a woman, and women cry easily.

SON. Mother?

MELENA. Yes?

SON. What's my father like? Is he a big man?

MELENA. [*Recovering quickly.*] Like one of the gods, my son! With a fine broad forehead and curling hair, a voice like the wind and the seas, a smile that can turn the greatest pain to happiness, straight limbs that shine in the sun—like one of the gods.

SON. Have you ever seen a god?

MELENA. Why, of course. I told you— I had a son by one.

SON. Now you're laughing at me. [*Then pointing off to the right.*] Oh, look! They're coming—the army—back from Troy. My father's coming home at last. Isn't he, Mother? Isn't he?

MELENA. [*Rising quickly and looking right.*] I don't know. I—don't know. Call one of them, and ask for Lysander, the shepherd. No! Don't! If he's there, he'll come to us. [*Turning away.*] Look and tell me: is anyone leaving the ranks?

SON. [*After a moment's pause.*] No! They're all passing by, Mother. They're all passing by!

[*The light fades, right. Once more the stage left brightens. JENNY is seen standing at the bus stop. She is crying softly. Presently her FATHER enters, stands left, watching her for a moment, and then comes behind her.*]

FATHER. [*Softly.*] Jenny.

JENNY. [*Startled.*] Uhh—Dad!

FATHER. Why did you leave the house?

JENNY. I couldn't stay there—not after . . .

FATHER. I understand, but come back with me now!

JENNY. In a little while. It sounds silly—like something from a book—but I need time . . .

FATHER. [*Gently.*] Of course, you do—and there's still hope.

JENNY. Hope?

FATHER. The telegram said, "Missing in action," Jenny. That's *all* it said.

JENNY. What more did it need to say? What more?

FATHER. But he might be alive.

JENNY. I don't feel that he is. I don't feel so.

FATHER. But think so, my dear! Try to think so.

JENNY. Alive? Alive for what? Alive to come home crippled, like those men you visit? His fine strong body in a wheel chair . . .

FATHER. Jenny!

JENNY. I don't understand. I don't know why things have to be . . . All this hatred, this suffering. Do you know? Do you understand?

FATHER. No—no, I don't.

JENNY. Bert didn't even understand why he went. And I don't. Doesn't anyone, Dad?

FATHER. [*Wearily.*] I don't know. I just don't know. Come home, come home with me now!

JENNY. [*Turning to leave with him.*] Yes.

[*There is a blackout, stage left, and the center lights come up again.*]

CHORUS.
> And so the cycle
> Is to a certain extent complete:
> Leaving "the unfinished" as
> The only completion known:
> Love and the spoils of love,
> War and the spoils of war.
> Neither do we understand,
> But both have always been.

FIRST WOMAN.
> Here is the moment for the philosopher
> To mint his new coinage of words.

SECOND WOMAN.

And, indeed, were we less clever,
We might also speak . . .

THIRD WOMAN.

Conclusions are the prerogative
Of the inexperienced.

FIRST WOMAN.

We have seen too much.

SECOND WOMAN.

And learned too little.

THIRD WOMAN.

Yet something surely remains to be said:

CHORUS.

More rich are men in their ignorance,
For in their not knowing they know much.
Yet all things seem to fade
Into that void which is the past.
While much might be said
By man in his sorrow,
Much in his darkness,
There is yet left to us
The ineffable beauty of man himself.
When did time begin for us?
The scalpel edge probing the earth
Has yet to answer.
And when assurance comes,
In the time of the great unfolding,
What then shall we know?
Even in that ephemeral span
That lies between the waking
And the yielding back to sleep,
We learn little.
But would we care
To know and understand
A time when time began?

FIRST WOMAN.

Before the Achaeans came from the mists?

SECOND WOMAN.

Before the beauteous laments
Awoke in the agonizing deserts?

THIRD WOMAN.

Before Germanic hoofs
Charged like thunder
Out of the unknown
Into the unknown?

CHORUS.

Timeless is time
In the dark
Of the world.

[*Gradually the light has faded, until the stage returns to the darkness of the beginning.*]

CURTAIN

SHORT PLAY PRODUCTION

1958-1959

BIBLIOGRAPHIES

NOTES ON CONTRIBUTORS

BROADWAY'S BOSSES

BY STANLEY RICHARDS

Although the general public (and, I daresay, a great many theatrical artisans) may be unaware of it, the American theatre is controlled by a small group of arbiters who decide what plays will be produced, how they will be produced, and when. These arbiters are not the drama critics of the New York dailies. The critics exert considerable force in establishing a success, but they do not indicate what is or is not to be produced in American theatres.

"The American theatre" is, of course, the Broadway theatre. By and large, what are seen in our road playhouses (what is left of them) and in the repertory, stock, community and university theatres, are merely warmed-over productions of past Broadway items. Occasionally, an untried opus will test its wings at one of the outposts of dramatic culture, but these experiments are too infrequent to be significant. This is lamentable, for a healthy theatre, to remain healthy, must encourage new forms as well as classics. But theatres outside of the metropolis depend on Broadway for survival. Schools throughout the country follow Broadway's lead. And Broadway is controlled by a baker's dozen of strong-minded, self-willed, and assertive individuals.

Just who are these controllers of American theatre? They hold two key positions.

Miss "A" is a famous playbroker. (Nearly all the leading playbrokers are women.) She controls the output of some of our top-ranking playwrights, as well as a slew of younger dramatists of promise. But "A" does have her preferences. As soon as a play that bears promise comes to her attention, she locks horns with the author and generously pours forth suggested revisions. In order to have the highly influential Miss "A" handle his property, the author returns to his desk and rewrites. Since "A" has had enormous success with a certain type of play, she diligently supervises the rewriting so that the play will contain most of the same elements that previously proved salable. Gradually the play is rebuilt to her specifications. The reconstructed play then goes to market and, with the benefit of "A's" prestige, is sold, cast and produced. It may not always materialize as a success. (As a matter of fact, during this past season, some variations on a single theme from one playbroker's stable folded like butterflies shorn of their wings.)

Miss or Mr. "B" is the theatre party agent. Theatre parties account for millions of dollars in advance sales, notably with large musicals. They also provide a crutch for many an ailing play. In short, theatre parties have their place in the theatrical world. But producers now submit manuscripts to party agents long before the signatures are dry on the author's contracts. If "B" disapproves of the play, it is an even bet that the play will be dropped by the disillu-

sioned producer. If the manuscript happens to win "B's" approval—
a manuscript by a topflight name writer automatically does—the producer will be able to finance his attraction through the guarantee of
theatre parties. He will also find it easier to engage a playhouse, in
these days of serious booking jams, for he has the promise of a captive
audience—for a few months, at the very least. After that, with God's
help and some strong promotion, his play may ride (or override) the
critical verdicts.

The theatre party agent must approve not only the script, but also
the star or stars. Many a player who seemed the playwright's ideal has
been passed by because of a party agent's arbitrary rejection. The
party agent has joined the dominating force of the American theatre.
These men may be exceedingly adept at wording contracts and selling
blocks of seats to playgoers, but certainly few of them are Brooks
Atkinsons or George Jean Nathans. The shoemaker may stick to his
last, but not so the play and party agent: they will have the whole shoe
or none of it!

Several years ago, an English dramatist who had been getting
deserved recognition at home approached me about getting a "hearing"
in the United States. I thought one of his short plays particularly good
and recommended it to the editor (not Miss Mayorga) of a collection of
one-act plays then being assembled. The editor shared my enthusiasm
for the play and arranged with the dramatist to include it in the
proposed volume. Then, somehow, an American agent became involved in the proceedings and persuaded the author to permit her to
handle the contractual transactions. And she did! For including the
play in the book (which included the work of ten or twelve other con-
tributors) she demanded $750 plus fifty per cent of the editor's royalties!
These terms were, of course, ludicrously unrealistic. Ironically, and
perhaps because of this highhandedness, the author has yet to be heard
from as a dramatist on this side of the Atlantic. His success in Great
Britain is assured, but the English theatre is not quite so much under
the dominance of ten-percenters.

We have heard complaints from critical and creative writers about
the paucity of contemporary short plays in our theatres and on television. Why are the topflight dramatists not writing as many one-act
plays as they once did? Simple! Their representatives have lowered
the boom on this form of dramatic art because the commissions from
short plays are considerably smaller than those from full-length plays.
This is understandable; but why deprive the American theatre of an
entertaining and age-old form of drama that has succored many of the
world's best dramatists?

If the playwright (like the short story writer) envisions an idea
within the framework of the short play, why stifle his creative faculties?
Indeed, many of our present dramas might have been considerably
more effective in the shorter form. The great sea plays of Eugene
O'Neill are enduring and noteworthy contributions to American dramatic literature. Free to write as he pleased, in any form he desired, and
without intrusive eyes peering over his towering shoulders, O'Neill gave

the American short play stature and serious import. Being an independent spirit, he never allowed himself the indignity of being influenced by outside forces. But then, when O'Neill composed his short plays, the theatre was not controlled by a few, and financial profit was not the keystone of dramatic success.

DRAMA AT HOME

BY PAUL SLOCUMB

Drama, like charity, can now begin at home. Thanks to some discerning individuals (more altruistic, I suspect, than commercial) it is possible today to hear recordings of some of the world's finest theatre classics and a smattering of contemporary dramas. The repertoire of recorded drama still is small compared with the more lucrative harvest of music, but the quality generally is of high value and interest. The recording companies are nosing in the right direction. Should the public respond via the purchasing dollar, the manufacturers will undoubtedly broaden their scope and step up their output.

CAEDMON, long a pioneer in this field, has transferred the lectern to the turntable, concentrating on readings from the classics and modern literature of superior quality—Yeats, Blake, Hans Christian Andersen, Dylan Thomas, James Joyce and others—as well as some of the all-time juvenile favorites. SPOKEN ARTS is also bringing famous playwrights and excerpts from their plays into the home. Arthur Miller, Paul Green, Moss Hart and Jean-Louis Barrault are only a few of the many eminent writers and actors who are now speaking from the turntable stage. These companies rely chiefly on the words, with their inherent drama or comedy, to please the listener.

For sheer production values and glittering casts, however, ANGEL RECORDS perhaps surpasses all others. Where in the world, other than for a record, could such a star-studded cast be assembled (and reimbursed) as that of ANGEL's full-length recording of Oscar Wilde's comedy, *The Importance of Being Earnest*: Sir John Gielgud, Dame Edith Evans, Pamela Brown, Celia Johnson, Jean Cadell and Roland Culver? Their mounting of Sheridan's Restoration comedy, *The School for Scandal*, is also notable; and Sean O'Casey's *Juno and the Paycock*, recorded in its actual locale, Ireland, is one of the most stirring and moving performances of this great twentieth-century tragicomedy.

Some years ago, DECCA instituted a series that held enormous promise for drama: *ANTA's Album of Stars*. These were, in essence, "great moments from great plays." One may question the insertion of scenes from *The Farmer Takes a Wife* and other plays of lesser caliber, but who will dispute the inclusion of moments from Chekhov's *The Sea Gull*, as played by Dame Edith Evans; from *The Barretts of Wimpole Street*, with Katharine Cornell and Brian Aherne playing their original stage roles; and from Lillian Hellman's *The Little Foxes*, with Tallulah Bankhead's coruscating portrayal of Regina? But the public, regrettably, did not respond; and the series, after two issues, was discarded in favor of Broadway's razzle-dazzle musical comedies. DECCA's first major entry, *Oklahoma*, started this boom—since picked up by other record companies—and some of the industry's greatest revenue is derived from these Broadway blockbusters.

Every now and again, an intrepid soul decides to record—for posterity rather than for fortune—an unusual dramatic presentation such as Samuel Beckett's controversial *Waiting for Godot* and Sir John Geilgud's *Ages of Man* (both COLUMBIA); Christopher Fry's abstruse and labored *The Lady's not for Burning* (DECCA); Archibald MacLeish's poetic parable, *J. B.* and Beckett's *Endgame* (both GROVE); and Tyrone Guthrie's production of Sophocles' *Oedipus Rex* (CAEDMON).

But why not the audience-attracting works of Eugene O'Neill, Maxwell Anderson, Tennessee Williams, Arthur Miller, William Inge, Paul Green and other masterful twentieth-century dramatists? Of these six, only Miller has been represented by a full-length recording of one of his plays: *Death of a Salesman* (DECCA). Surely there are many more scripts in the repertoire of modern American drama that warrant "waxing" after their regular Broadway and road engagements.

Looking even further, hasn't the time come for record companies to produce as well as reproduce? Many of the short plays written in the past several decades would lend themselves beautifully to recording. They are perfect in length, generally concentrated in story line, succinct in dialogue and characterization and bustling with ideas that would stimulate the listeners' minds and emotions.

With a bit of imagination and some prudent casting and direction, these short dramas and comedies could open an entirely new vista for the recording industry. The material is there: glance at some of it in THE BEST SHORT PLAYS anthologies dating from 1919 to the present! Some adventurous recording companies can tap this field, one of the few remaining sources of new dramatic material.

If drama in the home is to fulfill its vast potential for child and adult, it must experiment with the new as well as the old. It must discover as well as recover. In these respects, FOLKWAYS has been creating some astonishing dramatic values with a combination of paperback books, classical stories and impressive recorded productions, such as Sophocles' *Antigone* and Dante's *Inferno*. In fact, from a number of sources, it appears that turntable drama is becoming an exciting and intellectually stimulating medium of dramatic entertainment.

SELECTED PLAYS AND PLAY COLLECTIONS

ADOMOV, ARTHUR. PING PONG. Grove Press, New York.

ANDERSON, MAXWELL. FOUR VERSE PLAYS. Harcourt (Harvest), New York.

ANOUILH, JEAN. FIVE PLAYS. Vol. 2. Hill and Wang, New York.

AUDEN, W. H., and CHRISTOPHER ISHERWOOD. TWO GREAT PLAYS. Modern Library, New York.

BEHAN, BRENDAN. THE HOSTAGE. Grove Press, New York.

———. THE QUARE FELLOW. Grove Press, New York.

BEHRMAN, S. N. THE COLD WIND AND THE WARM. Random House, New York.

BETTI, UGO. THREE PLAYS. Grove Press, New York.

CARROL, PAUL VINCENT. IRISH STORIES AND PLAYS. Devin-Adair, New York.

CAWLEY, A. C., ED. EVERYMAN AND MEDIEVAL MIRACLE PLAYS. Dutton, New York.

CHAPMAN, JOHN. BROADWAY'S BEST, 1958. Doubleday, New York.

COMMITTEE ON PLAYLIST, ED. GUIDE TO PLAY SELECTION. National Council of Teachers of English. Appleton, Century, Crofts, New York.

CORDELL, RICHARD, and LOWELL MATSON, ED. THE OFF-BROADWAY THEATRE. Random House, New York. (Seven plays.)

COSTIGAN, JAMES G. LITTLE MOON OF ALBAN. Simon and Schuster, New York.

———. WIND FROM THE SOUTH. Simon and Schuster, New York.

DELANEY, SHELAGH. A TASTE OF HONEY. Grove Press, New York.

DENNIS, NIGEL. TWO PLAYS AND A PREFACE. British Book Center, New York.

ELIOT, T. S. THE ELDER STATESMAN. Farrar, Straus, Cudahy, New York.

ERNST, EARL. THREE JAPANESE PLAYS. Oxford, New York.

ETERNAL LIGHT. Series of radio and television dramas. Jewish Theological Seminary, New York. (Short plays.)

FITTS, DUDLEY, TRANS. ARISTOPHANES: LADIES DAY. Harcourt, Brace, New York.

GEDDES, NORMAN BELL. MIRACLE IN THE EVENING. Doubleday, New York.

GIRADOUX, JEAN. FOUR PLAYS. Hill and Wang, New York.

HAMMERSTEIN, OSCAR, II, and JOSEPH FIELDS. FLOWER DRUM SONG. Farrar, Straus, Cudahy, New York.

HANSBERRY, LORRAINE. A RAISIN IN THE SUN. Random House, New York.

HECHT, BEN. TREASURY OF BEN HECHT. Crown, New York.

HUGHES, LANGSTON. READER. Braziller, New York.

IBSEN, HENDRICK. THE LAST PLAYS. Hill and Wang, New York.

INGE, WILLIAM. THE DARK AT THE TOP OF THE STAIRS. Random House, New York.

KANIN, MICHAEL. RASHOMON. Random House, New York.

LINDSAY, HOWARD, and RUSSELL CROUSE. TALL STORY. Random House, New York.

LOGASA, HANNAH. INDEX TO ONE-ACT PLAYS. F. W. Faxon, Boston.

LUCAS, F. L., ED. WEBSTER: THE DUCHESS OF MALFI. Macmillan, New York.

MURPHY, SARA JANE. LUCIFER. *Keynote.* Wellesley College, Mass. (Short play.)

OBOLER, ARCH. NIGHT OF THE AUK. Horizon Press, New York.

O'NEILL, EUGENE. HUGHIE. Yale University Press, New Haven. (Short play.)

SAROYAN, WILLIAM. ONCE AROUND THE BLOCK. Samuel French, New York. (Short play.)

SCHULBERG, BUDD, and HARVEY BREIT. THE DISENCHANTED. Random House, New York.

SHAKESPEARE, WILLIAM. KING LEAR. Wolfit, Sir Donald, Introd. Folio Society, Ltd., London, England.

————. KING RICHARD II. Gielgud, Sir John, Introd. Folio Society, Ltd., London, England.

————. LOVE'S LABOUR'S LOST. Rogers, Paul, Introd. Folio Society, Ltd., London, England.

————. MIDSUMMER NIGHT'S DREAM. Richardson, Sir Ralph, Introd. Folio Society, Ltd., London, England.

————. OTHELLO. Brown, Ivor, Introd. Folio Society, Ltd., London, England.

SPIEGELGASS, LEONARD. A MAJORITY OF ONE. Random House, New York.

VAN DOREN, MARK. THE LAST DAYS OF LINCOLN. Hill and Wang, New York.

WINER, ELIHU. THREE HOURS BETWEEN PLANES. Samuel French, New York. (Short play.)

IMPORTANT BOOKS ABOUT DRAMA

AGEE, JAMES. AGEE ON FILM. McDowell, Obolensky, New York.

ALLEN, REGINALD, ED. FIRST NIGHT GILBERT AND SULLIVAN. Dial Press, New York.

BEERBOHM, MAX. MAINLY ON THE AIR. Knopf, New York.
BERNSTEIN, ALINE. MASTERPIECES OF WOMEN'S COSTUME. Crown, New York.
BOWEN, CROSSWELL. THE CURSE OF THE MISBEGOTTEN. McGraw-Hill, New York. (Biography of Eugene O'Neill.)
BOWERS, FAUBIAN. JAPANESE THEATRE. Hill and Wang, New York.
————. BROADWAY U.S.S.R. Thomas Nelson, New York.
BRAYBROOKE, NEVILLE. T. S. ELIOT: SYMPOSIUM FOR 70TH BIRTHDAY. Farrar, Straus, Cudahy, New York.
BRÉE, GERMAINE. CAMUS. Rutgers University Press, New Brunswick, New Jersey.
CHIARI, JOSEPH. THE CONTEMPORARY FRENCH THEATRE. Macmillan, New York.
CHINDAHL, GEORGE L. A HISTORY OF THE CIRCUS IN AMERICA. Caxton, Caldwell, Idaho.
CHURCHILL, ALLEN. IMPROPER BOHEMIANS. Dutton, New York.
CLARKE, MARY. SHAKESPEARE AT THE OLD VIC. Macmillan, New York.
CLURMAN, HAROLD. LIES LIKE TRUTH. Macmillan, New York.
CROY, HOMER. STAR MAKER. Duell, Sloan and Pearce, New York. (Biography of D. W. Griffith.)
DIXON, CAMPBELL, ED. INTERNATIONAL FILM ANNUAL. Doubleday, New York.
DONEGHUE, DENIS. THE THIRD VOICE. Princeton University Press, Princeton, New Jersey.
ENCYCLOPEDIE DU THEATRE COMTEMPORAIN. 2 Vols. Olivier Perrin Editeur, Paris.
ERNST, EARLE. THE KABUKI THEATRE. Grove Press, New York.
EWEN, DAVID. COMPLETE BOOK OF THE AMERICAN MUSICAL THEATRE. Holt, New York.
FALK, DORIS V. EUGENE O'NEILL AND THE TRAGIC TENSION. Rutgers University Press, New Brunswick, New Jersey.
FAY, GERARD. THE ABBEY THEATRE. Macmillan, New York.
FERNANDEZ, RAMON. MOLIÈRE. Hill and Wang, New York.
GARFIAS, ROBERT. GAGAKU. Theatre Arts Books, New York. (The music and dances of the Japanese Imperial Household.)
GIBSON, WILLIAM. THE SEESAW LOG. Knopf, New York.
GRANVILLE-BARKER, H., ED. COMPANION TO SHAKESPEARE STUDIES. Cambridge University Press, New York.
GREENE, DAVID H., and E. M. STEPHENS. J. M. SYNGE, 1871–1909. Macmillan, New York.
GROSS, FANNIE. SHAKESPEARE QUIZ BOOK. Crowell, New York.
GROSSVOGEL, DAVID L. THE SELF-CONSCIOUS STAGE IN FRENCH DRAMA. Columbia University Press, New York.
GUTHRIE, TYRONE, and ROBERTSON DAVIES. THE STRATFORD FESTIVAL. Clarke, Irwin, Toronto.
HARVEY, SIR PAUL, and J. E. HESSELTINE. THE OXFORD COMPANION TO FRENCH LITERATURE. Oxford University Press, New York.

HEWITT, BERNARD, ED. THE RENAISSANCE STAGE. University of Miami Press, Coral Gables, Florida.

HEWITT, BERNARD. THEATRE, U.S.A. McGraw-Hill, New York.

HOBSON, HAROLD, ED. INTERNATIONAL THEATRE ANNUAL. Doubleday, New York

HOWARD, LESLIE RUTH. A QUITE REMARKABLE FATHER. Harcourt, Brace, New York.

HUGHES, GLENN. THE PENTHOUSE THEATRE. University of Washington Press, Seattle.

HUGHES, ROBERT, ED. FILM: BOOK ONE. Grove Press, New York.

HUGHES, SPIKE. GREAT OPERA HOUSES. McBride, New York.

SOCIETY OF TRADITIONAL ARTS, ED. KABUKI. Auspices Institute of the Pacific. Kenkyusha, Lit., Tokyo.

LEVIN, HARRY. THE QUESTION OF HAMLET. Oxford University Press, New York.

LEWIS, ROBERT. METHOD OR MADNESS. Samuel French, New York.

LUMLEY, FREDERICK. TRENDS IN 20th CENTURY DRAMA. Rockliff, London.

McCARTHY, MARY. SIGHTS AND SPECTACLES. Farrar, Straus and Cudahy, New York.

McKEE, KEN. THE THEATRE OF MARIVAUX. New York University Press, New York.

MATHEWS, JOHN F., ED. SHAW'S DRAMATIC CRITICISM. Hill and Wang, New York.

MERCHANT, W. MOELWYN. SHAKESPEARE AND THE ARTIST. Oxford University Press, New York.

MITCHENSEN, JOE, and RAYMOND MANDER, ED. THEATRICAL COMPANION TO NOEL COWARD. Macmillan, New York.

OMAN, CAROLA. DAVID GARRICK. Hodder and Stoughton, London.

OPPENHEIMER, GEORGE, ED. THE PASSIONATE PLAYGOER. Viking, New York.

O'SHAUGHNESSY, MICHAEL. MONSIEUR MOLIÈRE. Crowell, New York.

POPE, W. MacQUEEN. NIGHTS OF GLADNESS. Hutchinson, London.

PRIESTLEY, J. B. THE ART OF THE DRAMATIST. Heinemann, London.

REDGRAVE, MICHAEL. MASK OR FACE. Theatre Arts Books, New York.

ROSENTHAL, HAROLD, ED. INTERNATIONAL OPERA ANNUAL. Doubleday, New York.

SCHILDKRAUT, JOSEPH. MY FATHER AND I. Viking, New York.

SCOTT, A. C. AN INTRODUCTION TO THE CHINESE THEATRE. Theatre Arts Books, New York.

SHARPE, ROBERT BOIES. IRONY IN THE DRAMA. University of North Carolina Press, Chapel Hill, N. C.

SHATTUCK, CHARLES H., ED. BULWER AND MACREADY. University of Illinois Press, Champaign, Ill.

SOBEL, BERNARD. THE NEW THEATRE HANDBOOK AND DIGEST OF PLAYS. Crown, New York.

Spectacles (Magazine of French Theatre). 198 Boulevard Saint-Germain, Paris VII, France.

STEVENS, FRANCES. THEATRE WORLD ANNUAL. No. 9. Macmillan, New York.

STIRLING, BRENTS. UNITY IN SHAKESPEARIAN TRAGEDY. Columbia University Press, New York.

TREWIN, J. C., JOE MITCHENSEN and RAYMOND MANDER. THE GAY TWENTIES. Macdonald, London.

Tulane Drama Review. Hill and Wang, New York.

WEST, E. J. SHAW ON THEATRE. Hill and Wang, New York.

WICKHAM, GLYNNE. EARLY ENGLISH STAGES, 1300–1660. Columbia University Press, New York.

WILLETT, JOHN. THE THEATRE OF BERTOLT BRECHT. New Directions, New York.

WILLIAMSON, AUDREY, and CHARLES LANDSTONE. THE BRISTOL OLD VIC. J. Garnet Miller, London.

WILSON, JOHN HAROLD. ALL THE KING'S LADIES. University of Chicago Press, Chicago. (Actresses of the Restoration.)

SELECTED DRAMATIC RECORDINGS

(All of the following are long-playing 33⅓ r.p.m. records)

AGES OF MAN. OL 5390, Columbia. (Sir John Gielgud reading from Shakespeare.)

ALICE IN WONDERLAND. TC 1097, Caedmon.

ANTIGONE. 9861, Folkways (English); 9912, Folkways (Greek).

APPLE CART, THE. TC 1094, Caedmon. (Noel Coward and Margaret Leighton in selections from George Bernard Shaw's play.)

BERNARD SHAW–ELLEN TERRY LETTERS. TC 1108, Caedmon. (Dame Peggy Ashcroft, Cyril Cusack.)

CHOCOLATE SOLDIER, THE. LOP 6005, RCA Victor. (Rise Stevens and Robert Merrill head the cast of the Oscar Straus operetta.)

CO-STAR. CS 101 through CS 115, Roulette Co-Star. (Dramatic readings by Cesar Romero, Fernando Lamas, Arlene Dahl, George Raft, June Havoc, Cedric Hardwicke, Basil Rathbone, Virginia Mayo, Tallulah Bankhead, Vincent Price, Paulette Goddard, Don Ameche, Jimmie Rodgers, Pearl Bailey, Maxie Rosenbloom, in which the listener reads from enclosed script scenes from plays and motion pictures opposite the "co-star.")

DANTE'S INFERNO. 9871, Folkways (English); 9977, Folkways (Italian).

DESTRY RIDES AGAIN. DL 9075, Decca. (Andy Griffith and Dolores Gray head the cast of Harold Rome's Broadway musical.)

ENDGAME. EVR 0003, Evergreen. (Full-length recording of Samuel Beckett's play, with original off-Broadway cast; text of play included with album set.)

FINNEGAN'S WAKE. TC 1086, Caedmon. (Cyril Cusack and Siobhan McKenna in scenes from the James Joyce novel.)

FIRST IMPRESSIONS. OL 5400, Columbia. (Polly Bergen, Farley Granger, Hermione Gingold and the original Broadway cast, in the musical version of Jane Austen's Pride and Prejudice.)

FLOWER DRUM SONG. OL 5350, Columbia. (Original cast interpretation of the Richard Rodgers–Oscar Hammerstein–Joseph Fields musical.)

GENESIS. TC 1096, Caedmon. (Judith Anderson reading from the Book of Genesis and other selections from the Old Testament.)

GIGI. E3641ST, M-G-M. (Leslie Caron, Maurice Chevalier and Louis Jourdan sing, from the sound track of the Alay Jay Lerner–Frederick Loewe award-winning motion picture.)

GOLDILOCKS. OL 5340, Columbia. (Original Broadway cast, with Don Ameche and Elaine Stritch, in a musical spoof of the early days of motion picture making.)

GONDOLIERS, THE. S3570 B/L, Angel Stereo. (Sir Malcolm Sargent conducts the Pro Arte Orchestra and the Glyndebourne Festival Chorus in a complete recording of the Gilbert and Sullivan operetta.)

GYPSY. OL 5420, Columbia. (Ethel Merman and original Broadway cast.)

GYPSY BARON. 3566 B/L Angel. (Elisabeth Schwarzkopf stars in the Johann Strauss operetta, with the Philharmonia Orchestra and chorus, under the direction of Otto Ackermann.)

HIGH BUTTON SHOES. CAL 457, RCA Camden. (Recently transferred to LP, this original Broadway cast recording features Phil Silvers and Nanette Fabray in leading roles.)

JUNO. OL 5380, Columbia. (Shirley Booth and Melvyn Douglas in the leading roles of Marc Blitzstein's musical adaptation of Sean O'Casey's Juno and the Paycock.)

LITTLE FLOWERS OF ST. FRANCIS, THE. TC 1112, Caedmon. (Read by Cyril Cusack.)

LORD BYRON'S LOVE LETTER. LM 2258, RCA Victor. (One-act opera, with score by Raffaello de Banfield and libretto by Tennessee Williams, based on the latter's one-act play of the same name.)

LOST HORIZON and TALE OF TWO CITIES, A. DL 9059, Decca. (The late Ronald Colman, with supporting casts, in scenes from two of his best remembered motion pictures.)

MARIA GOLOVIN. LM 6142, RCA Victor. (Original cast, from the Brussels Fair August 20, 1958, premiere, of the Gian Carlo Menotti opera.)

MEDEA. OL 3-104, Mercury. (Maria Meneghini Callas sings the title role in Luigi Cherubini's three-act opera, with La Scala orchestra and chorus under the direction of Tullio Serafin.)

MERRY WIDOW, THE. OSA 1205, London Stereo. (German libretto, with Hilde Gueden singing the title role in this complete transcription of the Franz Lehar operetta; chorus and orchestra of the Vienna State Opera, conducted by Robert Stolz.)

MIKADO, THE. 3573 B/L, Angel Stereo. (Gilbert and Sullivan's operetta, with Sir Malcolm Sargent conducting the Pro Arte Orchestra and the Glyndebourne Festival Chorus.)

MIKADO, THE. OSA 1201, London Stereo. (Peter Pratt, as Ko-Ko, and the D'Oyly Carte Opera Company. Isidore Godfrey conducts The New Symphony Orchestra of London.)

NERVOUS SET. OL 5430, Columbia. (Original Broadway cast.)

NOEL COWARD DUOLOGUES. TC 1069, Caedmon. (Margaret Leighton joins Mr. Coward in a complete adaptation of *Brief Encounter* and scenes from *Blithe Spirit* and *Present Laughter*.)

OH, CAPTAIN! OL 5280, Columbia. (Tony Randall and Jacquelyn McKeever, with most of the original Broadway cast, in the musical version of the English film, *Captain's Paradise*.)

ONCE UPON A MATTRESS. KDL-7004, Kapp. (Original cast of Phoenix Theatre production.)

PARADISE LOST. TC 1093, Caedmon. (Anthony Quayle reading passages from the John Milton classic.)

PLAY OF DANIEL, THE. DL 9402, Decca. (A twelfth-century musical drama, as presented at The Cloisters, New York. Noah Greenberg directs the New York Pro Musica musicians and singers.)

POETRY OF ROBERT BURNS, and SCOTTISH BORDER BALLADS. TC 1103, Caedmon. (Frederick Worlock and C. R. M. Brookes.)

RASHOMON. LPX 5000, Carlton. (Original music from the Broadway drama as composed and conducted by Laurence Rosenthal.)

RICHARD RODGERS AND OSCAR HAMMERSTEIN, II, A RECORDED PORTRAIT. 2E4 RP, M-G-M. (The tunesmiths in intimate conversation with Arnold Michaelis.)

SALAD DAYS. 5474, London. (A Bristol Old Vic original cast, seen recently off-Broadway with a Canadian company.)

SNOW GOOSE, THE. DL 9066, Decca. (Herbert Marshall and Joan Loring, with supporting cast, in the Paul Gallico story. Dumas' *The Count of Monte Cristo*, with Mr. Marshall and supporting actors, on reverse side.)

SORRY, WRONG NUMBER. DL 9062, Decca. (Agnes Moorehead re-creating her role in Lucille Fletcher's famed radio drama. The flip side features James Mason in readings from E. A. Poe's *The Tell-Tale Heart*, *Annabel Lee* and *Silence*.)

SUOR ANGELICA. G7115, Capitol. (Puccini's seldom performed one-act opera, with Victoria de Los Angeles in the title role.)

TALES OF HANS CHRISTIAN ANDERSEN. TC 1073, Caedmon. (Michael Redgrave, reading from *The Tinder Box*, *The Emperor's New Clothes*, *The Steadfast Tin Soldier* and *The Emperor's Nightingale*.)

THROUGH THE LOOKING GLASS. TC 1098, Caedmon.

TRISTAN AND ISEULT. TC 1106, Caedmon. (Claire Bloom reads the Bedier translation of the immortal lovers.)

TROUBLE IN TAHITI. E 3646, M-G-M. (Leonard Bernstein's

domestic opera in seven scenes, with Beverly Wolff and David Atkinson.)

TRUE STORY OF THE CIVIL WAR, THE. CRL 59100, Coral. (Raymond Massey narrates the Oscar-winning short documentary, transcribed here from the sound tract.)

VANESSA. LM 6138, RCA Victor. (Eleanor Steber, Regina Resnik, Giorgio Tozzi, Nicolai Gedda head a large Metropolitan Opera cast, with Dimitri Mitropoulos conducting the orchestra, in Samuel Barber's score, and the chorus, in lyrics by Gian Carlo Menotti.)

COMPLETE LISTING OF
REPRESENTATIVE ONE-ACT PLAYS
BY AMERICAN AUTHORS,
1919 AND 1937 EDITIONS
(Dates refer to earliest listing)

COMPLETE LISTING OF
BEST SHORT PLAYS, 1937-1959
(Dates refer to earliest listing)

Conkle, E. P. (cont.) — The Least One, 1951-1952
Muletail Prime, 1950-1951
Corwin, Norman — On a Note of Triumph, 1945
We Hold These Truths, 1942
Costello, Ward — A Wake for Me and Thee, 1948-1949
Daggett, James L. — Goodnight Please!, 1937
Darion, Joe; and George
 Kleinsinger — Archy and Mehitabel, 1957-1958
Dempsey, David — It Ain't Brooklyn, 1944
Devany, Edward H. — The Cow-Catcher on the Caboose, 1958-1959
The Red and Yellow Ark, 1957-1958

Dillon, Thomas Patrick; and
 Leary, Nolan — The Doctor from Dunmore, 1941
Donato, Pietro di — The Love of Annunziata, 1941
Dugan, Lawrence Joseph — Hospital Scene, 1939
Eaton, Walter Prichard — Period House, 1949-1950
Ferrini, Vincent — Innermost I Land, 1952-1953
Telling of the North Star, 1953-1954

Finch, Robert; and Smith,
 Betty — The Far-Distant Shore, 1945
Summer Comes to the Diamond O, 1940
(See also Smith, Betty)
Foote, Horton — John Turner Davis (television play), 1953-1954
Frankel, Doris — Journey for an Unknown Soldier, 1943
Gainfort, John — Going Home, 1949-1950
Never No Third Degree, 1938
The Maker of Laws, 1937

Goldschmidt, Walter; and
 Sinclair, Lister — A Word in Your Ear, 1953-1954
Green, Paul — Alma Mater, 1938
In Abraham's Bosom, 1957
Gurnel, A. J., Jr. — Three People, 1955-1956
Turn of the Century, 1957-1958
Harris, W. Eric — Twenty-Five Cents, 1937
Hawley, Esther M. — On the Way Home, 1944
Hayes, Marrijane and Joseph — The Bridegroom Waits, 1943
A Woman's Privilege, 1947-1948
Hecht, Ben — It's Fun to Be Free (with Charles Mac-Arthur), 1941
Miracle on the Pullman, 1944
A Tribute to Gallantry, 1943
Holland, Norman — Day Before Yesterday, 1949-1950
Farewell Appearance
 (with Stanley Richards), 1950-1951
Holm, John Cecil — Quiet—Facing the Park, 1943
Houston, Noel — According to Law, 1940
Howe, Carroll W. — The Long Fall, 1949-1950
Hughes, Babette — If the Shoe Pinches, 1937

Nash, N. Richard — *Parting at Imsdorf, 1940*
Rouge Atomique, 1954-1955
Neuenburg, Evelyn — *House Divided, 1942*
Niggli, Josephina — *Soldadera, 1937*
This Is Villa, 1938
Oboler, Arch — *Memo to Berchtesgaden, 1942*
O'Brien, Howard Vincent — *So Long, Son, 1942*
O'Dea, John D. — *Where Er'e We Go, 1943*
O'Keeffe, A. A. — *Slip Ahoy!, 1944*
Oliver, William I. — *The Stallion, 1957*
Packer, Barbara — *Patrick Brontë and the Saint, 1948-1949*
Turn Down an Empty Jug, 1950-1951
Perl, Arnold — *The High School, 1955-1956*
Mind in the Shadow, 1948-1949
Perrini, Alberto — *Once a Thief, 1955-1956*
Perry, Marjean — *A Trap Is a Small Place, 1952-1953*
Pollock, Channing — *"The Captains and the Kings," 1939*
Potter, Dan S. — *A Touch of Marble, 1958-1959*
Poverman, Helen — *Easy Money, 1958-1959*
Procunier, Edwin R. — *Two Sides of Darkness, 1958-1959*
Purkey, Ruth Angell — *Hangs Over Thy Head, 1955-1956*
Randall, William M. — *Tobacco Alley, 1937*
Reynolds, Rachel — *Until Charlot Comes Home, 1941*
Richards, Stanley — *August Heat, 1949-1950*
District of Columbia, 1944
Gin and Bitterness, 1958-1959
Half-Hour, Please, 1954-1955
O Distant Land, 1948-1949
Sun Deck, 1951-1952
Through a Glass, Darkly, 1947-1948
Tunnel of Love, 1952-1953
Riggs, Lynn — *A World Elsewhere, 1939*
Ringwood, Gwen Pharis — *The Courting of Marie Jenvrin, 1942*
Robinson, Marvin V. — *Exodus (dance drama), 1949-1950*
Rose, Reginald — *Dino (television play), 1955-1956*
Rosten, Hedda — *The Happy Housewife (television play), 1951-1952*
Rosten, Norman — *Concerning the Red Army, 1944*
Ryerson, Florence; and Clements, Colin
Saroyan, William — *Farewell to Love, 1938*
That's Hollywood, 1939
Hello Out There, 1941
The Hungerers, 1939
The Man with the Heart in the Highlands, 1957
Subway Circus, 1940
Schaefer, Lee — *The Little Flaw of Ernesto Lippi, 1953-1954*
Song for a Hero, 1954-1955
Schochen, Seyril — *One-Car Wedding, 1939*

Scholl, Ralph — *The Golden Axe, 1957-1958*

Seiger, Marvin L. — *Blue Concerto, 1955-1956*

Seiler, Conrad — *Good Night, Caroline, 1938*

Senior, Edward — *The Hunted, 1958-1959*

Shaber, David — *The Youngest Shall Ask, 1952-1953*

Shane, Maxwell — *We Refuse to Die, 1942*

Sheffield, John — *The Forgotten Land, 1953-1954*
The Imploring Flame, 1952-1953

Shore, Joseph; and Lincoln, Richard — *The Soldier Who Became a Great Dane, 1946-1947*

Shore, Joseph; and Williamson, Scott Graham — *Who Are the Weavers, 1947-1948*

Sion, Georges — *The Matron of Ephesus, 1950-1951*

Smith, Betty; and Webb, Chase — *Mañana Bandits, 1938*

Smith, Del — *They Asked for It, 1943*

Snyder, William H., Jr. — *Another Summer, 1953-1954*
The Departing, 1957-1958

Stein, Gertrude — *Brewsie and Willie, 1954-1955*
Doctor Faustus Lights the Lights, 1949-1950

Stein, Howard — *In Darkness, 1951-1952*

Stephens, John Peter — *The Changeling, 1952-1953*
Hugh of the Glen and His Clogs Are All One, 1951-1952

Stockton, Richard F. — *A Fabulous Tale, 1957-1958*

Stone, Weldon — *Cloud Over Breakshin, 1938*
Devil Take a Whittler, 1937
Rainbows in Heaven, 1940

Sundgaard, Arnold — *Equinox, 1941*
Mid-Passage, 1943
The Picnic, 1944

Thomas, Dorothy; and Slocumb, Paul — *Next-to-Last Rites* (television play), *1954-1955*

Thon, Frederick — *The Island, 1954-1955*

Tree, Jonathan — *The Fisherman, 1945*

Trevisan, Anna F. — *Easter Eve, 1947-1948*
Valley of the Shadow, 1950-1951

Waldau, Roy S. — *A Cabin by the Lake, 1954-1955*

Walsh, Norman — *Let There Be Farce, 1955-1956*

Welsh, Rae — *Let's Get Out of Here, 1957-1958*

White, Kenneth — *Freight, 1946-1947*

Wilde, Percival — *Mr. F., 1940*
Salt for Savor, 1953-1954

Williams, Tennessee — *The Lady of Larkspur Lotion, 1941*
The Last of My Solid Gold Watches, 1942
Mooney's Kid Don't Cry, 1940
Something Unspoken, 1955-1956

Williams, Tennessee (*cont.*)

Williamson, Scott Graham; and Shore, Joseph

Wilson, Dorothy Clarke
Wilson, Elizabeth

Wincelberg, Simon
Wishengrad, Morton

Woodress, Frederick A.
Woskoff, Verna
Young, Stanley

Zeiger, Henry
Zuckerman, Albert

27 Wagons Full of Cotton, 1944
The Unsatisfactory Supper, 1945

A Bed with the Others, 1948-1949
(See also Shore, Joseph)
The Return of Chandra, 1954-1955
Lord and Hawksaw Sadie (play with music), *1946-1947*
The Conquerer, 1954-1955
To the American People, 1945
The Camel and I, 1949-1950
How They Knocked the Devil Out of Uncle Ezra, 1946-1947
Impasse, 1948-1949
Castle in the Village, 1958-1959
A Bunyan Yarn, 1945
Farmer Brown's Pig, 1940
The Sound of Apples, 1957-1958
Five Days, 1955-1956
Blobo's Boy, 1958-1959

NOTES ON CONTRIBUTORS

Mayorga, Margaret. Miss Mayorga was born in New York City of parents also born in New York City. She received her M.A. in Drama at Adelphi College, including graduate studies in the Dramatic Seminar at Dartmouth College. While a student, she edited the first one-act anthology to be published in this country; this year's volume is her thirty-first anthology. She is also the author of the standard SHORT HISTORY OF AMERICAN DRAMA from *Ye Beare and Ye Cub* to *Mourning Becomes Electra.* Her theatre experience includes speech, acting, directing, producing, and teaching of playwriting (Writers' Conference, University of Colorado). She has a married son, an engineer; and a granddaughter. She has recently completed her first full-length play, entitled *A Woman's Place,* an American Commedia dell'Arte.

Conkle, Ellsworth P. Mr. Conkle is Professor of Drama (Playwriting) at the University of Texas and Guest Teacher of Playwriting at the Banff (Canada) School of Fine Arts. Educated at the Universities of Nebraska and Iowa, he studied at the famous Yale 47 Workshop with G. P. Baker and has held Rockefeller and Guggenheim Fellowships. Two of his plays, *Two Hundred Were Chosen* and *Prologue to Glory,* have been produced on Broadway. His published works include *Five Plays,* two volumes of one-act plays and numerous single one-act plays and articles.

Devany, Edward H. Mr. Devany, after six years of directing in community theatres and local TV stations, is now teaching direction and staging for TV at the School of Radio Technique in New York City. He studied playwriting with Lemist Esler at the Yale Drama School, and with Dr. Charles Glicksberg at the New School for Social Research. He is married and has one daughter. *The Cow-Catcher on the Caboose* is his third published play.

Inge, William. Mr. Inge was born in Independence, Kansas. He graduated from the University of Kansas and Peabody's Teachers College before joining the faculty of Stephens College, where he worked in the theatre department under the late Maude Adams. He then became art, music and drama critic for the St. Louis *Star-Times,* during which period he first essayed playwriting. His initial script, *Farther Off from Heaven,* was produced by Margo Jones at her famous Dallas Theatre in 1947. Following his debut, Mr. Inge returned to St. Louis, joined the faculty of Washington University and resumed playwriting. His Broadway plays have been *Come Back Little Sheba, Picnic, Bus Stop* and *The Dark at the Top of the Stairs.*

Potter, Dan S. Mr. Potter, a student at the Yale University School of Drama, is a newcomer to the playwriting field. *A Touch of Marble* is his first published play.

Poverman, Helen. Miss Poverman is a graduate of the Yale University School of Drama and a newcomer to the playwriting field. *Easy Money* is her first published play.

Procunier, Edwin R. Mr. Procunier is a member of Stanley Richards' Canadian playwriting workshop in Ontario. Although he has written several long and short plays, *Two Sides of Darkness* is his first published work.

Richards, Stanley. Mr. Richards is New York dramatic critic for *Players Magazine.* Many of his short and long plays have been published and produced, both on stage and on television, and nine of them have appeared first in this annual. He has been a writer in Hollywood for Universal-International and Columbia Pictures. He conducted the 1956, 1957, and 1958 summer seminars on playwriting in Ontario, Canada. His three-act play, *Beyond My Shore,* recently had its première in Sao Paulo, Brazil.

Senior, Edward. Mr. Senior is a graduate of the Massachusetts Institute of Technology; he took post-graduate studies at London University and the Sorbonne. He has written for television and the "little" magazines, and he is an associate of the Actor's Repertory Theatre Workshop in New York. *The Hunted* is his first published play. Another short play, *Nymphy,* has had successful productions.

Slocumb, Paul. Since World War II, Mr. Slocumb has been a writer and actor, in radio on the West Coast, and on stage at Laguna Beach. He toured for a season with a Children's Theatre, and had his own theatre for two seasons in Virginia. He writes long and short plays for stage and television, and has been represented in this annual and on Lux Video Theatre. He is record critic and Associate Editor for *Players Magazine.*

Woskoff, Verna. Miss Woskoff attended Antioch College and received her Master's degree in Drama from Columbia University. She has had radio scripts produced on WING in Dayton, Ohio, and WNYC in New York; has worked as production assistant with the New York Summer Shakespeare Festival; and has acted and directed for the Brooklyn Heights Players. *Castle in the Village* is her first published play.

Zuckerman, Albert J. Mr. Zuckerman attended Princeton and the Institut d'Etudes Politiques de Paris. He started writing plays while in the Navy. *Beer in the Backwash* was the first to be produced (by a small off-Broadway group). While working in the State Department in Washington, he joined a playwriting group; in 1958 he resigned from the department and entered the Yale School of Drama. *Blobo's Boy* is his first published work.